WHOSE VOICE?

WHOSE VOICE?

*Participatory research and
policy change*

Edited by
JEREMY HOLLAND with
JAMES BLACKBURN

with a Foreword by ROBERT CHAMBERS

INTERMEDIATE TECHNOLOGY PUBLICATIONS 1998

Intermediate Technology Publications Ltd,
103–105 Southampton Row, London WC1B 4HH, UK

© the individual authors; this collection Intermediate Technology
Publications 1998

A CIP record for this book is available from the British Library

ISBN 1 85339 419 X

Typeset by Dorwyn Ltd, Rowlands Castle, Hants
Printed in the UK by Bath Press, Bath

Contents

Contents

Contents

Acknowledgements

This book stems from an international workshop convened at the Institute of Development Studies, University of Sussex in May 1996. During the workshop, some 50 participants from 26 countries shared and reviewed recent experience with PRA and policy. Papers presented at the workshop form the major part of this book, Part 1 looking at Thematic and Sectoral studies and Part 2 reflecting specifically on Participatory Poverty Assessments. Part 3 of the book picks up on themes emerging during the workshop and attempts to draw together the verbal and written output of participants and others in exploring these themes.

We are extremely grateful to all the participants for making the original workshop such a success and for their subsequent contributions to the production of this book. To those participants whose papers appear in this book we are particularly grateful for their graciousness in accepting editorial condensing or restructuring of papers.

Sincere thanks are due to Katie Fawcett for her patient support, to Jenny Skepper for so often acting as intermediary, and to Meg Howarth for her editorial rigour. Finally, a special thanks to Robert Chambers for his expert co-ordination, analytical agility in moving between big picture and tiniest detail, and extraordinary enthusiasm, sustained from start to finish.

List of Tables

List of Figures

List of Boxes

Abbreviations and Addresses

Action Aid	Hamlyn House, MacDonald Road, Archway, London N19 5PG, UK
AKRSP-I	Aga Khan Rural Support Programme (India), Choice Premises, Swastik Cross Road, Navrangpura, Ahmedabad 380009, India
BA	beneficiary-assessment
CA	cropped areas
CBO	community-based organization
CEDEP	Centre for Development of People, PO Box 5601, Kumasi, Ghana
CI	cropping intensity
DANIDA	Danish Agency for International Development, Environment Secretariat, Ministry of Foreign Affairs, Asiatisk Plads 2, DK 1448 Copenhagen, Denmark
DRA	Data Research Africa, PO Box 37656, Overport, 4067, South Africa
GTZ	Deutsche Gesellschaft fur technische Zusammenarbeit, GmbH, Postfach 5180, D–65726, Eschborn, Germany
IDS	Institute of Development Studies, University of Sussex, Brighton BN1 9RE, Sussex, UK
IIED	International Institute for Environment and Development, 3 Endsleigh Street, London, WC1H ODD, UK
MCI	multiple-cropping index
MYRADA	MYRADA, 2 Service Road, Domlur Layout, Bangalore 560 071, India
NGO	non-governmental organization
ODA	Overseas Development Administration, 94 Victoria Street, London SW1E 5JL, UK
PA	poverty assessment
PAG	Participatory Assessment Group, PO Box RW 51080, Lusaka, Zambia
PAR	participatory action research
PDI	participatory development initiative
PDR	process documentation research
PIM	participatory irrigation management
PLA	participatory learning and action
PPA	participatory poverty assessment
PRA	participatory rural appraisal

RAT   rapid assessment techniques
RDP   South African Reconstruction and Development
             Programme
RRA   rapid rural appraisal
SARAR   self-esteem, associative strength, resourcefulness, action
             planning, and responsibility for follow-through
Sida   Swedish International Development Authority,
             Klarabergsgatan 23, 10525 Stockholm, Sweden
SSI   semi-structured interview
TRN   Tarai Research Network
UCBHCA   Uganda Community-based Health Care Association
UNDP   United Nations Development Programme, 1 United
             Nations Plaza, New York, NY 10017, USA
UNICEF   United Nations Children's Fund, UNICEF House, 3 United
             Nations Plaza, New York, NY 10017, USA
USAID   United States Agency for International Development,
             Washington DC 20523, USA
WWF   World Wide Fund for Nature
ZOPP   Zielorientierte Projektplanung (Objectives-Oriented
             Project Planning)

Foreword

ROBERT CHAMBERS

Whose Voice? presents a dramatic learning: it is that now, in the last years of the twentieth century, we have new ways in which those who are poor and marginalized can present their realities to those in power, and be believed, influence policy and make a difference.

The context

To many readers this will seem improbable. We live, after all, in a world of increasing polarization of power and wealth into North and South, into overclasses and underclasses. Materially, those in the overclasses have more and more, and are increasingly linked by instant communications. At the same time, the numbers in the underclasses of absolute poverty continue to rise. Among them, many millions have less and less, and remain isolated both from the overclass and from each other. Almost by definition, the poor and powerless have no voice. It may be politically correct to say that they should be empowered and their voices heard. But cynical realists will point to inexorable trends, vested interests and pervasive self-interest among the powerful, and argue that little can be changed.

The contributors to this book present evidence of new potentials to the contrary. They confront that cynicism with their own promising experience. They have found that there are new ways to enable those who are poor, marginalized, illiterate and excluded to analyse their realities and express their priorities; that the realities they express of conditions, problems, livelihood strategies and priorities often differ from what development professionals have believed; and that new experiences can put policymakers in closer touch with those realities.

These potentials come from participatory research in which the poor themselves are active analysts. This has a long pedigree, not least in the traditions of participatory action research and the inspiration of Paulo Freire and his followers. In the late 1980s and early 1990s a confluence of older streams of research together with new inventions evolved as a family of approaches and methods known as participatory rural appraisal (PRA). This has spread fast and wide. It is now often urban and frequently much more than appraisal. It has been applied in all continents, and many countries and contexts.

PRA stresses changes in the behaviour and attitudes of outsiders, to become not teachers but facilitators, not lecturers but listeners and learners. 'Hand over the stick', 'Use your own best judgement at all times' and 'They can do it' (having confidence in the abilities of local people, whether literate or not) are among its sayings. When well conducted, PRA approaches and methods are often open-ended, visual as well as verbal, and carried out by small groups of local people. They have proved power-ful means of enabling local people, including the poor, illiterate, women and the marginalized, themselves to appraise, analyse, plan and act. While some consider that PRA should always be part of an empowering process, others have used the methods for research, to learn more and more accu-rately about the realities of the poor.

As PRA evolved, it soon became evident that it had applications for policy. Thematic and sectoral studies were carried out and presented as reports to decisionmakers, sometimes in only days or weeks from the field-work. The World Bank, through trust funds from bilateral donors, initiated participatory poverty assessments (PPAs). Some of these used PRA methods to enable poor people to express their realities themselves. The insights from these thematic studies and PPAs were often striking, convin-cing and unexpected. A quiet revolution was taking place in parallel in different parts of the world, but it was too scattered for full mutual learning or for its significance to be fully seen.

Through support from Swiss Development Cooperation, an interna-tional workshop was convened at the Institute of Development Studies, University of Sussex, over the two days 13–14 May 1996, to share and review relevant experience with PRA and policy. Some 50 participants of 26 nationalities took part. The papers and discussions from that workshop, with Jeremy Holland as the main editor, provide the core of this book, updated and augmented by new material from this rapidly evolving field.

A related workshop a few days later drew together experience on the institutionalizing of participatory approaches. A companion volume, *Who Changes?* with James Blackburn as the main editor, similarly presents and analyses much learning from recent experience. It finds that PRA and related participatory approaches have presented many challenges – ethical, institutional and personal, especially as they go to scale with large organ-izations. It concludes with a bottom line that how good development is depends on what sort of people 'we' – development professionals – are. *Who Changes?* and *Whose Voice?* are part of a sequence of publications which draw on PRA-related experience.

In reading *Whose Voice?* there is excitement to be found, and a certain exhilaration. For one realizes gradually that there has been a break-through. Many questions are raised. Among these, certain insights and issues stand out and deserve comment, among these methods and ethics and the realities revealed.

Methods and ethics

With participatory research, and especially with PRA, methods and ethics are intertwined; issues raised are of time taken, expectations aroused and whose realities are expressed. Several writers agonize over whether the research process is exploitative. Participatory research is time-consuming for local people: PRA methods, especially the visual ones like mapping, diagramming and matrices, tend to be fun and to engage people's full attention, but sometimes for hours; and poor people's time is not costless. Expectations are also liable to be raised. After being helped to analyse their conditions, problems and opportunities, people often expect action, but with facilitators in a policy research mode, and not concerned with planning for action, follow-up may not be feasible.

No solutions can be universal, but two points are widely agreed:

○ *Transparency*: facilitators should make clear from the start who they are, what they are doing, and why, and what can and cannot be expected; often, even when nothing can be expected, local people will collaborate, not least because they find the activities interesting and enjoyable, and themselves learn from them.
○ *Selection for follow-up*: communities and groups can be chosen where responsible follow-up may be possible through an on-going programme.

A further concern is whose reality is being presented, and whose reality counts. Those most accessible to outsiders in communities are usually men, and those who are less poor, less marginalized, less excluded. Women are often continuously busy. Ensuring that the excluded are included, and that their reality is expressed, can demand patience, persistence, tact and inconvenience. The best times for poor women are, for example, often the worst times for outsiders.

There is then the question of how their reality is analysed, and into whose categories. (Researchers tend to fit material into preconceived concepts.) The Management Committee of the South African PPA set an example of best practice by going to pains not to impose their categories and constructs on the material. Instead, through card sorting, they allowed the categories and constructs to emerge from the material, and then to influence the structure of the report, which they wrote as spokespersons for the poor.

Realities revealed

Much of the power of PRA methods lies in what has been called group-visual synergy. Group activities include: making maps, lists, matrices, causal and linkage diagrams, estimating, comparisons, ranking and scoring, and discussing and debating. Realities are expressed in a cumulative physical and visual form, often democratically, on the ground. Typically, people become committed to the process and lose themselves in it. Visually, more diversity and complexity are expressed than can be put into words. Much in the contributions to this book was first presented visually.

The realities revealed in both the thematic studies and the PPAs are often striking. Once stated they seem obvious, but it is sobering to recognize that for urban-based professionals they have usually been new insights, or understanding presented with new force and credibility. To take examples in turn from the thematic studies:

○ In Nepal, in the Tarai (plains) area, the continuous introduction of irrigation and of new crop varieties led to yield increases, but was masking long-term declines in soil fertility.
○ In Guinea, contrary to officials' views, indigenous land-tenure systems persisted and were complex and diverse.

○ In The Gambia, 25 per cent of girls of school age were found to be overlooked at the village level because they were pregnant, married or about to be married; girls cared deeply and bitterly about the denial of education.
○ In Jamaica, poverty and violence are interconnected in complex ways, including area stigma, which hinders those from a neighbourhood with a reputation for violence from getting jobs; interpersonal violence is far more common than political or drug-related violence.
○ In India, local people understood the ecology of a national park better than conservation-minded professionals; excluding buffaloes in the name of conservation both damaged their livelihoods and led to a decrease in bird life in the park.

The PPAs were similarly revealing: in Ghana, infrastructure was found to be a higher priority for rural people than had been recognized; in Zambia, school fees had to be paid at the worst time of the year, coinciding with high incidence of sickness and hard work, and shortages of money and food; in South Africa, seasonal deprivation, urban as well as rural, was more significant than had been supposed; in Bangladesh, in a subsequent PPA sponsored by UNDP, enforcement of anti-dowry laws was a surprise priority of poor people. These are illustrative examples from reports rich in policy-relevant detail. The evidence is abundant that these approaches and methods, used well, elicit insights into previously hidden realities of the poor.

Whose Voice? deserves to be read, studied and acted upon by all who are concerned with poverty and policy, in whatever context, country or continent. Its lessons transcend the boundaries of professions, disciplines, sectors and departments. It indicates actions open to NGOs, governments and all agencies concerned with deprivation and with development. It shares seminal experiences, rather than set answers. It is for readers to select from these what makes sense for their purposes, and to go further themselves.

Let me hope that this book will encourage and inspire many others to join the pioneers who write here, to explore more of this new territory, and to share their experiences with the same disarming frankness. It may then be that the voices and realities of those who have been last – the poor, powerless, marginalized and excluded – will come to count and to change policy both in principle and in practice.

1

General Introduction

Whose voice?

The concept of 'participation' in development has become widespread. Notably, the Participatory Rural Appraisal (PRA) approach aims to create the conditions for local analysis of existing realities and local ownership of subsequent courses of action to change those realities. PRA aims to empower communities.

This book is based on the premise that relevant and sustainable policy-making requires local voices to be heard. Local perceptions and priorities must be listened to and addressed, and participation by 'beneficiaries' ensured early and meaningfully in decisionmaking at policy, programme and project levels. Sustainability in policy-making demands that those in power disempower themselves.

The question 'Whose reality counts?' has been posed and debated elsewhere (see Chambers, 1997) This book considers more specifically the participatory processes by which local voices are projected to policy-makers and local realities reflected in policy decisions. Underpinning these processes are highly distinctive philosophical and methodological conventions. Participatory approaches to policy analysis are open-ended, interactive, largely qualitative and interpretive, and seek diversity. They are promoted most notably for their post-positivist *qualitative explanatory power* in providing 'depth, richness and realism of information and analysis' (Chambers, 1994: 14). Participatory approaches provide space for local people to establish their own analytical framework and thus challenge 'development from above' (Mukherjee, 1995: 27).

What additional policy insights can such studies offer when compared with a 'conventional' empiricist approach rooted in the questionnaire survey? Most notably, conventional policy-focused research has been criticized for failing to assimilate local realities. As the Ghanaian proverb has it, 'The one who rides the donkey does not know the ground is hot'. This failure is manifested in several ways:

○ The priorities of policy makers may bear no resemblance to those of beneficiaries. Participatory research challenges preconceptions, 'help(ing) policy makers to move away from normative or stylized ways of thinking' (see Schoonmaker Freudenberger, Chapter 8).
○ Indicators of the success of policy intervention may be very different from those emphasized by local 'beneficiaries'. Just as priorities for intervention can be externally conceived and imposed on beneficiaries, so too can the criteria by which the success of interventions is judged.

Moreover, such criteria are restricted by the prevailing demands for quantifiable and 'objective' indicators of success.

o Participatory research can force policy instruments to become more sensitive by presenting disaggregated analysis within and between stakeholder groups. Communities are heterogeneous, characterized by differences of interest and inequalities of power; participatory research disaggregates and analyses difference (Welbourn, 1991). Differences of perception inevitably emerge between stakeholder groups. Triangulation of stakeholder opinion should ensure that these differences are considered.

o Explanations for the degree of success or failure of interventions cannot readily be elicited through conventional impact-assessment techniques. Participatory methods used flexibly, iteratively and sequentially allow for different groups within a community to articulate complex and non-quantifiable cause-and-effect processes. Preconceptions of the 'enabling conditions' for economic and social well-being are challenged by local interpretations of emerging constraints. Policy debates become grounded in local realities and local interpretations rather than in some 'objective reality' constructed from within the positivist research tradition.

What emerges is that participatory research has a potential and a role that goes beyond augmenting and complementing conventional research. It is able to explain (local perceptions of) the causes of trends that are described by official statistics. In doing so, participatory research can unearth surprises, information that is often counterintuitive.

For the same reason, the adoption of participatory approaches to policy formulation requires a shift in thinking, a change of attitude – a challenge that applies as much to the participatory theologians as to the positivist purists. This book looks closely at the steps that can be taken to strengthen the rigour of the participatory research process, while examining the means by which participatory research can relate methodologically to a conventional research paradigm.

How can local voices be amplified?

If we are to accept that local voices should be heard within the policy process, and we acknowledge that participatory research is able to make space for local voices to be heard, what are the issues that need to be addressed in order to project those voices effectively? This book addresses many key issues, some of which will need further exploration and elaboration.

'Scaling-up' local complex, cross-sectoral realities to simplified, sectoral policy frameworks is difficult. As a result, there is often a role for an intermediary institution to 'translate' local voices for the benefit of the policymaker, and the book examines this process in some detail. It emerges that researchers and intermediary institutions are empowered by the process. Rather than acting as technical components of a rational planning tradition, they are given 'agency'. In other words they are

2

politicized and play a transformative 'strategic-activist' role – 'kicking down doors and lighting fires'. Indeed, it is often not the report but the person who is the more important resource. Acknowledging this agency underlines the need for those representing local voices and advocating policy change to be critical, rigorous, hard-headed and realistic.

A problem with this scenario is that the process of analysis and abstraction tends to marginalize communities on the one hand and fail to engage the policymakers on the other. An alternative strategy becomes apparent through some of the case studies, one of bringing policymakers and local people together directly. This approach also faces problems raised by the behaviour and attitudes of the various stakeholders, including policymakers themselves. A gulf in context and language often exists between the two constituencies, reinforcing self-perpetuating attitudes. The book addresses ways and means of bridging that gulf.

In a third scenario, the activist role can overlap with a less confrontational but equally influential strategic approach to advocacy. This requires the patient building up of personal contacts, the recognition that some doors will open and others will not. Rather than 'representing the people', the intermediary acts strategically to ensure that participation itself becomes part of the policy framework.

Participation for policy analysis or policy analysis for participation?

The case studies presented in this book share the common distinction of the adoption of PRA methods for policy-focused research. Any discussion of participation in the context of policy-focused research unearths, however, a seeming contradiction between the requirements of policy research and those of a PRA-based exercise. 'Rapid appraisal' approaches using PRA methods can be a most effective mechanism for sensitizing policymakers to the needs, capacities and perspectives of the poor, yet although participatory research often provides a sounding-board for local people's voices to be heard, the tailoring of PRA methods to extract information to inform policy does not necessarily have a built-in component to ensure a local process of ownership and empowerment.

In contrast to the product-emphasis of policy-based participatory research, the central plank of PRA is the participatory process itself. The gulf between the open-agenda ethos of PRA and a focused (pre-defined) agenda often set by policy-led research underlines this distinction still further. The tension is ultimately between process and product in participatory research.

Given this tension, the book asks whether empowerment and policy analysis are mutually exclusive. If so, should PRA link solely to community empowerment or only to policy outcomes? One emerging answer is that it is more constructive to interpret this tension not in dualistic terms but in terms of a sliding-scale. Approaches such as rapid rural appraisal (RRA) and PRA can be placed on a spectrum, from product ('participation as an end') to process ('participation as a means'). The adoption of participatory methods for extractive ends implies a shift along this spectrum from process to product that forces the PRA community to re-examine the values underlying participatory approaches to development. Participation becomes a means rather than an end. Participatory tools are put to use to enlighten policy rather than necessarily to empower local people. The commonality that does exist between the case studies that follow is expressed throughout the book by reference to 'participatory research', meaning a mode of research that can fall anywhere on the spectrum identified above.

Definitional issues

A handful of terms have now become part of the jargon of the people engaged in trying to conceptualize and implement a more participatory form of development. Here we try to clarify our own understanding of some of the book's most common terms, or sets of terms: PRA and related methodologies; methodologies and approaches; and methods, tools and techniques.

PRA (participatory rural appraisal), and related methodologies

PRA has been described as a family of approaches, methods and behaviours to enable poor people to express and analyse the realities of their lives and conditions, and themselves to plan, monitor and evaluate their actions (Chambers, 1992). Much has been written on the various disciplinary and methodological streams which have contributed to PRA (Chambers 1992, 1994b).

In PRA, outsiders (researchers and/or practitioners who are not members of the community or group with whom they interact) act as catalysts for local people to decide what to do with the information and analysis they generate. Outsiders may also choose to analyse further the findings generated by PRAs, as is demonstrated through the course of this book. In either case, there should be a commitment on the part of the facilitating organizations to do their best to support or follow up on those actions that local people have chosen as a result of PRA, if local people feel that such support is needed. The question of what constitutes good, or ethical, PRA practice, and how abuse can be tackled, is explored in more detail in Blackburn with Holland (1997), as well as in Chapter 25 of this book.

PRA is only one of some 29 participatory approaches, or methodologies, which have been developed since the 1970s (Cornwall *et al.*, 1994). The number is growing. PRA has at its core a conviction

(1) that local people have the knowledge and ability to be the subjects of their own development, and
(2) that those who facilitate PRAs must pay particular attention to the way they behave when interacting with local people.

PRA is not in itself a methodology for community organizing or institution-building, although it can be used for these longer-term goals as well.

General Introduction

Methodologies and approaches vs methods, tools and techniques

In this volume, the terms 'methodology' and 'approach' will be used inter-changeably. Both refer to a particular school or current of research. Meth-odologies can be grouped according to their philosophical underpinnings. For example, PRA and PAR (participatory action research) share the same epistemological and ethical roots, even though their longer-term goals may differ. PAR sees itself as part of a broader movement of helping to shape popular movements pressing for social and political change; PRA is more concerned with the intricacies of recognizing the complex knowl-edge systems and rationales of local people, and providing them with the tools to design and evaluate their own specific projects. On the other hand, the philosophical basis of PRA and PAR can collectively be distinguished from methodologies allied to the positivist tradition of much prevailing empirical research, within which hypotheses about the nature of social relations can be empirically and objectively verified. These distinctions and their implications are discussed in greater depth in Chapter 23 of this book.

Methodology and approach are to be distinguished from *method*, which is a specific tool or technique. A method is not necessarily restricted to any one methodology. Mapping is, for instance, a particular method (or tool or technique) which is used in methodologies as diverse as PRA, PAR, agro-ecosystems analysis, farming systems research, RAP (rapid assessment techniques) and popular education.

Structure of the book

The contributors to this book attended a workshop on participatory research and policy convened at the Institute of Development Studies, University of Sussex on 13 and 14 May, 1996. They are from a range of backgrounds, including CBOs, NGOs, academia, consultancy groups, gov-ernment, and bilateral and multilateral institutions. Their contributions come in two forms: directly as chapters which were presented as papers at the workshop and indirectly through contributions to discussion groups that were held during the course of the two days. The views expressed are those of the authors and do not necessarily reflect those of the organiza-tions to which they are affiliated.

The book is divided into three parts. Each begins with a short introduc-tion presenting summary points of each of the relevant chapters; more detailed summaries are provided at the beginning of each chapter.

Part 1 explores thematic or sectoral case studies in which participatory methods, and in some instances participatory approaches, have been used to influence policy. The case studies – from Nepal, Zambia, The Gambia, Jamaica, Pakistan, India, Madagascar, Guinea and Scotland – are pre-sented on a crude sliding-scale of objectives, with policy output at one end and participation at the other.

Part 2 concentrates on PPA. This is an innovative approach, largely introduced to the World Bank through the external initiatives of bilateral donors, designed to bring local poverty and policy analysis into the policy process through the cross-sectoral lens of poverty. Discussions on PPA experiences in Ghana, Zambia, Mozambique and South Africa are presented, as well as more general reflections on the achievements and potential of PPA as a participatory policy-oriented research instrument.

Part 3 discusses key issues arising during the IDS workshop, and includes chapters by several participants. The issues arising include: the channels through which local voices are projected to policymakers; the role of advocacy in the policy process; the nature of the research process itself and its relationship with policy; the role of analysis in policy-focused research; and participation, policy change and empowerment.

PART 1

THEMATIC AND SECTORAL STUDIES

2

Introduction

The chapters in Part 1 discuss case studies of participatory policy-focused research, taking as their entry-point thematic or sectoral concerns. The case studies can be loosely disaggregated into two collections: in the first, the emphasis of the authors remains largely on policy output or 'product', in other words on information gathering; in the second, a concern with the participatory process itself outweighs to a greater or lesser extent the emphasis on research product.

Within this somewhat crude disaggregation, the first group of case studies underlines the extractive and analytical power of participatory research, with discussion highlighting its comparative advantage over more conventional approaches. These studies are also characterized by methodological pragmatism, pluralism and strategic thinking, driven by the imperative of improving both the quality of research product and increasing policy influence.

Chapter 3 demonstrates the way in which PRA methods can collect information: by triangulating data from other sources and by collecting data that have not or could not be collected using more conventional methodologies. Through detailed presentation of a research process and its results, Gill conveys how participatory methods can fill gaps in knowledge and provide rigorous and policy-relevant information. The use of PRA techniques by the Tarai Research Network in Nepal enabled research teams to establish trends in cropping intensity and causal explanations for these trends, information previously unavailable through official statistics.

As well as eliciting new information, the use of PRA methods unearthed counterintuitive or 'surprise' results. In some areas of the Tarai agroecological zone, for example, reforestation, rather than deforestation, is occurring as farmers become aware of the value of certain trees. Chapter 4 is also a clear recommendation of the comparative advantage of participatory research as an information-gathering exercise. Booth reflects on the use of 'interactive fieldwork' within a sectoral policy evaluation of the local impacts of user-fee introduction in basic social services in Zambia. As in Chapter 3, the research methodology adopted was sufficiently flexible and intensive to fill information gaps, with resulting policy recommendations addressing the quality and accessibility of health and education services.

Chapters 5 and 6 show how the entry-point of a sector or theme for analysis by local people provides a context-specific understanding of the causes and potential solutions to local problems. Kane, Bruce and O'Reilly de Brun (Chapter 5) demonstrate how a participatory research process was able to articulate the contextual barriers to girls' education in The Gambia, information which influenced significant revisions in Ministry of Education policy. Moser and Holland (Chapter 6) show how, through the entry-point of poverty and violence, a participatory study was able to facilitate local analysis of the factors that produce and reproduce violence. The subsequent design of the Jamaican government's Social Investment Fund reflected the analysis and concerns of local people.

The second group of case studies in Part 1 describes participatory research processes that are not designed simply or primarily to fill gaps in policy-relevant knowledge. While the comparative advantage of the participatory research tradition as an information-gathering mechanism continues to be stressed, there is an additional emphasis on using process to create new space for dialogue and negotiation. The shift of balance is away from product-driven participatory exercises whose objective is to influence policy towards exercises in which the process becomes as important and perhaps more important than the product.

By increasing the focus of attention on the research process itself, the authors widen and to some extent diffuse the debate as to the potential influence of a participatory approach. The distinction may be subtle but it is clear. Gujja, Pimbert and Shah's discussion (Chapter 7) centres on the role of participatory research in resolving wetland-management policy conflict. It is not the information gathered itself which provides the key to resolving conflict, but the inclusive nature of the research process. Based on case studies of community-wetland interactions in Punjab, Pakistan and Rajastan, India, they broaden the criteria for assessing the success of policy-focused participatory research to include the nature and extent of changes in attitudes and policy at higher levels.

Similarly, Schoonmaker Freudenberger (Chapter 8) shifts emphasis away from the search for pre-packaged solutions and recommendations, regardless of whether or not they come with a participatory stamp of quality and ethical acceptability. She reflects on the relative success of two distinct approaches to research aimed at influencing national land and resource policy in Madagascar and Guinea. Describing the process of using RRA for information gathering about local attitudes towards land and tenure, she argues that the more successful approach adopted was to integrate policymakers into the research process rather than trying to 'sell' them a packaged policy recommendation product.

Whether the research process ends up influencing policy is open to multiple interpretations, and cause and effect become harder to delineate as the research becomes decreasingly driven by the need for policy-tailored product. The prioritization of process over product is most evident, and the relationship between research process and policy outcomes most oblique, in the final case study in Part 1. Reflecting on PRAs conducted with a Scottish Highland village over community perceptions of local forestry ownership and management, Guy and Inglis (Chapter 9) challenge the linear causality often ascribed to policy-based research and its influence. They argue instead that PRA is part of a 'fuzzy' organic process of change in which cause and effect cannot easily be identified.

3

Using PRA for Agricultural Policy Analysis in Nepal: the Tarai Research Network Foodgrain Study

GERARD J. GILL

The Tarai Research Network (TRN) was set up in Nepal under the Ministry of Agriculture to address the problem of poor-quality official statistics and to provide accurate and up-to-date information for policymaking. Chapter 3 discusses one example of the TRN's work – the Foodgrain Study – showing how participatory tools were combined with more conventional survey techniques in order to elicit context-sensitive quantitative information. In presenting the results of the study, Chapter 3 shows how participatory research tools can be used to improve policy input in three ways: (i) participatory research results can be used to triangulate or cross-check the results of other empirical research and secondary-data sources; (ii) they can plug gaps in existing data resources, in this instance by establishing trends in cropping intensity; and (iii) participatory methods are better able to explore the causes of known or revealed trends, through eliciting farmers' own analyses and interpretation of events. While such an approach is acknowledged to be considerably less participatory than the process-based emphasis of PRA, Chapter 3 argues that eliciting analysis and extracting information at the local level are justifiable activities if they lead to locally beneficial policy outputs. By the same token, PRA-derived data should not be discounted on empirical grounds. Although more needs to be done to tackle issues of representativeness in such studies and formalize the analytical process, policymakers should take care to ensure that the best does not become the enemy of the good.

The Tarai Research Network (TRN)

Good policy analysis has a voracious appetite for sharply-focused, accurate, relevant and timely information. In Nepal, as elsewhere in the developing world, there are sometimes serious problems in trying to use official statistics to satisfy this need. These include inaccuracies, inconsistencies, data gaps and non-coverage of important variables. These drawbacks are compounded by data-collection and publication delays, which severely restrict the data's usefulness in a situation where immediate and pressing policy decisions must be made.

The TRN was established under the Ministry of Agriculture's Policy Analysis in Agriculture and Related Resource Management programme as a means of addressing these problems. Its aim was to provide a source of accurate and up-to-date information tailor-made to particular areas of

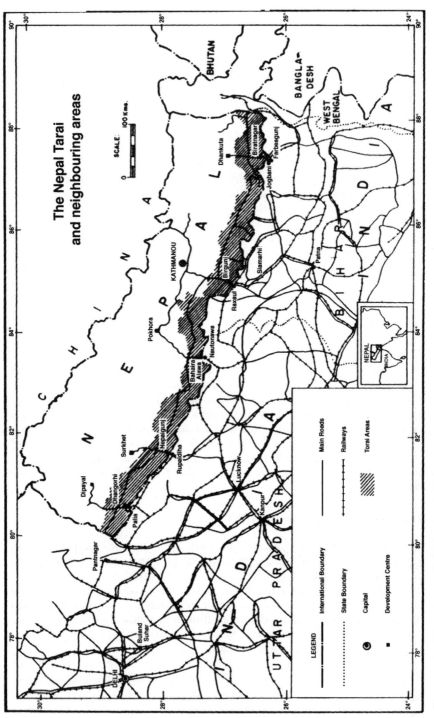

Figure 1.1 *The Nepal Tarai and neighbouring areas*

policy concern. As its name suggests, the TRN does not cover the entire country. There are three major agro-ecological zones in Nepal: the mountains, hills and the Tarai. The Tarai zone forms part of the northern flood plain of the River Ganges (Figure 1.1). It occupies 23 per cent of the country's surface area but has 47 per cent of the population, 53 per cent of cultivated area, 68 per cent of irrigated area, and 60 per cent of foodgrain production. It is the only food-surplus part of the country, so that its importance from a policy viewpoint is crucial.[1]

Members of the TRN were recruited from among professionals already living and working in the Tarai. They come from a wide range of backgrounds, including social science, extension services and agricultural science. They work for a range of institutions, from university campuses to extension and research organizations, and are based at various locations across the width of the Tarai belt. The number of members has varied: at the time of writing there are fifteen. They are engaged for policy analysis as and when required.

This chapter examines the largest study conducted by the TRN to date, an investigation into long-term trends in foodgrain productivity in Tarai districts. Official statistics and other secondary sources were used to establish trends, while PRA assessment with farmers aimed to establish the underlying causes. The findings of this study illustrate how PRA can be used in policy analysis, and provide examples of the type of insights that were obtained using this approach.

Why use PRA methods?

It is recognized that the approach used by the TRN is significantly less participatory than would be the case if the group were, say, an NGO about to launch a village- or area-development project. Given the nature of the exercise this is probably unavoidable. Network members are nevertheless encouraged by precept and example to feel and display attitudes of respect and understanding towards villagers, to be aware of 'who holds the stick'. The need for transparency in terms of what benefits the villagers can, and cannot, expect is constantly stressed.

It has to be accepted, however, that the type of exercise the TRN is involved in is basically extractive, in that villagers who provided the information can expect no direct benefit in return. At the same time, the underlying motive behind the exercise is to provide accurate and timely information to policymakers, and if this later feeds into better practice, some indirect benefit should ultimately accrue to the villagers who provided the information. The approach may be extractive, but it is not exploitative.

In view of the well-established problems of using questionnaire-based surveys with rural people, it was decided from the outset that the group would use the PRA approach when information was to be sought. The tools that typify PRA research have not, however, been regarded as sacrosanct, and other methods, including the questionnaire survey, have been used when appropriate.[2]

Initial guidance and training were provided by a team led by Jimmy Mascarenhas, then of MYRADA. The aim was to change members' attitudes before teaching them about tools and techniques. Network members were

---

Box 1.1   PRA methods and their application by TRN during the Foodgrain Study

Time lines. These were used to identify basic dates in the establishment and development of the village in question. The individual years in which significant events occurred (e.g. the establishment of a school) were later used as reference years to identify changes in agriculture such as evolving land-use patterns.

The 'Rupee-*Paisa*' system. Questions were put in the following form: 'Imagine the total area under villagers' jurisdiction in year x was like one rupee. How many *paisa* are under cultivation, forest, fallow, etc.'. The money analogy was used in conjunction with time lines and other tools, as indicated below.

Seasonality diagramming. This was used to establish seasonal rainfall patterns and relate cropping calendars to them. As usual, the seasonal calendar began by plotting the monthly rainfall pattern; the various cropping systems practised in the village were then added in the form of a set of cropping calendars. In some of the discussions other seasonal variables (such as food availability, fertilizer requirements, labour loads, source of irrigation water) emerged as very important from the farmers' perspective and where this was the case seasonal diagrams for these were also added. A good deal of information, including multiple-cropping indices, was derived from such diagrams and the associated discussions.

Trend lines. Since trends were of such central importance to the Foodgrains Study, trend analysis was used extensively. Figures for particular years were tied to the time line for the variables covered. In the case of land use, for example, the rupee-*paisa* system was used to estimate percentages under the different land-use categories at each point on the time line. Actual values were used for other variables, such as yields.

Semi-structured interviews. These were used to discuss the points emerging from the above diagramming exercises. In training sessions it was stressed that these diagrams are not outputs in themselves. Rather they are meant to serve as objects around which a meaningful discussion can be conducted.

---

educated first and foremost in the philosophy and processes of the participatory approach, then trained in the techniques of PRA. More specific training is provided whenever a new enquiry is launched.

For the Foodgrain Study, the process of devising the most appropriate methodology began with a dialogue among programme staff and others with considerable field experience of the participatory approach and/or substantial knowledge of the issues to be addressed. The methodology was further refined and then finalized in the course of field exercises in the Tarai. These involved discussions with local farmers and members of the network.

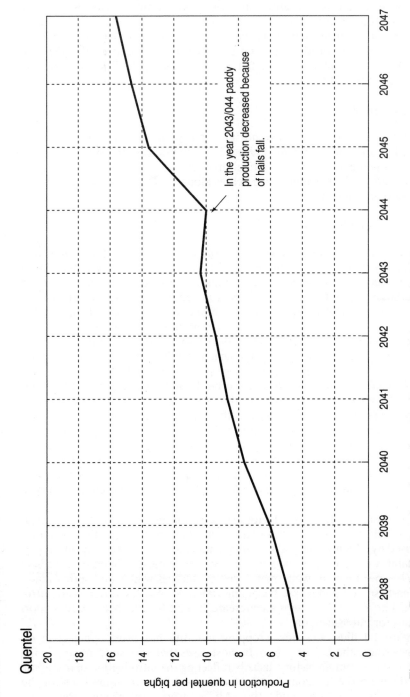

Figure 1.2 *Production trend analysis of paddy, Teghari Village, Kailali District*

The basic research tools were a set of participatory diagrams developed in the course of interactive group interviews with farmers (Box 1.1). These methods were used in sequence to explore causality. In a village in Kailali District, for instance, changes in the yield of paddy were tied to the village time line so as to produce a trend line. Discussion based on this diagram provided the explanation of the fall in production in (1987/88), namely hail storms (Figure 1.2).[3]

Summary results

The findings of the study of trends in Tarai foodgrain productivity are described in some detail in Gill (1996). The main points of the study regarding the two main components of agricultural productivity, namely cropping intensity and yield, are summarized below, along with the farmers' perceptions of underlying causes.

Trends in cropping intensity

Official statistics contain information on foodgrain area, production and yield, but not on cropping intensity.[4] This is obviously a vital component of land productivity, and estimation of changes in this variable was a major aim of the study. The information farmers provided through PRA methods made it possible to calculate trends in the multiple cropping index (MCI) in the various villages under differing production conditions. It transpired that cropping intensity has been rising for decades in most areas. Pushing farmers into higher-intensity cropping, as indicated by the land-use studies, is their knowledge that the land frontier is gradually closing in the Tarai. Forest areas suited to cultivation continue to be deforested and converted to agriculture. Further production growth therefore requires increasingly intensive use of the land. Figure 1.3 shows that the MCI tends to remain at around 100 per cent until all the available area belonging to the village in question is under agriculture, after which the index rises sharply. The picture is not, however, simply one of wholesale forest destruction, as many people believe. In a number of villages the study also uncovered the fact that some reforestation is now taking place, as farmers realize the economic potential of certain tree crops.

The most important 'pull' factor exerted on farmers is undoubtedly irrigation, which as it spreads throughout the zone has eased the constraints imposed by a highly seasonal rainfall regime. Another factor is the increasing availability of new crops and varieties. By far the most significant new cereal crop has been wheat, while new varieties, such as winter and spring maize and early season paddy, are becoming available. As new varieties are introduced into farming systems they create flexibility, and hence new opportunities for intensification.

Figure 1.4 illustrates how cropping intensity has been changing in six villages where there is irrigation. In most cases there is a sudden jump in the MCI at some point in history, usually reflecting the introduction of irrigation. The dates on the horizontal axis were derived from the time lines for the villages in question and the MCIs were calculated from the

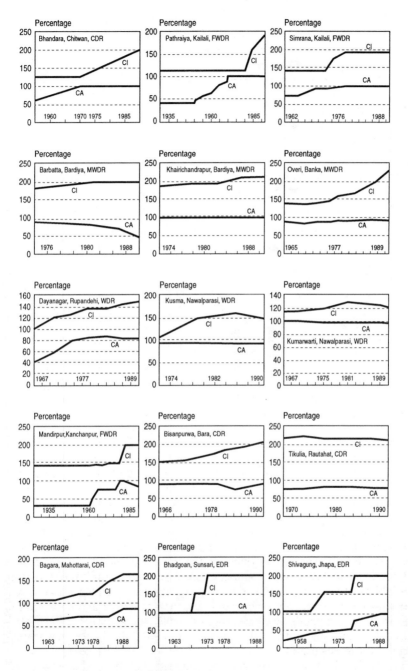

Note: The vertical axis measures multiple cropping index for CI and percentage of available area for CA.

Figure 1.3   *Trends in cropped areas (CA) and cropping intensity (CI) in Tarai villages (irrigated agriculture)*

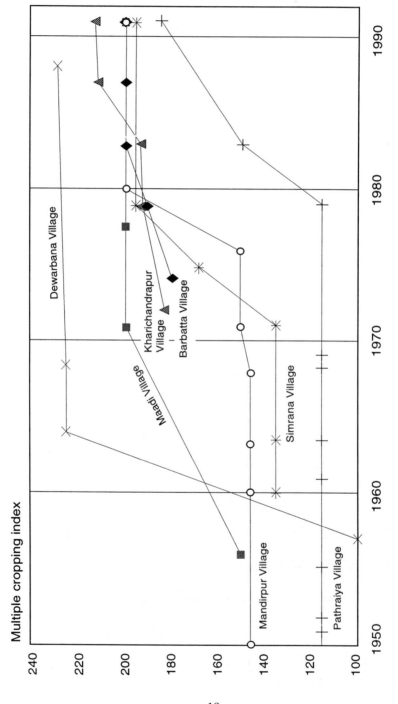

Figure 1.4 *Trends in cropping intensities (irrigated agriculture) in Tarai villages, 1950–92*

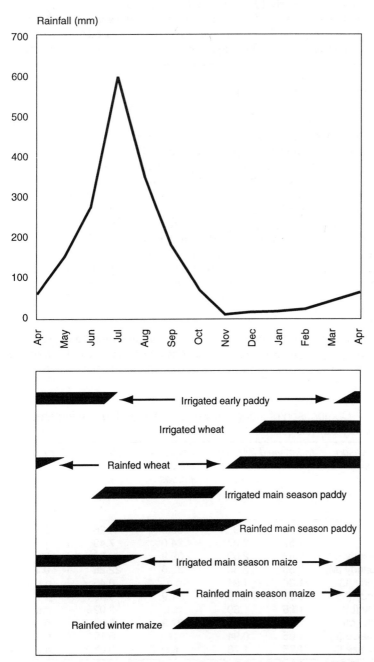

Sources: Rainfall: Ministry of Water Resources Data; Cropping calendar informant: M.B. Thapa.

Figure 1.5 *Monthly rainfall pattern in relation to foodgrain-cropping calendar, Chitwan District*

crop calendars. By the early 1990s the MCI averaged 171 per cent in villages with only rainfed agriculture. This is quite an impressive achievement, and it is difficult to see how such an average could be increased much further without better water control. The equivalent figure for villages with irrigation is 197 per cent, which is actually quite low, indicating inefficient water management (a condition widely reported by the farmers in areas with agency-managed irrigation systems).

Figure 1.5 provides an example of a cropping calendar, together with monthly rainfall distribution for one Tarai district, Chitwan. The connection between the two parts of the diagram can be seen on examination. For example, irrigated main-season paddy can be established (and therefore harvested) earlier than its rainfed counterpart, because it is not tied to early monsoon showers, which can be unreliable. Similarly, rainfed wheat has to be established immediately after the rainy season to take advantage of residual moisture, whereas irrigated wheat can go in later. The turnaround time between rainfed main-season paddy and rainfed wheat is very tight, and it is usually not possible to grow both on the same plot of land. Irrigation eases this constraint and thus makes increased cropping intensity possible. The availability of modern, short-duration wheat varieties has contributed to this process by making it easier to fit wheat into cropping patterns.

Yield trends

For a given variety and season, yields under irrigation would be expected to be significantly higher than under rainfed conditions, and the data from the PRA survey (Table 1.1) confirm this expectation in most cases. The

Table 1.1: Comparison of foodgrain yields under rainfed and irrigated conditions in Tarai villages

Crop and season (local/modern)[a]	Mean yield (MT/ha)		Irrigation effect (% increase)	Analysis of variance	
	Rainfed	Irrigated		F value	Significance (%)
Wheat (L)	0.64	1.03	60.9	4.26	5
Wheat (M)	1.67	2.07	24.0	7.49	1
Summer paddy (L)	1.43	2.00	39.9	4.66	5
Summer paddy (M)	2.53	3.38	33.6	22.26	0.1
Spring paddy (L)	1.80	1.91	n.a.	0.45	n.s.
Spring paddy (M)	2.10	3.19	51.9	9.49	1
Early paddy (L)	1.86	1.89	n.a.	0.02	n.s.
Early paddy (M)	2.72	3.48	27.9	6.03	5
Summer maize (L)	1.05	0.94	n.a.	0.19	n.s.
Summer maize (M)	1.75	1.78	n.a.	0.01	n.s.

Notes: Comparisons have not been made for other foodgrains/seasons because there are too few observations to produce meaningful results; [a]L = local variety; M = modern variety; n.s. = not significant at the 5% level; n.a. = not applicable (because yield difference is not statistically significant).

Table 1.2: Comparison of yields of local and modern foodgrain varieties in Tarai villages

Crop and season	Mean yield (MT/ha)		Modern-variety effect (% increase)	Analysis of variance	
	Local varieties	Modern varieties		F value	Significance (%)
Wheat	1.03	2.07	101.0	19.92	0.1
Summer paddy	2.00	3.38	69.0	76.71	0.1
Spring paddy	1.91	3.19	67.0	65.95	0.1
Early paddy	1.89	3.48	84.1	68.98	0.1
Summer maize	0.94	1.78	89.4	25.57	0.1

Note: Yield comparisons have not been made for other foodgrains/seasons because there are too few observations to produce meaningful results.

introduction of modern varieties would also be expected to increase yields for a given crop and season. The statistical analysis confirms this view, indicating that the contribution of varietal change is even greater than that of irrigation (Table 1.2).

Comparison of the yield figures in this table with those based on official estimates indicates that the two sets are mutually consistent. The main difference is that, unlike the official statistics, the figures from the PRA study partition the crop by season, type (local/modern) and production environment (irrigated/rainfed), and therefore provide a basis for further insights into trends and their underlying causes.

With modern varieties increasingly tending to replace local ones, and irrigation replacing rainfed agriculture, both of these trends have strongly beneficial effects on yields. The analysis of yield trends within crops and varieties produces, however, a very different picture, and one with worrying long-term implications.

In a situation where varieties with higher-yield potential are replacing those with lower potential, one would expect a situation similar to that found in Kusma Village, Nawalparasi District, depicted in the top left-hand segment of Figure 1.6. Here, yields more than doubled when the switch was initially made, and continued to grow until by the early 1990s they had virtually doubled again. However, there were many more villages where the pattern resembles those in the other five segments of Figure 1.6.[5] That is, when the switch is made initially yields are boosted, and in some cases continue to grow for some time, but in most cases a decline sets in, either immediately or after a time lag, until the modern variety often yields less than it did at the beginning, and in some cases even less than the local variety did at the time the substitution was made originally.

Table 1.3 quantifies yield trends where these are statistically significant. (In all other cases there is no significant trend.) The table also indicates average yields in each decade since the 1950s or 1960s. Clearly these figures are not encouraging, especially in the case of rainfed agriculture, where every foodgrain shows either zero growth or a negative growth rate. In each of the cases shown, average yields have been dropping consistently

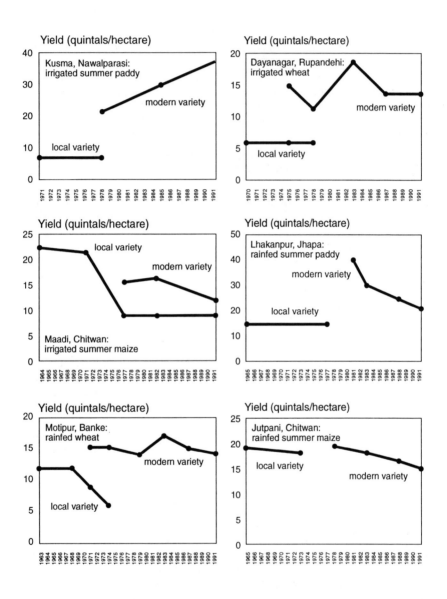

Figure 1.6   *Yield effects of switching from local to modern varieties in Tarai villages*

Table 1.3: Trends in foodgrain yields in Tarai villages

Crop/season (local/modern)[a]	Average yield in decade (MT/ha)					Trend statistics	
	1950s	1960s	1970s	1980s	1990s	r^2	Annual growth rate[b] (%)
1. Rainfed agriculture							
Summer paddy (L)	2.16	1.88	1.72	1.64	1.47	0.0565	−0.78[0.05]
Wheat (M)	n.d.	2.62	1.91	1.54	1.41	0.0997	−1.91[0.01]
Early paddy (M)	n.d.	3.60	2.63	2.40	2.25	0.7610	−1.63[0.01]
Summer maize (L)	n.d.	2.56	1.45	1.23	0.83	0.2096	−3.72[0.05]
2. Irrigated agriculture							
Early paddy (L)	1.50	1.71	1.81	2.01	2.40	0.1527	+1.36[0.05]
Summer paddy (M)	4.37	3.78	2.98	3.44	3.06	0.0868	−0.85[0.05]

Notes: [a] L = local variety; M = modern variety; [b] growth rates calculated from the logarithmic functions; superscripts in this column indicate level of statistical significance ($p<0.05$ or $p<0.01$); n.d. = no data.

from decade to decade over a period of 30 or 40 years. Even in the case of irrigated agriculture the picture is not all that encouraging.

This finding seems at first to contradict the picture revealed by analysing the official data, namely that yields have been increasing at a modest rate over roughly the same period as that covered in Table 1.3. The apparent contradiction can, however, be resolved by further examination of the PRA data. Yield growth is being maintained by farmers switching to a superior production environment (irrigation) and/or a superior technology (a modern variety), whose effects are mutually reinforcing. Because not all villages, or even all farms in a given village, make the switch at the same time, the result is a succession of upward shifts in production at the micro level which aggregate to produce modestly increasing yields at the macro level. The shift is being made, however, in contexts where productivity is already tapering off or even diminishing, so that any gains are purely temporary. (In diagram-matic terms the macro-level situation is similar to that depicted in the bottom left-hand corner of Figure 1.6).

These upward shifts have been masking the fact that yields in almost all situations are declining; as the potential for making more such shifts is used up, it will become increasingly difficult for Tarai farmers to maintain even the present modest level of growth in yields unless further new technologies are introduced, popularized and properly supported.

Farmers' views on productivity trends

Although there was some degree of differentiation due to local factors, farmers' explanations of foodgrain-productivity trends were broadly consis-tent across the entire Tarai belt. There are four common denominators: soil fertility, water availability, plant genetics and crop husbandry.

Soil fertility

Almost all Tarai farmers noted that the natural fertility of the land is declin-ing and that there is a dearth of organic matter in the soil. In some cases the link with deforestation was specifically mentioned ('the area was recently forested, so the soil is new and fertile'; 'as the forests have been cleared the organic matter content of the soil has also decreased'). The farmers' preferred solution is to add humus in the form of compost and manure, but an indirect result of deforestation is that they cannot get it in sufficient quantity. This is happening because deforestation has reduced the supply of both fuel and fodder, so that fewer animals can be kept and what dung is available must be used for fuel.

Further light was thrown on the linkages between yields and deforestation by villagers in Banke District, who reported that immediately after deforestation yields are fairly low because of the presence of so many tree roots and stumps in the soil, making it difficult to plough and level the land. The gradual clearing of such obstructions and the elimination of low spots (which cause waterlogging) increases yields, at least until such time as the depletion of organic matter begins to take its toll. This may form part of the explanation for the non-linear yield trends found in some parts of the Tarai.

The link between yield trends and chemical fertilizer was widely noted, and one of the most common complaints was that it was often impossible to get sufficient fertilizer on time. On the occasions where yields were said to be increasing, this was usually associated with increased fertilizer use. However, in a number of cases it was reported that it is now necessary to apply increasing amounts just to maintain yields at existing levels, and farmers in one village reported that after using chemical fertilizer for a number of years the land became exhausted and infertile. Interestingly, no-one reported the price of fertilizer as a problem, thus confirming previous findings that fertilizer demand at existing prices remains to be satisfied.

Despite continuing supply difficulties, farmers in some areas did report that fertilizer is becoming rather more widely available and that use is increasing, with farmers in one village in Rupandehi quantifying the change. The situation is, however, basically one of any increases in supply being unable to keep pace with demand growth.

Water availability

Lack of adequate water was mentioned frequently as an explanation for stagnant or declining yield trends, especially in villages with only rainfed agriculture, but also in irrigated areas. In one village it was specifically mentioned that yields of modern varieties were stagnating under both rainfed and irrigated conditions, although at different levels. In a number of irrigated areas problems were reported with the quantity of water made available and its timely distribution to the fields.

The most serious water problem is drought, which was repeatedly mentioned as a cause of falling yields. There were often severe droughts in the years immediately preceding the survey, and this may have affected farmers' perceptions because the problem loomed large in their minds. It is also quite possible, however, that decreasing rainfall is in fact a longer-term trend, as trees do induce rainfall, and deforestation can therefore reduce precipitation. A related problem is the hot westerly winds, which farmers in some districts report as an increasing nuisance. These affect particularly the wheat crop, causing it to dry out and shatter, leading to yield loss. This, too, could be a direct consequence of deforestation.

Plant genetics

It was widely reported that yields of local varieties of all three major foodgrains are stagnant or declining. This is especially true under rainfed conditions, but there were reports of this even with irrigation. Yields of older modern varieties (which form the majority, especially in the case of paddy) are also deteriorating, as they degenerate and become susceptible to disease. Shortage of modern-variety seeds was also recognized by the farmers as a problem and frequently reported as such. This is, however, not so much the case in the far-western Tarai because of availability of supplies from India. In other parts of the zone, rust was reported as an increasingly serious problem with the wheat crop, as varietal resistance to this disease breaks down.

Crop husbandry

A factor mentioned increasingly as one travels westward in the Tarai is that paddy yields have increased in number with the shift from direct seeding to transplanting. Frequently the changeover to transplanting accompanies a shift from local- to modern-paddy varieties, and farmers recognized that both changes have a positive impact on yields. A similar situation occurs in some areas with maize. This is a crop which was previously sown broadcast in many villages, with no secondary cultivation. Improved management is now underway in some places through the introduction of post-emergence practices such as weeding and 'earthing up'.

In many villages it was reported that both population growth and falling average farm size have increased both labour availability and the need for more food, so that the process has been accompanied by intensified farming and higher yields. Technological shifts such as the introduction of transplanting and secondary cultivation reflect increasing labour availability and growing food requirements. In other villages, however, the other side of this particular coin was highlighted, with falling yields being attributed partly to a decline in cultivation standards, which in turn reflect falling labour supply.

Other factors

Increasing losses to insect pests and birds were fairly widely reported, but not as often as one might expect, perhaps because there is no very obvious trend. In the area around the Royal Chitwan National Park, in both Chitwan and Nawalparasi districts, farmers reported losses to wild animals, particularly rhinoceros grazing on crops like wheat (and, of all things, chili peppers!). This highlights an important policy issue, the need to reconcile the interests of wildlife conservation with those of local farming communities.

Given the fact that yields of local varieties are either falling or stagnant, some people may find it surprising that they continue to be produced. Part of the explanation is the scarcity of high-quality modern varieties to replace them. There are other reasons also, however, particularly tastes and preferences: many farmers reported that they grow modern varieties for sale and local varieties for home consumption. Another reason given for the continued use of local varieties is that they are more drought resistant than most modern varieties, and farmers in a number of villages have reported that they are particularly attracted towards modern varieties that are both short season and drought resistant.

Conclusions

The information that emerged from the PRA exercise looks very useful from a policy perspective. This is particularly so because so much triangulation is automatically embedded in a study of this type, which uses both PRA information and secondary sources to examine different aspects of the same set of issues. For example, the yield figures and trends as reported by farmers can be checked against the official statistics. When this was done the two sets of figures were found to be highly consistent. Similarly, the findings from the PRA that for a given variety in a given production environment the general picture is one of zero-yield growth, or even yield decline, were checked against results of long-term response trials on experiment stations in the Tarai (and in other parts of the Gangetic Plain); again the two sets of findings were mutually consistent.

The information on trends in foodgrain-cropping intensities is new, and fills an important gap in our knowledge of the subject. What has been learned about the sourcing of new varieties in India carries important implications for the national agricultural research and extension system. The farmers' point about the inadequacy and unreliability of fertilizer supplies confirms existing views and points to knowledge gaps that should be filled by further research. This finding in fact helped set the agenda for future work by the TRN, research that has since been carried out.

Probably the most exciting insight to emerge from the PRA exercise is the way that it became possible to reconcile the apparently mutually contradictory perceptions of slowly increasing aggregate foodgrain yields in a situation where yields of particular varieties in particular production environments all seem to be stagnant or declining.

Some important questions clearly remain to be answered after a study of this nature. Village-sample selection was to a large extent governed by logistics; as more resources become available more could be done to ensure that the sample of villages could not be challenged on the grounds of non-representativeness. Another crucial issue concerns data analysis. The standard PRA approach of analysing information in iterative steps together with the people who provided it is not possible in a situation where the study covers a zone 800km in length and 34000km² in area. A major difficulty was that of finding an efficient means of handling the mass of information that emerged from the study in a situation where there are few paradigms and no models. In this case computer graphics were used extensively. These produced some useful insights, as did the application of standard statistical tests to the data. It is not entirely clear, however, how valid it is to use such tests on this type of information. More has to be done in formalizing the analytical side of the work, and it is important that statisticians and others be involved in the discussions.

Having said all this, it is important also to take care that the best does not become the enemy of the good. Policy decisions have to be made, whether there are data or not. Even deciding to do nothing is to decide. If the information obtained in this type of exercise is sometimes rather rough-and-ready, it is better for decisionmakers to have such a broad-brushstroke picture of what is happening than to have no picture at all.

4

Coping with Cost Recovery in Zambia:
a sectoral policy study

DAVID BOOTH

Chapter 4 summarizes the results of the Zambia cost-recovery study, which looked at the local impacts of the introduction of user fees in basic social services. The study formed part of a series of exercises examining the potential for 'interactive fieldwork' to influence 'macro-policy' issues by illuminating their 'micro' implications. The research revealed a large gap between policy-in-principle and policy-in-practice and proposed policy change addressing the future quality and accessibility of health and education services. As a sectoral study with a distinctive origin and some special concerns, the Zambia case study illustrates especially well certain themes that ought to be considered if the potential of such interactive fieldwork is to be realized. These include: the relative emphasis within PRA between principles and techniques; the importance of learning from other traditions through triangulation; the need to build analytical capacity for policy studies; the extent to which policy-oriented appraisal can be genuinely participatory; and the importance of the institutionalization of participatory assessment.

Background

How do poor people respond to and contend with the introduction of user charges in primary health-care facilities, or with a sharp increase in fees down to the base of the school system? How might Zambia's policies be reshaped so as to reduce the human costs of the 'community co-financing' principles being applied in these two sectors while conserving any benefits? Does PRA, on its own or in combination with other traditions of interactive fieldwork, give us the basis for conclusions that are sufficiently vivid, authoritative and timely to make a difference to policymakers and practitioners concerned with such issues? These were the main questions tackled in a 1994–5 study by a Zambian team under John Milimo and myself (Booth *et al.*, 1995).

The study was rich in learning relevant to the theme of 'PRA and Policy'. Some of this may be regarded as a chapter in the story of the Participatory Assessment Group (PAG) in Zambia, a story which includes exploiting the possibilities of PRA in national poverty assessments, and carrying out participatory beneficiary assessments (PBAs) on donor-supported micro-projects, as well as sectoral policy evaluations of this sort. This chapter summarizes briefly the research experience and its results, and raises several key issues that need to be pursued further if participatory research is to become an effective and acceptable policy instrument.

The experience

The study was commissioned by the Swedish official agency Sida. It was intended as an input into Sweden's policy dialogue with the government of Zambia, and also as one of a series of studies designed to explore the possibilities of using interactive fieldwork in combination with desk studies to illuminate 'macro'-policy issues by exploring their 'micro' implications.[1] The work brought together an experienced Zambian anthropologist, John Milimo; a team of younger Zambian men and women who had been trained in PRA; a British PhD candidate in health anthropology working in Zambia (Ginny Bond), and an academic sociologist from the UK (David Booth). Fieldwork was conducted in two urban and two rural sites (two weeks each) as well as in Bond's rural research site. Mapping and ranking exercises with focus groups were combined with wealth ranking and interviews in clinics, hospitals, schools and homes.

Analysis of the results confirmed the worst expectations of specialists in Lusaka on the exclusion of the poorest, and revealed a big gap between policy-in-principle and policy-in-practice regarding exemptions from charges for the destitute and those with infectious or chronic diseases. It confirmed the importance of quality as well as cost of service and suggested that it would be rational to charge for treatment, not consultation. There was a need for a comprehensive social safety net in health and education, and proposals for making a workable one were explored.

The resulting report was printed by Sida and presented to a public seminar in Lusaka attended by ministry planners, NGO representatives and donors (but not, despite our efforts, by the press). John Milimo, who sits on various government advisory committees, fed the results and one immediate policy suggestion to an influential health-finance group. The findings may (and may not) have been a factor among others in the decision to withdraw charges in rural areas facing drought emergencies. It is not known how, if at all, they figured in bilateral relations between Sweden and Zambia, but the report was well-received in Stockholm, was used as a background document for Sida's Task Force on poverty reduction and may have helped shape a set of guidelines on user charges prepared within the Special Programme for Africa.

Some lessons

The central message from the cost-recovery study is, of course, that 'rapid' interactive fieldwork of the PRA type has great potential as a lever towards sectoral policymaking that is more realistic about grass-roots conditions and/or more sensitive to the needs, capacities and perspectives of poor people. A little more controversially, our experience also suggests the following propositions and questions:

(1) PRA is likely to be useful for sectoral policy learning only if emphasis is placed on its generic principles – for example, learning reversal, optimal ignorance, offsetting biases, triangulation – and not if it is treated in practice mainly as a technical repertoire. During the course of the study, the research team tried out a limited range of mapping

and ranking exercises, but only some of these were helpful in exploring the issues of concern. More technique could easily have produced less understanding. One wonders: *are trainers always aware of this danger?*

(2) Especially if it is to develop as an instrument of policy analysis, PRA must not become an exclusive approach which blinds practitioners to opportunities for triangulation involving other traditions of work, such as past and ongoing agricultural, economic or anthropological research. The research team would surely have made many mistakes and produced shallower recommendations had we not been able to draw on Milimo's long experience and Bond's research results, much of this of the slow-maturing academic sort. This raises the question: *do PRA practitioners always do enough to capitalize on resources of these kinds?*

(3) Using PRA for policy analysis implies building a capacity for analysis going well beyond the needs of project appraisal/assessment. This is a training need that ought to be planned for. We operated with a fairly strong division of labour, using preparatory and analysis workshops to minimize but not close the gap between fieldwork and report writing. More people need to have the capacity to handle both dimensions. An important question is: *do current training plans for PRA teams take this sufficiently into account?*

(4) The transition from rapid rural appraisal (RRA) to PRA is a less natural step if national or sectoral policies, rather than local needs and local plans, are the focus. Making the fieldwork engender a genuinely empowering experience for the local people concerned may not be possible in such cases (in which eventuality, this should be recognized). The best that can be achieved may be to make the exercise a learning and not *dis*empowering experience, by providing some kind of report-back. In the Zambia cost-recovery study, we were in a position to do a little on these lines, thanks to the formation of the PAG.[2] A question here is: *should at least some form of report-back to study communities be considered mandatory?*

(5) Institutionalized participatory assessment capabilities are going to be better than ad hoc arrangements on several counts: they are better-placed for optimal learning and building participatory networks, as in the example just given; and they are more likely to be listened to, assuming they get a reputation for quality work. On the basis of the Zambian cost-recovery experience, we wonder: *are there stronger channels from participatory work into the corridors of power in other countries? What other general principles apply to the strengthening of such links?*

5

Designing the Future Together: PRA and education policy in The Gambia

EILEEN KANE, LAWRENCE BRUCE AND
MARY O'REILLY DE BRUN[1]

Chapter 5 describes the experience of applying participatory research to issues relating to girls' education in The Gambia. Underlying the research project, the authors' concerns included: how to generate useful and convincing information for policymakers while leaving something behind for the community; how to build a sustainable training component that goes beyond cookbook replication of methods; and how to ensure cross-sectoral policy implementation necessary to guarantee successful outcomes for girls' education. The research exercises illuminated existing socio-economic and socio-cultural barriers to girls' education, information which influenced significant revisions in Ministry of Education policy and which are summarized in the chapter. In addition, community involvement in the PRA process encouraged previously muted voices to be raised and heard in village discourse, perhaps for the first time. Initial concerns about the implications of 'provoking' communities to reassess sensitive issues appeared unfounded; 'internal barometers' within communities influence what can or cannot be placed on the community agenda. Chapter 5 concludes by emphasizing the role of PRA in a long-term process of facilitating information flows, both by challenging the 'expertise blindspot' through raising the value of community opinion, and by encouraging open and honest dialogue between a range of interest groups within communities.

The problem

Nearly a billion adults in the world today cannot read and write and 300 million school-aged children are not in school. Two-thirds of those who cannot read and write are women; 60 per cent of children not in school are girls. Research has shown that investing in girls' education is the single most important investment which countries in the South can make to improve girls' futures and their quality of life (Thomas, in Stromquist and Murphy, 1995; Schultz, 1989). Most donor agencies and governments are now seriously concerned about improving girls' school access, retention and achievement, but are hard pressed, both in terms of information and resources, to identify the operative constraints in a particular region and to identify, among the myriad prevailing strategies, the most helpful interventions.

Experience has shown that in the right circumstances, RRA/PRA can be the most effective strategy for producing valid, timely information and appropriate, sustainable action. It seemed to us, the authors, from our very different perspectives, that a careful use of this approach might help to provide data on problems and suggest possible options to policymakers and planners, and at the same time help communities to address some difficulties which are far more effectively dealt with at local level.[2] The chapter gives an account of our[3] experience of an ongoing project in The Gambia, with some additional lessons from Eritrea and Mauritania.

Challenges

In all our projects to date, we have had several basic challenges. Some of the issues which concerned us with this project were:

○ how to adapt the methods to the study of educational problems;
○ how to see whether they worked, while operating in a situation in which we had nothing to bring to the community except a common trial-and-error learning experience (no funds were allocated for implementing any community initiatives which might emerge);
○ how to generate information for policymakers while simultaneously leaving something useful behind for the community;
○ how to do all of this in communities which had not asked us to come (but which, for the most part, cooperated most enthusiastically);
○ how to relate our findings to policymakers and planners who were more comfortable with quantitative studies;
○ how to handle the issue of 'representativeness' which many people mistakenly think cannot be a feature of so-called qualitative methods;
○ how to aggregate data across communities, using a more participatory approach to help individual communities develop action plans which were unique to their circumstances;
○ how to give something back to the community in what have been, so far, data-collection missions;
○ how to leave behind a trained body of people who could carry on something better than a cookbook replication of the approach;
○ how to incorporate appropriate training in theory, in order to enable PRA practitioners with little experience or status to make effective cases to policymakers and donor agencies for the use of PRA; and
○ how to get multi-sectoral cooperation when working with one ministry; for example, installation of wells, which is not a Ministry of Education function, can release girls from time-consuming water-bearing tasks.

We addressed some of these challenges by:

(1) Incorporating PRA methods with other methods such as surveys. Ideally we would have used PRAs to create better surveys, from which we would then have identified issues and areas worth pursuing further through PRA approaches, thus using them iteratively. As it happened, time constraints were such that we used them simultaneously, so they complemented, reinforced and sometimes contradicted one another, leading to new challenges. The use of surveys, although not so important in The Gambia, satisfied planners' hunger for numbers, 'objectivity', 'instruments', etc., while providing us with methodological triangulation.

(2) Combining cluster sampling and non-random purposive sampling in order to benefit from the quality of random sampling with the depth of

understanding provided by deliberately selected cases.[4] We also used the community map (made by local people) as a sampling frame, and the well-being card sort (eliciting local people's categorization of 'well-being' and their disaggregation of community members, using cards, according to this categorization) as a reference for other techniques, in order to ensure that people from a variety of social categories were represented in whatever groups we were working with. For example, when separate focus groups formed, we needed to know if there was an even socio-economic spread in each group.[5]

(3) Standardizing ways of recording by numbering each technique: for example 'No.23: Solutions/Sources of Help Matrix with Women'. If researchers chose to work with that technique, it was then called '23' and recorded on a standardized form. In addition, we found that we could aggregate certain items by scoring the order and weighting of items presented in matrices,[6] for example community educational priorities. At the same time, people were free to explore unique community perspectives, and develop an iterative sequence of techniques appropriate to each local situation.

(4) Insisting on including an adapted community-action plan component, in which we worked with the community to assess options for problems which they themselves could address, helped local people to identify and access community resources, create an action plan and mobilize for action. What we have been asked to do, in every country in which we have worked, involves what the theologically correct would call RRA, albeit in a participatory mode. In this project we recognized the importance of siting an essentially extractive process within a broader community action plan.[7]

Some of these challenges we have tackled more successfully than others. Even among the successful outcomes, we realize that sometimes good will and serendipity were factors that may not be easily replicable elsewhere.

Background and sequence of events

The project began with the anthropologists. PRA's practical data-economizing approach to some standard anthropological methods appealed to the methodologist in us; its emphasis on participatory approaches to constructing an understanding appealed to the penitent in us (we had seen too many hit-and-run, extractive forays by social scientists, even in Ireland, and had, in our time, ourselves carried them out); and probably best saved for another occasion, its fascinating, *à la carte* paradigmatic base – phenomenology, post-positivism and critical theory all rolled into one, as needed – appealed to the outlaw in us. Also, as teachers, we have specialized in demystifying research, and were drawn to the fact that PRA methods could be shared with people who had no research background.

We approached the World Bank with the idea of using this approach to address some of the current issues in girls' education. Our first undertaking was funded in November 1993 as a one-month World Bank, Ministry of Education and UNICEF project. The brief for Eileen Kane and Mary O'Reilly-de Brun was to train 13 Gambians in various research techniques, including RRA/PRA, carry out research in both the Greater Banjul area and in rural communities throughout The Gambia, analyse the material, produce a study on constraints on, and options for, girls' education, and make recommendations for action. All but the last task were completed within the month; the study, 'Bitter Seeds', took two additional weeks. We also made a video, 'Invisible Voices'.

In the next stage, with the same sponsors, we returned to The Gambia in May 1994 to work with 4 of the original 13 Gambian researchers to develop a process for creating community action plans, and carried out the process in two villages. Out of this came a report, 'Tender Shoots'. The Bank also funded us to make a training video, 'Groundwork' and an accompanying manual.

During this period, the ministry and the World Bank were considering the findings of these reports, and began to implement some of them. One, which arose from community seasonal calendars, was the need to change the timing of school fees payments; these currently fell due during the 'hungry season'.

Interest within the World Bank began to increase. The Economic Development Institute, as part of its world regional seminars on girls' education, incorporated a pilot PRA-training workshop for senior educators, planners and administrators. We were invited to run this, and chose The Gambia as the site for the 17 trainees from Anglophone Africa.

One of the trainees was Omar Faye of Busura, brother of the chief of a village in which we had used PRA and now an enthusiastic advocate of it as a community development strategy.[8] We invited the people of his village to teach the trainees some of the methods. We had visited the village on a day when 350 girls were being circumcised, including Omar's daughter. Omar pointed out how much school time newly-circumcised girls missed, and the health dangers ('the knife they use on the first they use on the last'). He asked if we could use our training workshop exercises to plan a community-awareness programme. 'I want my daughter to be the last', Omar said. A video, 'Two-Way PLA',[9] shows the villagers teaching us that day, and how we adapted the rest of the workshop to meet his request.

The methods we used have been subsequently illustrated in a video and manual, and in *Seeing For Yourself: research handbook for girls' education in Africa* (World Bank, 1995b). For the most part, we adapted standard PRA methods, integrated into a sequence which maximized the iterative process.

Findings, learnings, insights

Rights, privileges and constraints

Our first-phase study, 'Bitter Seeds', was so named because, if we learned one incontrovertible fact, it was that girls who were denied access to primary education spoke bitterly and poignantly about that experience. They were perfectly well aware of the opportunities they would not have and the futures they dared not hope for. It became clear that, although 'education for all' is the official aim, from a cultural perspective education for boys is a right (which some are denied) while education for girls is a privilege which has to be hard-earned. Given the economic situation of The Gambia, and prevailing sociocultural attitudes and practices, for many girls education remains a dream that is well-nigh impossible to realize.

'Bitter Seeds' highlighted key problems associated with girls' education as perceived by communities themselves. We discovered that the high cost of schooling functions as a trigger in decisions about girls' education: when financial constraints dictate difficult choices about which children to send to school, sociocultural considerations about girls' perceived lower intellectual ability, dangers to female virtue, the questionable marriageability of educated girls, potential return on investment, and several other factors (all of which could be countered in isolation and in the absence of financial constraints) come into play. The resulting decision is invariably made in favour of boys. Even locally categorized 'poor' families, who send the highest percentage of boys to school, send the lowest percentage of girls. Education, perceived as a way out of the poverty trap, is rendered more accessible to boys than girls.

We discovered that teenage girls who were pregnant, married or about to be married constituted an 'invisible' segment of the community. While admiring a social map drawn in the sand, a little boy asked 'Where's the girl in that house? Why didn't you put her in?' and the men nearby replied: 'She's fifteen, she's about to be married'. Checking, we discovered that 25 per cent of the girls in the village were missing from the map. This pattern of exclusion was repeated in every village studied, and social maps adjusted accordingly.

This invisibility of girls is echoed in other sociocultural factors which influence girls' participation in education: the lack of female role-models, markedly gender-biased textbooks, too few female teachers. Endless hours of labour in compound and field restrict girls' study time. Their workload is heaviest (and boys' at its lightest) throughout the most intense period of schooling: preparation for exams. Girls fail and drop through the education net.

Even where women are visible, in media, government or business, negative lessons are often taken from their lives. Similar conclusions are drawn, too, from the lives of educated local girls who fail to find employment which warrants the investment in their education. Seen as failures on whom education was wasted, the girls themselves are understandably bitter. They also become targets for anxiety among elders about girls losing traditional values: in one village, a girl plaintively pointed out that wearing short skirts was a fashion, adopted by educated and uneducated alike, and not the 'fault' of girls like herself who go to school. An interesting outcome of this intervention was the suggestion that school uniforms might be designed in line with everyday traditional local dress and produced locally by women's groups.

Developing community action plans

We named the second phase of the study 'Tender Shoots'. As we spent more time in the community it seemed to us that even bitterness may sometimes give way to hope, that tender things can grow from difficult beginnings. The case studies indicated that communities are capable of devising and assessing socially acceptable and culturally sensitive 'best-bet' initiatives to address their educational problems, that innovative ideas come from all sectors of the community, and that engagement in the PRA process builds community confidence and promotes general sensitivity to issues of girls' education. Even without any external financial support being promised to the communities, people were willing to mobilize their resources to address education problems, resources like time, energy, labour, interest, concern. In one community, young girls identified a current constraint to school attendance and drew the new cartoon problem: 'No Toilet Door'. They presented this at a community meeting. The following day, researchers noted that young men had made and hung a new door. That is positive action.

We began to see that one of the main benefits to the community of engagement in the PRA process was that it offered people a chance to hear, perhaps for the first time, the voices of those who are often 'invisible' and are certainly not foremost in decisionmaking processes. We were reminded continually that we were dealing with economic *and* cultural factors which inhibit girls' educational participation. We were confronting directly attitudes, beliefs, pride, prejudice and power. A delicate task.

A group of teenage women in Busura decided to form a special association to discuss the problem of teenage pregnancy, to advise each other and to 'try to put a stop to it'. This seemed to be subtle-speak for 'try to stop the men harassing us'. Hot and heavy debate ensued. We became concerned: is this process promoting attitudinal change too fast? What have we started here that we may not be able to support? But our questions simply betrayed our tendency to attempt, yet again, to control the process. If the community had decided *en masse* to discuss the problem, to argue and shout about it, then they were ready for it. Later, in team discussion, we agreed that the selection of a delicate-enough issue like teenage pregnancy by each focus group in Busura indicated that the community as a whole seemed ready to handle an open-forum debate on the topic.

Although villagers may at first have expressed surprise at the girls' initiative and their independent stance, the overall consensus was that this was a positive move. For a group of young girls to take this kind of power into their hands is intriguing, and it would be interesting to be able to assess the strategies they might use to integrate this action into the web of tradition and expectation which presently supports their life.

Confirming the insight that communities have an internal barometer with regard to what can or cannot be safely placed on the community agenda, we found that in the second case-study village, although every focus group agreed that teenage pregnancy was a problem, in not one was it selected for discussion at the level of the community meeting. The villagers, unlike in Busura, were simply not ready to deal with the topic publicly, or perhaps not in the presence of the team.

PRA and gender sensitivity

What else did we learn? That PRA is not automatically gender-sensitive; gender-sensitive participatory research is most often attributable to the personal consciousness and commitment of those facilitating the research, rather than to the methodology itself. We noticed on many occasions the tendency for women to remain in the background and men to take centre-stage, particularly at all levels of the decisionmaking process. For example, the most discussed problems on the community agenda in Busura were teenage pregnancy and early marriage, closely related issues, yet when it came to community ranking of six priority problems, the elder men vociferously prevailed and these two concerns were relegated to fifth and sixth position. Women, however, raised the largest number of practical initiatives – which in itself acted as a corrective.[10]

We became conscious that the gender imbalance within the community was exacerbated by a lack of gender-consciousness among team members. On one occasion, a male facilitator was taking feedback; automatically, he faced the men, with his back to the women, who could not see the charts and who tried in vain to get his attention. We agreed later that training in gender-sensitivity would benefit PRA teams and that integration of gender analysis into the PRA process was a must.

It is also worth noting that gender-sensitive programmes would be able to capitalize on indications that men were beginning to take more responsibility for their part in teenage pregnancies, or were prepared to acknowledge the imbalance in male and female workloads, both of which are central issues in the development of opportunities for girls.

Allied with this is the importance of having both female and male local facilitators who clearly understand how information is disseminated at community level. Relying on a sole source of information is always bound to be risky, as we discovered. When we were planning to take World Bank-PRA trainees to be taught by local people, village men, who tended to make decisions for the entire community, decided upon a 'suitable' time for our visit. What we innocents did not know was that this time was highly disruptive for the women of the community, who were hosting female initiation and circumcision ceremonies for the neighbouring villages. Imagine our dismay when we discovered why the local women were acting a little ruffled as they taught our visitors how to do seasonal calendars, and then hurried back to the bush for their private ceremonial activities. We were in danger of seeming both dismissive and ignorant of local events and priorities but for some skilful facilitation work.

Institutions and information flows

Accessing various local institutions and informal information networks brings a wider variety of people into the PRA process, and local facilitators can best assess the quality and representativeness of the information being shared. As translators of the needs and realities of local people, the latter must be able to articulate this information in an accurate and reflective manner. We have seen too much local expertise lost to inadequate translation.

Accessing external expert advice is another important part of this type of PRA activity. Our experience suggests that it would be advisable to set up a data-bank of information based on the advice required for the types of options which surfaced in the community action plans. This would allow the facilitators to bring the necessary advice with them, and present it as an integral part of the options-assessment process. It would also be advisable to link in with all the relevant donor agencies active in The Gambia to avoid unnecessary duplication of effort in data collection and analysis; useful information-exchange networks might evolve.

Training and theory

We learned, with one training group after another in communities in The Gambia, Eritrea and Mauritania, that PRA is fun, exhausting and exhilarating in equal measure. These processes can bring together diverse ethnic groups, can regularly bridge the gender, poverty and marginality gaps to engage local people in a productive and energizing dialogue with each other and with policymakers.

We have also learned that theory is an important part of training, and we were baffled that many people attending the workshop on PRA and policy at IDS Sussex were antagonistic to the idea ('We don't need theory'; 'focusing on theory is what led the social sciences to become irrelevant'; and 'people will create their own theory').[11] However, we stick to our guns; deriding theory will not make it go away. This is a difficult point for anthropologists. We know that there is no such thing as 'pure' theory, because theory is affected by, and affects our local world, and we know that PRA is not atheoretical; its paradigms, while broader than most, are western (despite the claim that PRA arose in the South) and it draws from methods firmly grounded in both post-positivism and phenomenology.[12]

As facilitators, we take great care to let people know that they can alter the methods, the sequence, the applications or, indeed, discard some altogether and replace them with new ones. Not to introduce them to the rest of the package smacks of paternalism; how are people to know that they are free to create new paradigms if they do not know that paradigms exist, are debatable and can actually benefit from input from competing cultural perspectives and cognitive systems? How are they to know that challenging the ones we are using and substituting others is a legitimate exercise? Are we just helping people to engage in low-level tinkering with research tools, or are we also equipping them to understand the fundamental assumptions underlying PRA so that they can fight back if they like, add some different viewpoints, or even help us to make sense of the stewpot of contradictory paradigms from which we now draw? Do we want them to be able to participate in our international meetings, if they wish, and contribute to the literature on the same footing as those of us who now attend them, or do we want them to be craftspeople: paralegals rather than lawyers, paramedics rather than doctors?

For those of us who are westerners, what about our own learning? The point has been made that [all human beings] are struggling to apprehend, organize and interpret their perceptions of reality through models that have to some greater or lesser extent been rendered inadequate. How are we to make them more useful, except by discussing idea systems with our partners everywhere?

This may seem an academic issue, but it has practical consequences, particularly for people who are functioning in isolated areas, without extensive PRA-support networks, and perhaps trying to work in a hostile bureaucratic environment. They are often not well-equipped to deal with sceptics (just saying 'it works!' is rarely enough) and they find it hard to make a persuasive case for PRA to officials who are often themselves prisoners of outdated western notions of 'science' and resistant to anything other than a survey. The people we have exposed to PRA in The Gambia, Eritrea, Senegal, Mauritania and Mali can match beginning practitioners anywhere; they have the necessary technical competence, the enthusiasm and the commitment. We intend, in future, however, to take them further along the road, so that they can leave us at the crossroads, if they wish, and know why they are doing so.

Potential for policy

One of the most significant outcomes of our work was the sheer potential for policymakers. Appropriate government incentives and donor support for community initiatives could be designed along the lines of the community action plans produced by local communities, which provided tentative community-specific blueprints for sustainable development in the area of girls' education. For example, women in Missera suggested starting a communal farm. They would divert one-half of the income derived from the sale of the farm produce towards school costs for girls: uniforms, lunches, books etc, but to farm effectively, they needed farm inputs, pesticides and materials for fencing. Acquiring these was beyond their capabilities. This is where government and donor agencies can support local initiatives and make the ideal of 'partnership in development' a reality – but were any policymakers listening?

What triggered the changes in education policy?[13]

Yes, we were listening, and trying to work out how best to respond to the insights emerging from the PRA process.

For many policymakers, it has been quite a leap to perceive locals as experts in their own right, and potential partners in development projects. For us here in the Ministry of Education, PRA has been central in bringing this perspective forward. Beginning in the rural community and building on what local groups define as important problems and workable solutions, PRA enables us to tap into both external and internal resources and expertise in such a way that education initiatives designed on this integrated basis have a much better chance of success.

The Ministry of Education has taken part in PRA activities because it has realized that even the best strategies will achieve only modest results unless local communities, community-based groups and the people as individuals play increasingly assertive roles in defining, managing, implementing and monitoring the development efforts that affect their lives. In this regard, the 'Education For All' mid-decade review of The Gambia's Education Policy[14] placed a strong emphasis on community participation and involvement in institutional and regional education management through existing local structures.

The revelations and findings of these PRA studies have helped us at the ministry level to rethink and reshape the education-policy objectives in line with the aspirations of the Gambian communities. A Girls' Education Programme, designed to increase girls' enrolment in primary school, was adopted by the ministry. The programme was conceived as a series of measures to:

○ increase the proportion of women in the teaching force;
○ support the development of unbiased educational materials;
○ actively encourage girls to enrol in science, mathematics and technical courses; and
○ incorporate family-life education programmes into the junior-secondary school curricula.

The PRA process and findings also made it possible to re-examine specific segments of the education policy that deal with girls' education within the context of primary-school enrolment, retention and performance. The revised policy for renewed education included the following measures:

○ *The entry age to primary school will be lowered from seven to six by the end of the policy period.* This will allow more girls, particularly in rural areas, to complete the basic cycle before reaching the traditional marriageable age of fifteen.
○ *The teaching force for grades 1–6 will have an increased proportion of qualified female teachers. The ministry, in collaboration with The Gambia College School of Education, has introduced remedial programmes (Remedial Initiative for Female Teachers (RIFT) for female students with lower academic performances both in their school-leaving examinations and in the college's selection examination for the Primary Teacher's Certificate programme.* This represents a response to the need for female role models, yet the PRA revealed that many rural parents prefer female teachers to teach their girls. The studies also showed that the security of girls in school is increased by the presence of female teachers.
○ *School facilities will be planned and expanded through an assessment of the educational needs of the country, ranging from the establishment of new primary schools to the location of junior- and senior-secondary schools.* This addresses the PRA insight that not having a school within easy reach of home deters girls' enrolment as parents are concerned about their daughters' safety.
○ *In order to increase and improve quality and relevance in the Islamic Education (Madrassah) system, the ministry will harmonize its curriculum with the national curriculum and extend teacher-training opportunities to potential Madrassah teachers.* The preference for Islamic education was highlighted by many rural parents. The Madrassah attracts a significant number of children, especially girls.
○ *The ministry will pursue objectives through a largely decentralized process, involving beneficiaries (in other words, girls and community members) as principal actors in planning, implementation, monitoring and evaluation of the Girls' Education Programme.*

○ *Implementation of interventions will be pursued through ongoing policy dialogue on key issues affecting girls' education and by launching an advocacy and social mobilization campaign.* The ministry recognizes that the success of development interventions will depend on the degree to which local groups and communities are:
  i) enabled and permitted to organize, participate in and influence development priorities;
  ii) have access to natural and financial resources; and
  iii) participate in the generation and extension of productive technologies.

○ *In line with the government-initiated Strategy for Poverty Alleviation (SPA), the Girls' Education Programme will be coordinated by actors at the national, divisional and community levels through broad-based education sub-committees.*

○ *An Information, Education and Communication (IEC) package with PRA methods is being developed in order to further and promote constituent relations between communities, development partners and government, and encourage policymakers to be more responsive to the priorities of the people.* Under the SPA, programmes to promote local capacity-building have been launched through the participatory development initiative (PDI) mechanism. The PDI encourages local communities to be more assertive, to rethink their own roles, to organize their own activities better, to clarify their priorities, and to link up with similar organizations which can help them design and implement their priority programmes.

○ *In response to the barrier presented to parents by school fees and costs, there will be a 50 per cent reduction in tuition fees at the junior-secondary school level.* In addition, user charges (school fund, textbook rental etc.) at the primary level are now payable after the harvest in January/February when rural parents can better afford to meet these costs. Relaxing the requirement that girls wear uniforms – through a change in the Education Act – has encouraged greater participation of girls in schooling. Reflecting insights gleaned from the PRA process, the new policy encourages parents to become involved in the design of locally-appropriate uniforms, especially for girls.

Designing the future together

Projects designed 'outside' the community forum, without the participation and continuous involvement of villagers toward whom the project is directed, have all too often failed. One of the main reasons for this lack of success was the 'blindspot' about expertise.

The adapted PRA process revealed that rural communities have a wealth of experience and knowledge in all areas of development, especially where these concern their own livelihood. The hidden problem was that no-one had sought their opinions, no-one enquired about their problems in educating the girl-child, no-one explored how they might go about solving their community problems, no-one asked what their community development aspirations and priorities were, and no-one asked what resources were at their disposal which, if efficiently utilized, could bring rewarding changes in their lives.

These were exactly the areas explored in the two Gambian communities of Busura and Missera, where PRA methods were used to mobilize community action for girls' education. The PRA approach was able to initiate honest and straightforward dialogue with a cross-section of the communities. It relied on the knowledge and expertise of the villagers to reveal and prioritize their own educational problems. The village elders opened up (a rare phenomenon); young men gathered around to discuss issues affecting parents' willingness to send and retain girls in school; the women converged on their traditional credit clubs (*Osusu*) to discuss their daughters' education; girls in the primary schools sat together to chat about why they were considered as threats to village society; and, most importantly, all these groups sat together to discuss at length the community's educational problems.

The girls (voices of the powerless) spoke for the first time about actions they wanted to embark on regardless of whether their elders were around. The village elders endorsed the action-oriented initiatives proposed by the young men, who would have taken unilateral instructions from the village elders, a long-held tradition within the village environment.

Overcoming the expertise blindspot has proved positive, and we might expect that as soon as local know-how is requested villagers participate eagerly. This is usually the case, but we cannot afford to ignore the impact of development history nor the legacy of poverty. Many communities suffer from a lack of confidence, low community-esteem, and do not experience themselves as empowered to make decisions, put forward suggestions, or implement courses of action. We are still working toward empowerment and away from a dependency mentality.

Nevertheless, people were obviously fired up by their experience of and participation in the PRA process. Surrounding villagers commented that:

> We are the luckiest to have the team and to learn new ideas with them. We have seen our problems and discussed them as one body which we have never done before. I hope we will put into practice all we have learned here and give our girls the chance to benefit from it (Missera men).

The hope for a better future must not be overestimated. Villagers will need encouragement to face the difficulties they are bound to encounter when struggling to put new solutions in place. Hope alone will not suffice. On-going interest and support from the Ministry of Education and others, monitoring and evaluation of community action plans, and appropriate financial support are clearly needed to ensure that the human energy which fuels community initiatives is not allowed to dissipate.

To the policymaker amongst us, it is clear that the PRA process should not be a one-off approach, but a repeating experience building on previous insights and research findings. This would enrich the interaction and relationships of change agents and the communities where future interventions are planned. These processes, once mastered and strengthened, should be replicated in other communities. To do this, more researchers need to be trained in PRA methodologies for community mobilization. All sectoral boundaries are open to these processes. Most importantly, once these methods are established in these sectors, they should complement one another. For instance, imagine women's communal farms and gardens using their produce and proceeds of sales to finance the education of the girl-child and in the process improving the nutritional standards of the community children.

The potential of rural communities as partners in development has always been underestimated by the policymakers. The impact of policies geared towards the education of the girl-child has, for a long time, consequently fallen short of expected outcomes. Sectoral policies should attract and win the support of rural communities with a bottom-up approach. Interventions should be designed in consultation with rural local experts who would then be in the forefront of making these interventions operational. PRA creates the atmosphere for this to happen.

6

Can Policy-focused Research be Participatory? Research on violence and poverty in Jamaica using PRA methods[1]

CAROLINE MOSER AND
JEREMY HOLLAND

Chapter 6 presents the results of a participatory study of local perceptions of urban poverty and violence in Jamaica carried out in 1995 using PRA[2] methods. The study was undertaken because of a growing preoccupation with the issue of urban violence in Jamaica. It presented the opportunity for the World Bank, in its support of a participatory methodology, to move beyond poverty assessments and address a new development concern, the issue of violence.

The research exercise was conducted in two stages. PRA activities in selected representative poor urban communities elicited local people's conceptions of poverty and violence, and their prioritization of problems and solutions. Triangulation was then used to elicit and reconcile the diverse views from various stakeholders, including representatives of local businesses, NGOs, the police and the church.

Chapter 6 highlights two important questions that concern the use of participatory methodologies in policy-focused research: (i) how participatory can the research process be; and (ii) who ultimately 'owns' it? It describes how the analysis and synthesis of the PRA data aimed to retain local perceptions while presenting information in a form accessible to policymakers. This included:

○ *interpreting local analysis in terms of the relationship between urban violence and its erosion of two key assets, labour and social capital, both perceived by local communities as vital for reducing poverty; and*
○ *some aggregation and categorization of local perceptions in order to establish policy priorities of specific relevance to the design of the Jamaican Social Investment Fund.[3]*

Finally, Chapter 6 reflects on the procedures that were followed best to disseminate policy proposals emerging from the research process, a process which raised a notable internal contradiction: attempts to disseminate highly sensitive information in a participatory and effective manner to the widest possible audience can be constrained by the need to preserve the anonymity of vulnerable participants. The questions and contradictions raised by this study, concerning as they do the relationship between PRA and policy, may be of relevance to PRA researchers, whose insights into such issues are welcomed by the authors.

Context and definitions

At the outset it is necessary to mention briefly background information concerning the research context, as well as to provide a number of definitional clarifications relevant both to the PRA and to this chapter.

The study, which was carried out during September–October 1995, was undertaken as a consequence of consultation between the Jamaican government and the World Bank revealing a growing preoccupation with the issue of urban violence in Jamaica. It was commissioned for two different but linked World Bank policy-related operational initiatives: (i) to provide preliminary data on poverty and violence for the Jamaican Urban Poverty Study being undertaken by the Human Resources Operations Division in Latin American Department 3; and (ii) to assist in the identification of the sub-project menu for the proposed Jamaican Social Investment Fund, under preparation by the Jamaican government in collaboration with the World Bank Resident Mission in Jamaica. The fieldwork was completed in five weeks, followed by four weeks for data analysis, and the study ended with a diversity of dissemination activities in November 1996.

Box 1.2   Social Funds and poverty reduction

A Social Fund is a mechanism through which resources are channelled, according to pre-determined selection criteria, to demand-driven projects proposed by public, private or voluntary (formal or informal) organizations. Individual sub-projects are not designed at the time the Social Fund is established.

The typical objectives of a Social Fund are:

o to mitigate recession and adjustment-related social costs or to address emergencies such as natural disasters or wars;
o to improve living conditions of the poor through speedy provision of basic economic and social services; and
o to strengthen decentralized delivery mechanisms by supporting local (governmental and non-governmental) organizations that are responsive to local needs and to build institutional capacity at the local level.

Social funds are typically created as new agencies, often outside the realm of a ministry, with a relatively high degree of independence with regard to normal bureaucratic procedures. Social funds can be viewed along a spectrum with varying degrees of demand-driveness, autonomy, execution responsibility, community participation, and each financing varying sectors and activities.

To date the World Bank has supported about 30 major social funds in twenty-four countries amounting to a total of somewhat less than US$1 billion.

Source: Carvalho, 1994.

Two definitional issues can be raised deriving from the design of the study:

(1) It was undertaken within a policy-focused[4] context, in particular relating to the design of the upcoming Jamaican Social Investment Fund, and consequently was firmly grounded in a specific framework (see Box 1.2). This raises questions concerning the contextual frameworks within which PRAs are undertaken, and whether it is useful *a priori* to distinguish between:
   - a policy-focused PRA whose objective, i.e. product, is to influence policy; and
   - PRA processes that in themselves end up by influencing policy.

(2) It was undertaken on an issue of great sensitivity – violence. Communities were selected for fieldwork so as to be broadly representative of a range of poor community types found in urban Jamaica, rather than to be specific case studies in themselves; violence is an island-wide, rather than an isolated phenomenon restricted to the five study areas. The delicate nature of the topic meant that community anonymity was a pre-condition, guaranteed from the outset of the study, with pseudonyms used throughout. This raises a second question of concern: how does PRA remain a participatory process while accommodating sensitive information, the identity of which can increase the vulnerability of its participants?

Who defines the objectives of the study?

In commissioning a study of urban violence the World Bank did not stipulate that this should be undertaken using PRA methodology; indeed, as with most 'sector' work to date, the Bank assumed this would be completed from secondary-data sources. A number of factors assisted in convincing the World Bank staff member responsible for the research design of the particular advantages of participatory methodologies: the growing recognition of PRA as an important research tool for shared learning between local people and outsiders (Chambers, 1992); the increasing prioritization in World-Bank country poverty assessments 'to include within the analysis the views, perceptions, experiences and preferences of the poor themselves (World Bank, 1994: ii); the possibility of collaboration with researchers at the University of the West Indies (UWI); and the critically necessary financial support from a donor to undertake a PRA study.

In Jamaica, where the impact of violence is felt at all levels of society, its importance as a contributory factor to, and outcome of, urban poverty, has not been clearly identified, while the voices of the poor themselves are rarely heard. The study therefore presented the opportunity for the Bank to move beyond poverty assessments in its support of participatory methodology to address a new development concern, the issue of violence, not previously explored in this way.

The specific objective of the exercise as defined by the researchers was better to understand the complex processes that produce and reproduce violence in urban poor communities and that have an impact on the

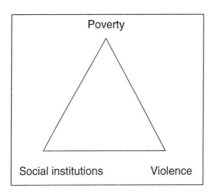

Figure 1.7   *Framework for analysis: the poverty–violence–institutions nexus*

poverty and well-being of community members. The study framework, through a nexus linking violence, poverty and social institutions (see Figure 1.7), clarified that violence cannot be looked at in isolation, but has to be understood in terms of causal relationships. An understanding of the inter-relationship of these three elements was seen as potentially important for the design of appropriate policy recommendations. The framework recognized that people's perceptions of their poverty were not necessarily based on static, fixed-income measurements or captured by poverty lines, but more frequently related to vulnerability – to complex aspects of 'well-being' and 'livelihood security' – that include survival, security and self-respect (Chambers, 1989: 1). Vulnerability referred not only to individuals but also to households and communities (Moser, 1993a).

Is the product more important than the process?

The study was implemented in two distinct stages: (i) the team conducted research in five poor urban areas using a variety of PRA tools; (ii) focus-group discussions were conducted with other stakeholders including representatives from NGOs, women's groups, the police, lawyers and the church. The adoption of participatory methodologies within a policy-focused study raised two questions:

○ how participatory can the research process be; and
○ who ultimately 'owns' the research process?

The fieldwork in the five poor areas was participatory in a behavioural sense – to the extent that we (the researchers) were not dominant in the research process. Community participants were handed the 'stick of authority', presenting, analysing and interpreting their own reality in the field (Chambers, 1992: 19). In following the PRA principle of 'devolution of impetus' 'onto those whose livelihood strategies form the subject for research' (IIED, 1994: 1), we tried to ensure 'transfer of ownership' by, for instance, leaving visuals with their authors and faithfully reporting participant analyses in our field reports.

It could be argued that the PRA process contributed to the product. At the same time, community ownership of the day-to-day research process, particularly on the part of local indigenous leaders, both men and women, possibly contributed to a greater sense of empowerment around the knowledge of the appalling problems violence generates in such communities. As Table 1.4 shows, a number of different PRA methods were used by community members to explore a diversity of issues relating to the violence–poverty–social institutions nexus.

Table 1.4: PRA tools used during research process to explore the poverty–violence–social institutions nexus

PRA tool	Examples of issues raised
Transect walks	Ice breaking: high-visibility systematic walk through community with 'gatekeeper(s)', critically important to dispel suspicion of outsiders Encouraged participants to discuss and raise issues, both spatial (e.g. identifying gang 'turf' boundaries) and non-spatial
Participatory mapping	Spatial characteristics within the community of perceived importance highlighted and listed/ranked/discussed (e.g. location of police station; wealth of different households within a street)
Listing	Types of problems perceived by different groups Specific types of violence perceived by different groups, aggregated to show the frequency with which each type of violence was mentioned Characteristics of wealth and well-being (those who 'have it' and those who 'don't have it') Characteristics of 'good men' and 'bad men' Dreams and solutions
Ranking and scoring	Prevalence and importance of: types of violence; types of weapons; types of employment Wealth or well-being ranking
Seasonality mapping	Trend analysis of violence in general or of specific types of violence Activity schedule – seasonality analysis of police harassment; of different sources of income generation
Time lines	Perceptions of significant changes within the community or of community characteristics – relating to different types of violence and their intensity
Causal impact diagrams	Analysis of unemployment, area stigma, domestic violence, teenage pregnancy, lack of education, and their relationship to violence
Institutional Venn ('roti') diagrams	Analysis of relative importance and nature of individuals and institutions within the community and their inter-relationships, particularly important in identifying 'good' social institutions and 'bad/dangerous/violent 'social institutions'

What role does triangulation play in policy-focused PRA?

In the context of a policy-focused participatory research process, triangulation goes beyond cross-checking information. To reconcile diverse views of different constituencies in the final analysis, triangulation includes and compares the different perceptions of distinct interest groups both within and outside communities. Focus-group discussions were conducted with a number of interest groups to elicit differences of perception. As the following examples illustrate, there were often radical differences in terms of both priority problems and their causes. Triangulation ensured that such diverse views could be incorporated into the overall analysis:

o a local-business focus group prioritized 'the wrong work attitude' as the main reason for a lack of employment amongst the urban poor. In contrast, participants in urban poor communities prioritized area stigma and a general lack of employment opportunities;

o a women's NGO focus group prioritized gender relations and domestic violence in their interpretation of violence in Jamaican society. Community participants, on the other hand, presented a broader picture in their typologies of violence, and highlighted the importance of interpersonal violence beyond family members; and

o a focus group of police officers complained that because the urban poor treated their major criminals as heroes, they were unwilling to help the police arrest them. Amongst community participants, however, there was an almost unanimous disaffection with the role and influence of criminals in their areas.

Who provides the framework for analysis?

Participatory research using PRA methodology generates extensive descriptive data, both the daily field notes, diagrams and drawings, as well as the field-team reports written at the end of each stage in the process. In the Jamaica study, participants from the five different communities provided important perceptions and insights into the problems of violence.

Once fieldwork was completed, development of a framework for the analysis of this data proved a tremendous challenge with an inherent tension between the necessity:

o to remain true to participants' perceptions and not impose outsiders' categorizations;

o to synthesize results in a form accessible for policymakers; and

o to provide, where appropriate, indicators to measure perceptions of problems.[5]

The following section highlights different stages in the process as well as identifying a number of critical decisions made during analysis.[6]

Stage 1: presentation of descriptive data

The study purposely did not *a priori* define violence as a problem. It sought to identify: (i) the extent to which communities themselves perceived it as a problem; (ii) the priority given to violence relative to other problems; and (iii) the gravity of different types of violence. In aggregating the listings of perceived problems to gauge the frequency with which they were raised, however, categorization based on a five-fold asset vulnerability matrix (Moser, 1996) was introduced.

In listing the frequency of perceptions of types of violence in four of the five communities some 25 self-defined types of violence were distinguished by different focus groups, dramatically illustrating the importance of better understanding the phenomenon's complexity in poor urban communities in Jamaica. Here again, categorization was introduced to systematize the data, in this case into six main groupings of violence, based on well-known local categories.

This allowed policymakers to grasp clearly one of the most important counterintuitive results of the research, namely that in terms of frequency, interpersonal violence is far more pervasive than political or drug violence, although the latter are more commonly cited by politicians and the media as a problem.

Stage 2: analysis of the PRA findings

Analysis of the causal relationship between violence, poverty and social institutions – clearly separated in the report from the descriptive findings – was undertaken in terms of the relationship between the different assets of the poor and violence – how each asset related to violence, and how violence in turn eroded or consolidated it. Two assets in particular were addressed: (i) labour as an individual asset; and (ii) social capital as a community asset.

Labour as an asset
Lack of work and of employment opportunities in all communities was perceived as a direct cause of poverty; this in turn was considered to affect levels of economic violence directly. Area stigma, largely an outcome of

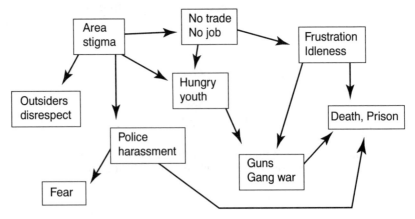

Figure 1.8 *Impacts of area stigma, analysed by a group of youth, Campbell Town*

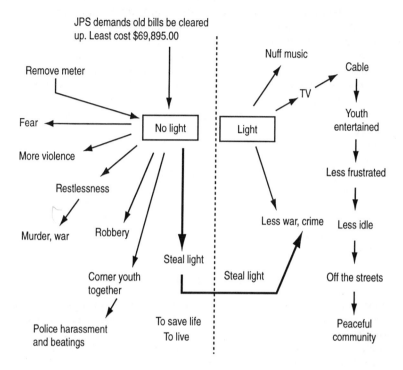

Figure 1.9   *Impact analysis of 'light' (electricity) and no 'light', prepared by a group of youths, Campbell Town*

violence, was seen universally by all communities and groups as affecting their local work force, which suffered discrimination as a result (Figure 1.8). In addition, local people argued that access to employment was restricted because of local businesses closing down or moving out, and by the effect on physical mobility of turf wars and the reluctance of buses and taxis to operate in the areas. Physical access to social infrastructure was similarly, restricted by gang war, with access further limited by schools and health centres closing down, closing early each day, or being looted or vandalized. Lack of access to electricity was, moreover, perceived by one group of youths as exacerbating levels of frustration and violence (Figure 1.9).

Important gender differences were identified in terms of men and women's perceptions of the impact of unemployment. Young men in particular perceived high unemployment as leading to frustration and idleness which in turn leads to an increase in gang violence, interpersonal conflict and domestic violence. Young women believed that high unemployment leads to greater dependency on a man for income as a survival strategy; this in turn increases domestic violence.

Social capital as an asset

The significance of examining social capital as an asset within poor urban areas in Jamaica related to the importance of social institutions not only for social cohesion but also for economic development. The PRA showed the extensive nature of social institutions, ranging from informal bodies, such as families and households, through local associations (around such recreational activities as sport, music and dancing) to formal organizations concerned with political, religious and educational matters. Institutional 'roti' diagrams identified the range of institutions (both individuals and organizations) considered important in a community, as well as providing ideas as to their inter-relatedness, relative importance, and whether they were negative or positive.

A distinction was made between social institutions with either hierarchical or horizontal relationships (Putnam, 1993). These provided very different avenues to reduce poverty and violence, as well as interacting differently with violence. Analysis showed that widespread fear was an indirect consequence of violence and war, permeating both social and spatial aspects of community life, thereby eroding stocks of social capital. This has important implications at the level of both social relationships and social associations.

Stage 3: presentation of community solutions to problems of violence

To elicit perceptions of solutions in the PRA, focus groups listed their 'dream community'. Responses were mixed, but fell into two broad categories: on the one hand were ideals for the future, on the other hand concrete solutions. In synthesizing results in a form accessible for policymakers, these were separated for the purposes of this analysis. Concrete solutions were aggregated into the different sub-project categories of the upcoming Jamaican·Social Investment Fund.

This categorization allowed three important messages to reach policymakers, with implications for changes in the design of the social fund sub-project menu:

(1) that peace, articulated as unity or the end of war, was universally ranked highest by focus groups in all five communities;
(2) that while a small number saw the need for strong leadership or greater political involvement as part of this dream, far more conceived the issue in terms of a range of empowering characteristics such as 'uplifting themselves', 'gaining respect' or 'changing attitudes';
(3) that projects and programmes that bring people together and build social capital were the most frequently stated solutions provided by focus groups. This is indicated by comparing the aggregate listing of 'social-assistance' type interventions (Table 1.5) with those types of intervention included in existing sub-project menus for social funds (Table 1.6).

The aggregation of recommendations revealed that social-assistance interventions – such as community-based activities, centres for counselling around violence and programmes to improve relations with the police – were recommended more frequently than any one of the existing social fund types (i.e. those addressing social infrastructure, economic infrastructure and income generation).

What dissemination procedures best ensure that all voices are heard?

Because they were not predetermined, the dissemination procedures proved to be an important stage in the PRA process. A number of different, but complementary procedures were tested across the widest group

Table 1.5: Aggregate listing of community recommendations for building social capital

Type of solution	Focus group				Total
	Children	Young men	Young women	Middle-aged/ elderly	
Social-assistance intervention (total)					64
Community-based activities:					35
– community/youth/day-care centres		6	4	5	
– youth projects	1	4		2	
– drama group				1	
– literacy classes			1		
– voluntary work/self help				2	
– Citizens' Associations etc./ Neighbourhood Watch		1	1	7	
Safe centres and staff for counselling around violence:					14
– parenting skills to deal with children		2	1	4	
– youth involved with gun violence		1	1	1	
– community relations				1	
– drug addiction		1		1	
– family planning				1	
Programme to improve relations with the police/reduce police harassment	1	3	1	2	7
Soup kitchen/lunch money/school-fees assistance			1	2	3
Military training for youth	1			1	2
Job-placement programmes that teach youth how to present themselves for jobs				1	1
Prisoner-rehabilitation programmes				1	1
Return subsidy on basic food items				1	1

Source: PRA field notes from Greeland, Campbell Town, Park Town, Zinc City and Maka Walk.

Table 1.6: Aggregate listing of community recommendations for project intervention

Type of solution	Focus group				
	Children	Young men	Young women	Middle-aged/ elderly	Total
Social-infrastructure projects (total)					55
Training/Training Centre	1	9	6	11	27
Education/schools/school equipment		5	3	5	13
Sports fields/playing area/sports centre for both boys and girls – provision, rehabilitation and equipping		4	1	4	9
Health clinic/nurse/family planning			3	2	5
Police station			1		1
Economic-infrastructure projects (total)					56
Provide housing		2	2	7	11
Water supply and sanitation		1	2	4	7
Community rehabilitation of rented/ captured housing and zinc fences, and reclamation of open lots		1	1	5	7
Telephone installation		2	1	4	7
Street repairs		1	2	2	5
Drainage/gully repair		2	2	1	5
Reliable garbage collection		2	1	2	5
(Legal) electricity			1	3	4
Fix up physical environment/'war zone'	1			1	2
Street light installation				2	2
Systems to ensure transport can move through communities				1	1
Income-generating projects (total)					32
Provide work		8	5	13	26
Programme to provide incentives for business to work in inner-city areas		1	1	1	3
Community-level workshops, e.g. welding				1	1
Shopping centre				1	1
Business centre				1	1

Source: PRA field notes from Greenland, Campbell Town, Park Town, Zinc City and Maka Walk.

possible, thus ensuring the most effective a link between the research and policymaking stages of the process.

While the policy-determined context of the study ensured that Jamaican Social Investment Fund staff were briefed at different stages of the process, a priority consideration was to reach a broad audience of policymakers. At the same time, considerable constraints were recognized as working against the participation in the dissemination process of the urban poor themselves, given the precondition of community anonymity. This meant that open participation of potentially vulnerable community members was not possible; in addition, the divided nature of Jamaican society meant that previous initiatives for the poor to talk directly to policymakers had been highly conflictive.

To attempt to cope with both constraints, two stakeholder workshops were run almost as a continuum of interest groups ranging from community members through to senior government policymakers. The UWI's stakeholder workshop, held on the university campus, included: individuals from the research communities who attended in their own right but were unable to act formally as spokespeople for their anonymous communities; Jamaican members of the research team who in a sense acted as their sole representatives; other local researchers; and NGOs. A second stakeholder workshop, held in a city hotel, was organized by the World Bank for members of communities, a number of researchers and NGOs, and included a considerable number of policymakers from a wide diversity of government ministries, the business community, police, church and donors.

A third dissemination mechanism was the use of the local media. Research-team members participated in a number of press briefings, as well as in a highly popular peak-hour morning local radio phone-in show. Finally, those able to influence policy were targeted and briefed, including members of the government's social-policy think-tank, prime ministeral-level advisers and opposition leaders.

Conclusion

In reflecting on the research exercise conducted in Jamaica, two questions are raised, neither of which yet has a clear answer.

(1) It is evident that important policy-relevant results emerged from this micro study, yet what changes in policy and action occurred as a result of this process? At a macro level, research results showing the importance of rebuilding social cohesion in enabling economic growth challenge orthodox policy prescriptions that emphasize macro-economic indicators and investment in human capital. The macro-level policy implications will be fed into a wider urban poverty study being undertaken within the World Bank, and have been disseminated through various media to policymakers within the country.

At the project level, the research conveyed clear messages from local voices which had direct relevance to the design of the upcoming Jamaican Social Investment Fund, and the policy messages were heard, because of the demand-driven nature of the exercise. The findings specific to the design of the social fund were presented and discussed with the fund's co-ordinators, whose enthusiasm and expressed need for the research had been evident from its inception. Consequently, four key features of the social fund, including the sub-project menu and key procedures within the sub-project cycle, were designed to prevent as far as possible further erosion of social cohesion as well as to consolidate and build upon existing stocks of social capital (Moser *et al.*, 1996):

○ The social-fund menu incorporated innovative interventions which aim to provide support, training and space for the building of collaboration and trust.

○ The social fund recognized the importance of community-level institutions by seeking to work with existing local bodies (both formal and informal), and provide technical assistance where necessary, rather than create new 'project committees' as undertaken in some social funds. Projects must, moreover, be sponsored by a community group in order to restrict the influence of individual-led, hierarchical institutions.

○ The social fund recognized that communities must be involved in the identification of sub-projects, with a small in-house capacity developed to undertake participatory needs assessment, and train interested NGO and local-government entities in participatory approaches and methods.

○ The social fund recognized the implications of violence for contracting and disbursement procedures, with local groups vulnerable to co-option by political interests and gangs. In areas where fears of co-option and violence outweigh institution-building objectives, the project sponsor can therefore, as part of the sponsor agreement, authorize the Social Fund to contract on its behalf and direct funds directly to the executing agency.

(2) Can the process be repeated? Local participation in social funds has often been limited to the implementation stage, with implications for the long-term sustainability of projects. The Jamaican exercise enabled a greater degree of local input into the design stage of a social fund through community participation in the analysis of problems and prioritization of types of project interventions. The Jamaican Social Investment Fund also recognized the importance of continuing participatory-needs assessment for sub-project identification. The current Belize Social Investment Fund also reflects this concern by giving PRA a more systematic place in the social-fund process. Participatory exercises will allow local people not only to voice their concerns and negotiate their priority needs but will feed this into the project preparation process for submission to the social fund, resulting in early and direct involvement of local project 'beneficiaries' in the project cycle. It will be interesting to see whether this shift of emphasis to process in policymaking becomes institutionalized in future social funds.

7

Village Voices Challenging Wetland-management Policies: PRA experiences from Pakistan and India

BIKSHAM GUJJA, MICHEL PIMBERT AND MEERA SHAH[1]

Chapter 7 focuses on the community-wetland interactions of two sites of international importance for conservation: the Ucchali wetland complex in the province of Punjab, Pakistan; and Keoladeo National Park in the state of Rajastan, India. PRAs, involving key government and WWF staff, were carried out in several villages neighbouring each wetland in response to local opposition to existing wetland-management policies and the threat of worsening conflict between villagers and conservation authorities. The PRA exercises revealed that severe restrictions on the use of protected-area resources by local communities, such as the banning of grazing in Keoladeo National Park, were ecologically unsound as well as a threat to local livelihoods. Furthermore, local people had not derived any benefit from the growth of tourism in the protected areas.

A framework for assessing the influence of PRAs on policy and action is presented. This is based upon three sets of inter-related criteria that help evaluate: (i) the outsiders' performance in designing and running the PRA training and fieldwork; (ii) the extent to which emerging recommendations are followed up on the ground; and (iii) the extent to which higher-level policy change, with accompanying devolution of power and planning, has been influenced. Both PRA exercises proved to be successful in terms of the first set of criteria, yet to date have not demonstrated significant influence on changes at local or higher-policy levels. Such exercises should not ultimately be judged on their ability to remedy poorly designed and insensitive protected-area schemes, but instead on their ability to address the underlying concerns of local people, namely their opposition to existing unequal and in some instances illegitimate access to resources. It is these inequities that perpetuate the conflicts which the proposed joint-management schemes attempt to mediate. The greatest challenge for policymakers is for PRAs to be conducted with local communities in protected areas before these are formally established. Such a measure would encourage joint management, reduce potential conflict, and promote ecologically sound practices.

The context

The management plans for the Ucchali wetland complex and for Keoladeo National Park were drawn up by following western scientific principles and the internationally agreed guidelines of the RAMSAR Convention (Convention on Wetlands of International Importance especially as Waterfowl

Habitat). In both cases, however, effective protected-area (PA) management has been hampered by the passive or active opposition of local communities living in and around the wetlands. The threat of worsening conflict between local people and conservation authorities created a context in which consultations for effective wetland management with local communities were seen as necessary by government departments and conservation organizations (such as the WWF).

Participatory rural appraisals (PRAs) were carried out in several villages neighbouring each wetland. These were conducted in order to build up pictures of natural-resource endowments; the means by which they were managed; and the socio-economic make-up of communities. In each case the purpose was threefold:

(1) to assess the social impact of the PAs' management on local communities and make the assessment available to all stakeholders;
(2) to revise the PA-management plans in the light of the interactive dialogues between local people and outsiders; and
(3) to initiate a dialogue on the policy reforms needed to involve local communities as equal partners in wetland conservation.

Both PRAs were designed to involve key government and WWF staff in experiential learning. Throughout the training workshops and appraisals it was constantly emphasized that participation is not simply the application of a method, but is instead part of a process of dialogue, action, analysis, conflict resolution and change.

New insights experienced by outsiders

Keoladeo National Park (KNP), India

This wetland ecosystem was designed some 150 years ago by the local ruler to attract water birds for shooting. KNP is a RAMSAR site, a world and heritage site 'protected' under national-parks policy (see Box 1.6, p.62). This wetland is internationally known and is a major tourist destination in India. The PRAs with the local communities have raised five main issues which are directly or indirectly related to implementation of national-parks policy.

(1) *Local people perceived that the grazing by buffaloes inside the wetlands is part of the ecosystem management.* Grazing contributes to the health of the ecosystem and thus helps attract migratory birds, the very purpose of the park. But policies on national parks ban livestock grazing. Grazing has been a traditional right for centuries and villagers argued that it is needed to sustain their own lifestyle as well as the biodiversity of the wetland. 'Scientific' evidence, based on expensive studies, also suggests that the grazing inside the wetland area is required to control the water weeds (see Boxes 1.3 and 1.4).
(2) *Local people did not approve fodder collection on moral and economic grounds.* Collection of grass is not permitted under the national policy, yet the authorities need to spend on grass cutting and on the fire services to prevent fire.

Box 1.3 Buffaloes and wetlands

'The traditional major primary consumers of the wetland of the park, the buffaloes, should be brought back to control the unchecked growth of Paspalum distichum'.

Source: Summary of recommendations of 'Keoladeo National Park, ecological study', Bombay Natural Society, 1991.

Box 1.4 Policies and local perceptions

1a: Grazing
'Arguing against the new policy the local communities maintain that they have used this park for grazing their livestock, particularly buffaloes, for centuries. Although the damage caused by grazing during the last several decades could be a point of discussion, the banning of grazing in Keoladeo National Park is not based on any scientific study or report recommending it. It is because these wetlands are declared as National Parks that a ban on grazing inside becomes automatic, irrespective of its merits or demerits. This is precisely what is being challenged by the local communities'.

1b: Grass and fire
'We believe in God. It is a sin to set fire to standing grass, specially when there is no fodder for the cattle'. (A village woman during the exercise)

Source: Participatory Management Planning for Keoladeo National Park, WWF report on the PRA workshop held at KNP.

---

(3) *Local people did not see any benefits of tourism.* Recent policy changes and restrictions on access have encouraged the view that the park is now being managed to attract the tourists, particularly from outside the country. Local people expressed some resentment towards the tourist industry because it captures most park benefits. This will have implications for policy on tourism.
(4) *According to local people, the park gets priority access to water from the nearby dam.* They believed that their water rights had been violated. The policy on water distribution was also challenged by the local community.
(5) *Local people challenged the violation of their traditional rights to visit the temples inside the parks, particularly in certain areas.*

Ucchali complex, Pakistan

The Ucchali complex is an internationally well-known area for wetland conservation. This site is located in the Salt Range of north-central Punjab,

Pakistan. The complex is a combination of three interdependent wetlands: Ucchali, Khabbaki and Jalar. Khabbaki lake was declared a RAMSAR site in 1976. Following the 1991 RAMSAR mission, it was proposed to declare the total Ucchali complex as a RAMSAR site. The wetlands cover about 1243 hectares and are managed as protected areas under the Punjab Wildlife Act (1974). The following PRA findings have major policy implications for wetland management:

(1) *The profound mismatch between locally lived experiences of wetland histories and the perceptions of outsiders.* External organizations and professionals have either assumed that lakes Ucchali and Khabbaki are natural features of the landscape or have not internalized evidence invalidating this belief. According to villagers, Lake Khabbaki is a disaster flood zone rather than a lake. The wetland is of very recent origin, formed by heavy rains over the last 50 years. It sits on prime agricultural land owned by neighbouring villagers. Conservationists' failure to understand the relatively recent social and ecological history of the wetlands has led to the neglect of the prior land rights of local people, creating conditions for conflicts between the state and local communities.

(2) *The boundary conditions and inclusiveness of the villagers' analysis were wider than those of the natural scientists hitherto involved in the wetland-management planning.* The scientists tended to focus on species of special concern for international conservation and the wetland habitat itself. In contrast, the villagers explored the connections between forests in the watershed, land-use history, livelihoods and the White-headed Duck's only overwintering site in Pakistan. Complex issues such as patterns of migratory-bird activity, changes in water quality, rates of sedimentation, relationship between groundwater levels and wetland presence were monitored locally and often well understood. Villagers established causal links between recent outside interventions and the detrimental effects on avian species of international importance, such as the negative impacts of the introduction of exotic fish species (carp and tilapia) on White-headed Duck populations and the strong lights of a newly opened military base which interfere with the orientation and landing behaviour of immigrating bird species on Lake Ucchali.

(3) *The interactive dialogues with the members of the three different villages revealed many contrasts between the social make-up of each village and the lakes' ecologies.* This local-level diversity suggests that standard and undifferentiated approaches to wetland-management planning and implementation are inappropriate. There is a need to combine the general validity of the ecological principles on which management plans rest with the site-specific knowledge and innovations of local communities.

(4) *Farmers who had lost land and/or traditional rights over resources could not appreciate the value of vague 'long-term' conservation benefits for society or humanity.* In their view, conservation benefits accruing from the successful management of the wetlands should be immediate and quantifiable, with villagers getting a fair share or fair compensation for loss of productive resources.

(5) *To avoid further conflict there is a need to incorporate proposals made by villagers into the existing management plan, clarify legal matters (i.e. rights on land under the lake water) and encourage linkages between local communities and government departments to facilitate the emergence of joint-management schemes.*

(6) *Existing policies regulating access to and use of wetlands declared as RAMSAR sites are major sources of conflict and need to be reformed* (Box 1.5).

Box 1.5 The management of Khabbaki lake in the Ucchali complex as an example of coercive conservation

Khabbaki lake is classified as a wildlife sanctuary and is managed as a protected area under clause 16 of the Punjab Wildlife (protection, preservation, conservation and management) Act (1974) which reads as follows:

16 (2) The 'Wildlife Sanctuary' shall be set aside as undisturbed breeding ground for the protection of wildlife and access therefore to the public shall, except in accordance with the rules, be prohibited and no exploitation of forest therein shall be allowed except for reducing fire hazards, epidemic or insect attacks or other natural calamities.

16 (3) No person shall:
  i. enter or reside;
  ii. cultivate any land;
  iii. damage or destroy the vegetation;
  iv. hunt, kill, or capture any wildlife or fire any gun or other firearm within one mile of the boundaries;
  v. introduce any exotic species of animal or plant;
  vi. introduce any domestic animal or allow it to stray;
  vii. cause any fire; or
  viii. pollute water in a wildlife sanctuary.

provided that government may for specific purposes as are deemed expedient, authorize the doing of the aforementioned acts (other than those mentioned in clause iv).

Policy implications

The two exercises at Ucchali and Keoladeo raised several issues which are directly related to major policies on wetland conservation, in both India and Pakistan as well as elsewhere.

(1) The national-parks policy in India is categorical in 'banning' livestock grazing (Box 1.6). Such policies are not unique to India and are based on an assumption that people and livestock damage biodiversity. People who lived for thousands of years were evicted after an area was declared a national park. In India alone, over half a million people

---

Box 1.6   National parks and livestock

'No grazing of any livestock shall be permitted in a national park and no livestock shall be allowed to enter therein grazing except such livestock is used as a vehicle by a person authorized to enter such a national park'.

(Punjab Wildlife Protection Act, 1972, Section 35 (7), India)

---

have been displaced because of such policies. At Keoladeo, local communities directly questioned the national policies. Though they might also be fighting for their traditional rights, villagers argued that grazing by livestock inside the wetland is needed for the maintenance of biodiversity and the health of migratory birds. Whilst the scientists and experts also concluded after an expensive and decade-long study that grazing is needed for the park, they did not suggest any changes in national-park policies.

(2) Tourism is considered good for the nation and its economic growth. Often many policies promoting tourism are based on an assumption that it will help the local people. The outcome of the PRA seriously questions such an assumption and the related policies:
  ○ the net loss to local people in establishing the national park is significant;
  ○ tourists are in fact subsidized to visit the park; and
  ○ tourism revenue accrues to social groups that do not experience any conservation costs or burden.

(3) The Ucchali experience clearly led to a questioning of the RAMSAR Convention and its policies of declaring internationally important wetland sites. The PRAs revealed that the local people own part of the Ucchali wetlands. The lakes are gradually expanding and people are losing their private lands, yet where people own part of the wetland, the RAMSAR-site declaration made by the Government of Pakistan is clearly against its own policy of protecting private property.

(4) The concept of wise use of wetlands has been around for the last ten years, but in practice, 'wise use' is defined, implemented and evaluated by government experts and international consultants. The PRAs indicated clearly that if an opportunity is given to the local communities, they can carry out these tasks. Wise-use policy should be based on the people's priorities, knowledge and management systems.

Changes in policy and action

The degree to which the PRAs have encouraged shifts from normal top-down practices can be assessed in terms of three sets of interrelated criteria (Box 1.7). Cluster A is made up of factors that help evaluate the outsiders' performance in designing and running the PRA training and rural appraisals. Cluster B focuses on how well the recommendations that emerged through initial appraisals are followed up on the ground, for example, have local institutions been strengthened? Cluster C refers to higher-level

---

Box 1.7   Three sets of criteria to evaluate the impact of PRAs

Cluster A. This normally includes the following:

○ identification of the problems in a particular area which can be addressed through PRA:
○ selection of suitable institutions, resource persons etc;
○ workshop design;
○ conducting the PRA workshop;
○ report writing;
○ publication; and
○ people and institutions requesting for copies and referring to the publication.

This stage is successful in most, if not all, cases to a reasonable degree. The experience and the outcome of the workshop are also interesting for the institutions which conduct and host the PRA exercise.

Cluster B. This is the follow-up of the PRA exercise. The workshops and the exercises will come up with a series of recommendations including:

○ redesign of the plan;
○ extension of the benefits to the local community;
○ inclusion of community representation;
○ strengthening of local institutions; and
○ building the capacity of local people to conduct the work and monitor progress.

Some if not all of the PRAs are likely to lead to this stage. This will solve some of the issues in development and conservation which cannot be addressed by other methods. This stage will also strengthen local people's confidence that outside institutions will function to their benefit.

Cluster C. This represents the ideal situation and includes the following:

○ the PRA experiences are used to advocate bigger policy changes;
○ institutional changes at a higher level;
○ empowerment of local communities;
○ democratisation and decentralisation of planning;
○ questioning the knowledge systems advocated by western and urban institutions.

This stage is a great opportunity as well as a challenge to the institutions and individuals engaged in the PRA. Radical changes in the approaches of the institutions presently involved in PRA could occur. In some specific cases, policy changes advocated could threaten the very basis of existence and rationale of the institutions engaged in the PRA.

---

policy changes that are needed for the devolution of power and planning to the local level.

Both the Ucchali and Keoladeo experiences with PRAs have been highly successful in terms of Cluster A criteria: local-government officials and NGO staff were trained; information was exchanged with local communities in a confidence-building mode; the usefulness of PRA methodologies was demonstrated for conservation; and reports and other outputs had a positive impact on international fora.

In terms of criteria B and C, we are acutely aware that answers to the following questions are at this juncture not so positive:

○ So what? Did it change anything on the ground?
○ Did people derive any substantial benefits except, maybe, the pleasure of meeting some outsiders from exotic places?
○ Have steps been taken to share resources and conservation benefits more equitably?

It is, however, too early to say if wildlife-conservation policies at a national level will change to allow for:

○ differentiated approaches to highly site-specific situations, e.g. the three lakes forming the Ucchali complex;
○ the recognition of prior rights and the granting of rights of access and use to some PA resources (e.g. grazing resources in Keoladeo National Park, India); and
○ the adoption of enabling legislation for joint protected-area management in Ucchali and in Keoladeo National Park.

A central challenge facing policymakers is to consider these people–park conflicts more historically and to try to resolve them more imaginatively. Huge differences in the scale of opposing stakes and claims were revealed as village voices reconstructed the local social and ecological histories of the wetlands. In and around Keoladeo National Park for example, the needs and rights of the tourist industry are not comparable with those of the resident communities. Whereas private firms need only worry about increases in their profits, local people's stakes hinge around issues of basic subsistence and adequate nutrition. The manner in which non-resident parties got their stakes in the first place can, moreover, no longer be ignored in the light of information gathered during the PRAs. Both tourism in Keoladeo National Park and private-owned fishing in the freshwater lake of the Ucchali complex take place precisely in those areas from which previous residents have been expelled and denied their prior rights of access and use.

PRA exercises should not be limited to conflict resolution and/or extending some monetary benefits to the poor local communities. The experiences emerging out of PRAs in different countries, though at present limited, suggest that a major policy shift in the conservation of natural resources is required. Existing policies are not only counterproductive, they are also becoming very expensive mistakes. PRAs or similar processes should ideally lead to new, socially acceptable policies.

Policy reforms need, therefore, to acknowledge that some stakeholders' claims to resources are illegitimate: they ignore previously existing rights of long-time local residents. Enabling policies for joint protected-area management will need to address larger questions of land alienation and land scarcity (Ucchali) and grazing rights (Keoladeo). For the villagers, these are the crucial issues. Should they be left out of the policy reform, inequities will perpetuate the conflicts which the proposed joint-management schemes attempt to mediate. It is against these yardsticks that the ultimate success or failure of these PRAs should perhaps be judged since, in both wetland contexts, village voices are calling for these profound policy changes.

A still-greater challenge for policymakers is to ensure that the initial location and planning for PAs are based on local peoples' knowledge, analysis and priorities from the start. Whilst clearly useful, the PRAs described here should not be seen merely as examples of what governments could do to patch up poorly designed and socially insensitive PA schemes. Instead, we hope that these examples argue in favour of a radically different participatory approach in which local people exert more democratic control over the early formulation of PA policies and management plans. In both policy and practical terms, their realities and voices must count more than those of outside professionals and their national or foreign-based institutions.

Costs and benefits

The PRAs require considerable preparation and planning by professionals working in the conservation organizations, but the overall cost of completing one exercise is relatively cheap. In each case the benefits were training, capacity building and the revision or preparation of protected-area management plans.

PRA exercises are cheaper, faster and should, in principle, be more humane than others; the conventional-consultant approach is usually very expensive and disempowers local people by extracting their knowledge.

Both wetland-site exercises have drawn key staff from government departments into the process, by no means a small achievement. The training process for the officials creates new possibilities for the further spread and scaling-up of these participatory approaches. The growing demand in WWF to conduct more such PRA exercises is, moreover, a clear indication that this approach is seen as highly relevant to address conservation issues in different contexts.

Learning from the process

The most important lessons learnt about the PRA process include:

○ Outside professionals from government and WWF got first-hand experience of the ground-level impacts of PA policies and management schemes. The experiential learning in villages provided, to some extent, a moment in their professional lives to reflect on the perverse impacts of standard approaches to PA design and management. A better understanding of the villagers' knowledge and own readings of the landscape and local history also helped demystify expertise. The value judgements,

65

biases and ideologies behind conservation expertise, top-down planning and national policies for wildlife protection were partly or fully exposed through dialogues with villagers.

○ The national-policy implications for wetland management in developing countries were effectively raised at an international level through the showing of a video describing the participatory appraisals carried out (in India) at the Meeting of the Conference of the Contracting Parties of the RAMSAR Convention (Brisbane, Australia, 19–27 March 1996). In the recommendations of this international meeting, both the Ucchali and Keoladeo national-park experiences were mentioned as 'models for active and informed participation of local people in the wise use of their wetland resources'. The contracting parties (country governments) were called upon to facilitate from the outset the participation of local and indigenous people in the management of wetlands.

○ Lastly, the PRAs and the villagers' voices are important in stimulating heightened awareness of the variety of alternative futures and alternative-policy frameworks towards which conservation and natural-resource management can be steered. Villagers' analysis often questions deeply and moves beyond the assumptions of current protected-area management policies to illuminate what is possible and what is not. Through village voices, conservation becomes a central political question linked with enduring debates over the distribution of wealth and power. By framing the policy issues in this way, local people challenge conservationists and policymakers to rethink the distribution of land, economic rights and ecological responsibilities in and around protected areas. This process is long overdue and we hope that future PRAs in this area will further contribute to it.

8

The Use of RRA to inform Policy: tenure issues in Madagascar and Guinea

KAREN SCHOONMAKER FREUDENBERGER[1]

Chapter 8 explores issues emerging from RRAs carried out in Madagascar and Guinea to assist the countries' respective governments in considering changes to their national land and resource-management laws. The RRAs were carried out with assistance from the Land Tenure Center of the University of Wisconsin. A series of case studies was conducted, interspersed with regional workshops designed to disseminate the results to a range of stakeholders. A national policy review was scheduled at the end of this process to consider the implications of the research findings for policy changes. The chapter argues that for RRAs to lead to effective input into the policymaking machinery and immediate follow-up by local support agencies, both personnel from the relevant ministries and representatives from local NGOs must be involved in the RRA process from the beginning, as was the case in Guinea. There are, however, constraints that can make the process less effective: the problem of how to sample in order to achieve representativeness; the relatively high cost of PRA exercises and subsequent dependency on external donors that it brings; the difficulty of challenging the attitudes and assumptions of policymakers when including them in the research process; and the need to ensure credibility through methodological rigour. Chapter 8 concludes that it is much easier for policymakers to make decisions without *information from RRAs, given that RRAs are most likely to expose competing interests, challenge assumptions, and reveal complexities that make decisionmaking very difficult.*

Background

Over the past five years I have been involved in several initiatives to use RRA to inform policy decisions at the national level. In two of the cases (Madagascar and Guinea, from which I will draw examples) the governments were considering changes in the national land or resource-management laws. As part of its development-assistance package, the United States Agency for International Development (USAID) financed the services of the University of Wisconsin's Land Tenure Center (LTC), to provide technical assistance to the governments as they carried out their reviews.[2]

LTC felt strongly in both of these cases that it did not want to follow the standard donor/technical-assistance approach that typically involves proposing a prepackaged solution to the host-country government and then carrying out a series of activities intended to persuade the government to adopt that approach over any of the others that has been proposed.[3]

Instead, it wanted to set in place a process of reflection and analysis that would help government officials, first, better to understand the local realities in their country and, second, to come up with their own solutions to tenure and land reform, solutions that one fervently hoped would be firmly rooted in those realities rather than copied from standard European or American land codes.

How RRA was used

In both Guinea and Madagascar, the projects' organizers planned a series of case studies using RRA[4] that were carried out in sites scattered around the country. Each RRA study lasted typically from 7 to 10 days and employed a wide range of tools and techniques including (but not limited to) participatory maps, transects, Venn diagrams, wealth rankings, historical and classification matrices, bean quantification, and semi-structured interviews.

In Madagascar, the key policy question was related to the management of lands around national protected areas. A key element of Madagascar's National Environmental Plan (NEP) is a concern to protect better the resources of these nature reserves. In order to do this, it was believed that people living near these reserves had to have more secure access to and control of land and natural resources around the parks. Behind this was the hypothesis that security of tenure leads to increased agricultural production and that increased security decreases pressure on protected areas (see Leis and Gage, 1995). One proposal being widely advocated was to title private lands around the parks in order to increase tenure security. LTC's prior experience suggested that private titling might not be the most appropriate solution in this setting and that there are other modes, such as reinforcing indigenous systems of tenure security, that should also be considered. Its staff proposed a series of studies better to understand issues of tenure security in this context and to assess the appropriateness of titling and its potential impact on populations and natural resources. RRA case studies were carried out in seven study sites around four of the protected areas over the course of a year.

The government of Guinea was more generally concerned with land issues. In 1992, a new Land Code was adopted (not, unfortunately, as a result of any participatory process) but there were no ancillary texts to explain in practice what the provisions of the code meant and how they would be applied. While many people were concerned that there had been no participatory process of study and reflection before the code was adopted, it was felt that there was still considerable latitude in the interpretation of its decrees, with a possibility of making these more responsive to local concerns. To provide further information to policymakers who would be deciding on the texts and their enforcement, a series of eight RRAs (one peri-urban and one rural in each of four regions) was proposed. The case-study sites were deliberately selected to represent a range of ecological and social conditions.

In both Madagascar and Guinea, the field studies were interspersed with regional workshops that presented the findings of the studies from that

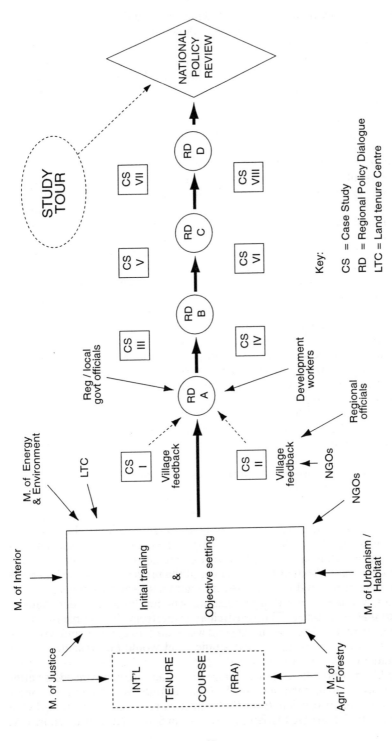

Figure 1.10 *The RRA process in Madagascar and Guinea*

Key:

CS = Case Study
RD = Regional Policy Dialogue
LTC = Land tenure Centre

region (or protected area) to interested parties, including local government officials, extension workers and project personnel (Figure 1.10). The purpose of these workshops was multi-fold. First, it was an opportunity to share the results of the studies with a larger audience. It was hoped that this would build a more informed group that would be more receptive and more sympathetic to whatever policy recommendations came out of the research at the end.

Second, the regional policy workshops offered the possibility of putting the isolated case studies into a somewhat larger context. One of the problems with using RRA for policy work is the problem of sampling. Nobody was trying to suggest that the two or three case studies from any region could possibly represent the myriad of situations present in that zone. What we could do was to present an interesting case that almost always raised some critical issues. At these local policy workshops, the case studies were presented as examples of the kinds of resource-management issues that existed in that region. The participants were then asked for their feedback: Was this typical of their experiences? What other examples had they seen of similar issues in the region? What had they seen that might contradict or add other perspectives to the study? This process helped to cross-check the information that had been collected and to assess whether the case was indeed more or less typical of the zone. The workshops also contributed additional information to the study, all the while keeping the discussion anchored in local realities.

At the end of the series of case studies and regional policy dialogues, in each country a national policy review was scheduled to assess the results of the entire process in order to expand the dialogue to a much larger group of people and to begin much more systematically to consider the implications of the research findings for policy changes. In the case of Guinea, however, USAID withdrew its support before a national policy review could be convened.

A key difference: composition of the research teams

While the two projects took similar approaches, there was one notable difference: the composition of the research teams. In both cases the majority of the researchers were from the country in question; LTC staff and consultants facilitated the process and provided methodological and research guidance throughout.[6] In the case of Madagascar the Malagasy team members were selected at the beginning of the process for their experience with tenure issues and resource management, and their willingness to endure tough conditions and a demanding schedule over the year that the field studies took place. The researchers came from diverse backgrounds (both academia and development) and were hired to conduct and write up, with LTC staff, the series of case studies that would be presented to the government.

The Guinea project took a different and, I am now convinced, a better approach. The team members for the Guinea study were all mid- to upper-level government officials from the ministries responsible for writing the texts and implementing the land code. This included Agriculture/Forestry,

Energy and Environment, Urbanism and Habitat, Mining, Interior and Justice. The team members were selected in an interactive process between USAID, LTC and the ministries involved. Emphasis was placed on selecting people who expressed an interest in the process, who would play an active role in policy deliberation and/or implementation, who had the personality to work well in a team and were willing to adopt the respectful and open-minded approach necessary for effective RRA research, and who expected that they could make room in their schedules to carry out a series of four 2-week RRAs (approximately one every 2–3 months) over the course of the year. Nine people were identified who met these criteria. They went through an initial training in RRA and tenure concepts and then participated in each of the regional RRA case studies as they took place. At the beginning, LTC staff served as team leaders; over time, various members of the team showed their aptitude and interest in taking leadership and became increasingly involved in guiding the case studies. In addition to this core of team members, in each region two or more local government administrators were included in the teams.

In both Guinea and Madagascar, the teams also included NGO representatives, some of whom were selected from national headquarters but at least one of whom came from the zone where the case study was carried out. This was important to diversify the perspectives on the team but also helped to ensure that information collected in the studies could be put to immediate use by local development practitioners working in the area. Since the benefits to the local population of the policy assessment were distant at best, and nonexistent at worst, participation by NGOs working on local resource-management questions increased the chance that participating villages would gain some direct benefits as a result of the studies. In fact, there were numerous examples of this in both Guinea and Madagascar. In some cases the NGOs stepped in to respond to specific needs identified in the studies, in others they refined and improved their projects in light of information gathered.

The difference in the approaches taken in Madagascar and Guinea was, essentially, that in Madagascar a team of outsiders presented their results to government officials, asking them to review the information and incorporate their findings into policy decisions. Their success was thus dependent on the willingness of key government actors to accept the credibility of the information and to internalize it in their deliberations. The LTC team was still in the position of trying to 'sell' its information and approach, even if it was not trying to sell prepackaged policy recommendations.

In Guinea, the research was done by 'the government', or at least by an influential subset of important decisionmakers. While there was still a critical need to disseminate the information more broadly and to persuade a larger group of people to act upon it, there was a core group that had been through the whole process, had been deeply touched by what had been learned and was convinced of the importance of the information and its use in the group's policy deliberations. Most important, it was not LTC that had to persuade anyone of anything; rather Guinean government officials had the task of convincing their own colleagues, based on their own experiences.

In both cases the process appears to have had significant results, though it is too early, especially in Guinea, to make any definitive assessment of the impact. In Madagascar, the pilot programme to title lands was brought to a halt until the situation could be studied further. This was, admittedly, not entirely due to the results of the LTC research. The initial red flags were issued by villagers themselves who met titling agents as they arrived in their village with guns and machetes. This unexpected challenge did, however, create a substantial demand for the LTC case studies which from the villagers' perspectives, explained, among other things, how titling would destroy their indigenous management systems.

In Guinea, the cancellation of the national policy review casts doubt on the formal review process that was to culminate the year-long research effort. It cannot be questioned, however, that the process has had a profound effect on the perspectives of the government functionaries who participated. Nearly all began the process with the attitude that customary tenure systems no longer existed in Guinea, having been eradicated by the politically repressive practices of the Sékou Touré regime and replaced by 'modern' legal systems. This assumption was challenged from the first case study and, over the course of the year, most of these functionaries became fervent advocates of the idea that customary tenure systems had to be taken into consideration in revising the texts and implementing the land code.

Reasons to use RRA to inform policy discussions

RRA can help to bring village perspectives to the debate

Policy debate most often takes place between high-level people of different opinions or people at different levels of government. Rarely is the perspective of people at the grassroots level heard explicitly in these discussions. By focusing on local realities, RRA helps policy analysts to move away from normative or stylized ways of thinking that dominate most policy debates and to focus on the real impact that policies have or might have on local people. RRA is an effective method of listening to what local people have to say and looking at issues from their perspective. Reports from these studies can add another dimension to the discussion and help to anchor the debates in local realities.

Equally important, however, is the fact that villagers who have gone through a systematic RRA analysis that addresses the impact of policies or proposed policy changes on their lives are generally better able to discuss their views in a coherent and systematic fashion that policymakers can understand. This facilitates their ability to express clearly and stand up for their own rights and interests. Village RRA participants themselves frequently put forth the view that, while obviously they had in some sense 'known' all the pieces of the information that was delivered to the team, they had never considered it systematically or contemplated its implications. In at least one case, in Guinea, following the RRA study villagers confronted local authorities whom they felt were abusing their rights on land redistribution and demanded that they cease. They were supported in their claim by higher-level government officials who had been on the research team, and it has been reported that the questionable procedures have stopped, not only in that village but in the region.

RRA challenges preconceived notions and particularly those that are the product of western or formal education systems

While many government officials have their roots in rural life and may still have relatives in villages, most have spent years (if not decades) in formal educational systems that belittle indigenous knowledge and 'backward' customary systems. In many cases, the principal frame of reference for these officials is not the local reality in their own country but rather western, urban approaches. They have been taught not to listen to their own cultural intuition, and often to despise the traditional and customary practices of rural people. Some people are so entrenched in these western/ 'modern' ways of thinking that no amount of alternative exposure can expand their horizons.

For many, however, participation in RRA is a liberating experience that allows them to reactivate instincts, cultural ties and personal indigenous knowledge that have been long buried. Most of the officials with whom we worked in Guinea, for example, must have 'known' at some level that customary tenure systems continued to exist in rural areas – almost all hold land in rural communities or have close relatives who do so – and yet they have been so oriented toward formal systems regulated by laws, codes and decrees that these had become their reality in spite of their experiential knowledge to the contrary. Despite the inevitable discomfort involved in the initial phases of challenging long-held assumptions, many ultimately seemed to find the process a liberating one, as it exposed, acknowledged and legitimized a reality that they had so long been forced to deny.

Reasons to include policymakers as members of the RRA research team

The learning process is more effective

While spending two weeks in an RRA study, or eight weeks in a series of studies, may not be the cheapest way for policymakers to learn, there is little doubt in my mind that it must surely be one of the most effective. Policymakers have benefited and will continue to benefit from RRA reports prepared by research teams for their consideration, yet learning is infinitely more profound and more lasting when it comes from their own experiences as members of a study team. In most cases, when reading a report, people absorb information that fits into or expands their prior views only marginally. Rarely will they allow such information to challenge their deeper assumptions; before doing so they are more likely to dismiss the report and the study on which it was based on one ground or another. In contrast, from the first day of the RRA, policymakers with whom I have worked have begun questioning, reflecting and debating at deeper levels as they confront, in person, real situations that challenge orthodox views.

One lesson that has become apparent in working directly with policymakers is the importance of extending the experiential learning through RRA over a considerable period of time. While one RRA can open

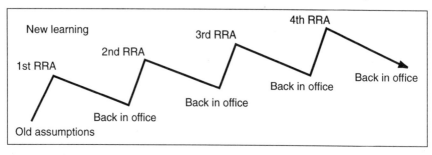

Figure 1.11 *Policymaker learning curve*

people's eyes to new information, rarely is it sufficient to move them into new ways of thinking. This requires a more cumulative and reinforcing process. We have noticed that almost all the officials with whom we have worked have been very excited by the information they gain during the course of an RRA study and the analysis that immediately follows. Often, the nature of their discourse changes dramatically during this period. Equally predictable, however, is the fact that when they return to their office and the dominant paradigm of their workplace and colleagues, they tend to ratchet back a few notches and fall into old habits and ways of thinking. By the time we meet them again some months later, many of the old assumptions have at least partially taken root, though few revert totally to their earlier dogmatic views. The learning process, then, is something like the trend line shown below (Figure 1.11) where there is progressive learning, but the greatest gains are evident only after the several field experiences.

There is clearly a trade-off between exposing more policymakers to local realities by including them in RRAs or including fewer people, as we did in Guinea, but working with them over an extended period of time. Instead of taking eight people through the series of four RRAs, we might have instead selected new team members each time, thereby working with 30 or more policy people over the year. Having never attempted the latter I cannot assess the relative efficacy of the two approaches, but I am sure that the amount of learning of those involved would have been significantly less in the latter situation. Certainly, the more deeply entrenched the assumptions that are being challenged, the more important it is to prolong and reinforce the process.

Mutual perceptions of policymakers/bureaucrats and villagers may change dramatically

In a case such as Guinea, where relationships between villagers and government authorities have been overwhelmingly adversarial in recent times, the opportunity for the two groups to sit down and discuss serious issues face to face was eye-opening for both sides. One comment that arose frequently during the feedback sessions the team held with the villages was that villagers were astounded that the officials were so 'human', so approachable and so willing to listen. In later discussions, the government officials expressed equal disbelief about the hospitality and sophistication of the village populations with whom they had worked. While the benefits cannot be measured in the short term, surely these types of interactions can only be beneficial in promoting more approachable and responsive political systems?

The credibility of the study and its results are increased

The issue of RRA credibility in general will be addressed below. Suffice it to say here that officials who have participated in well-run RRA studies rarely question the validity of the information gathered. They may tear out their hair in confronting the difficulty of acting on such complex information, but they are unlikely to question its veracity. Many became fervent defenders of the studies and their results in front of their more sceptical colleagues.

Problems that arise in using RRA to inform policy dialogues

Sampling

One of practical issues that invariably arises when RRA studies are used to inform policy debates is the small number of sites that can be sampled by these intensive, qualitative methods. It takes resources – time, money and, especially, energetic, inquisitive researchers – to do good RRA. In my experience, it is not possible for a person to maintain enthusiasm, energy and a creative approach through a string of consecutive RRAs. Even two in a row can be a strain; the returns after three become questionable, given the fatigue of the researchers. A time of rest, reflection and recuperation is needed before the teams can go out again.

What this means, in practice, is that unless large numbers of people are brought into the process, which raises other issues of quality control and the comparability of results across sites, the number of sites that can be sampled is limited; even if multiple teams are dispatched continuously, the number of sites will still be infinitesimal compared to the total number of villages in most countries. It is impossible to satisfy those who doubt anything that is not based on statistical significance

While this issue continues to plague me, I have found that in practice it poses more of a conceptual than a real problem. In fact, in the studies with which I am most familiar (most of which have sampled less than a dozen sites), the results have been extraordinarily useful for decisionmakers. The key is not to view RRA sites as producing information that can be directly extrapolated to a larger population. The relevant question is, instead, 'what types of information are we getting and what sorts of issues are arising that need to be factored into the policy debate?'.

In the case of the Guinea study, for example, the local tenure systems varied dramatically from site to site; perhaps the most impressive finding from the eight sites was the immense diversity that was observed. It was, clearly, not possible to extrapolate from one or a few sites to say that 'local tenure rules concerning X resource are the following'. What was clear, however, was that in each of the sites there was strong evidence that some sort of local/customary/traditional tenure system was very active. If the national policies failed to take these systems, and their tremendous diversity, into consideration, the consequences would be serious. Since policymakers had begun the study process denying that local tenure systems existed, and therefore had no intentions of even considering them in writing the new texts, this was in itself a major finding. The studies were, given the conditions in any one site, then able to go on to anticipate the types of impacts that might occur if certain measures were or weren't implemented in the new laws.

While RRA is highly effective at getting qualitative information and, specifically, understanding the reasons why people behave in one way or another – which should be a critical concern in policy discussions – it is without question less effective than other research techniques in understanding the scope of certain practices across a region or country. When used to inform policy, it is thus often most effective when it is combined with these other techniques. Depending on the type of information being sought, this can be done using quantitative surveys which can address key questions across a broad population sample or remote-sensing techniques (e.g. satellite imagery or aerial photography) to detect issues such as land-use patterns across broader areas. Combining these various methods gives policy analysts a much greater range of information. Surveys and remote sensing are effective at providing rather superficial information across large areas or populations; RRA can go into much greater depth, but in just a very limited number of sample sites.

Cost

While RRA is generally touted to be cost-effective relative to more drawn-out research methods, it must be acknowledged that the costs of doing a series of well-conceived and implemented RRAs across several regions and involving a sizable number of people is high. While precise costs will vary enormously from country to country and depend especially on arrangements to pay or provide daily allowances for the research staff and government officials (usually the most expensive item in the RRA budget), we have found that a budget of US$7–10000 per RRA is not unusual. When this is multiplied by two more teams each conducting 4–6 studies over the course of the year, as well as various policy workshops at the regional and national levels, the overall expense of gathering this type of information is by no means insignificant. LTC's projects to conduct a year's worth of studies and policy workshops have generally run to the order of $250,000. This covers the above-mentioned expenses, as well as the time of LTC researchers in the field, consultants and trainers, and local research assistants who have been essential to addressing the myriad of logistical issues that such a process entails.

The expense often means, however, that one of the major donors is involved. This in turn implies a certain political agenda and, at the least, dependence on that donor's continued interest. When this interest flags, as was the case in our Guinea study, the entire process becomes vulnerable to the whims of the funder. Having said that, the fact that policymakers are intimately involved throughout the process does help to mitigate any damage. Even if formal, funded policy reflections are halted due to the donor's withdrawal of financial support, the personal learning of the participants continues to have an impact as they carry out their routine administrative and decisionmaking responsibilities.

Difficulties of working with policymakers/bureaucrats

I have presented a heartfelt exhortation to include policymakers directly in the research process, but I am the first to admit that this is not the easiest way to do things. While I have certainly had the good fortune to work with upper-level decisionmakers with whom the entire experience has been a delight, just as often there have been substantial problems.

Some of the problems are logistical. It is hard to pull people away from their routine work to carry out a series of field studies. To the credit of the Guinean participants, I must say that in Guinea the project had remarkably consistent participation, but this can be a major problem. More difficult in this precise case was the fact that government entirely reorganized its ministerial structure part way through the research year. Our carefully selected representatives of key ministries no longer worked for those ministries, or their functions had been changed dramatically. Certain of the team members no longer had direct responsibility for land and resource decisions.

The more difficult problems have, however, been related to attitudes and assumptions. There is no question that it would be easier to work with a hand-picked team of people who already had ample experience in research, tenure issues, participatory approaches, etc. While most of the policymakers with whom we worked had some village roots, there were a few who had never spent a night in a village. Sometimes it seemed as though team members were spending more time defending their ministerial interests and trying to impose their own assumptions on the rest of the group than listening to what villagers were telling us. This situation improved enormously as the process advanced and in the end I think all agreed that the benefits of working directly with policymakers far outweighed the difficulties and challenges that the approach entailed.

While the government officials brought many skills to the RRAs there were several areas where there were consistent gaps that were filled by LTC counterpart researchers, both expatriate and local. The most notable weaknesses were in analytical and writing skills. While the government participants became stronger in these areas over the year, continued LTC support was critical. Over the course of the project, the relative strengths and weaknesses of all the parties involved became clearer and the entire process became stronger as people worked from their strengths and improved, or where necessary deferred to others, in their weaker areas.

Credibility of qualitative methods

The purpose of conducting these RRA studies was to inform a policy debate and to turn policymakers' attentions to the implications of their decisions on rural populations. But research can only have this impact if the results are viewed as credible and worthy of consideration.

Unfortunately, as soon as the RRA results contradict the orthodox perspective or challenge entrenched interests – because RRAs tend to question assumptions and prevailing paradigms this is often the case – the reaction of the challenged party is invariably to question the methodology and impugn the reputation of the researchers. In most cases this involves questioning the small number of sites and the credibility of information that is obtained by informal tools such as participatory mapping, as opposed to precise cartographic representations.

I do not in the least resent people challenging the way RRAs are done, although I do not particularly like the fact that all qualitative methods are often assumed to be defective while all quantitative methods are considered trustworthy. In fact, I think that given the many poor RRAs that try to pass themselves off as quality research, people are fully justified in questioning how the methods have been used. This means, however, that the teams have to take extraordinary precautions in their use of the methods so that they will be in a position to defend their use of the methodology persuasively.

Being able to do this requires that deliberate and systematic steps are taken to ensure that: (a) methodological principles are followed with the greatest attention; and (b) the process is well documented. In my experience, when I have taken the trouble to explain the careful means by which the sites were selected and the teams' scrupulous attention to reducing bias through triangulation of team members, village respondents and the use of diverse tools, most discussion of the methods is dispatched, allowing people to focus again on the substantive results of the work. To the extent that information from other methods (e.g. surveys or remote-sensing techniques) can be brought in to corroborate the qualitative findings, this helps to assuage the doubters further.

Finally, in more than one instance, villagers themselves have leapt to the defence of the research team. We have tried to make it a practice to invite representatives from the sites studied to at least the regional workshops held to discuss the results. In one case, when one of the functionaries in attendance began to rail against the team and suggest that the findings from the study could not possibly be accurate, an elder of the village rose with great dignity and proceeded defiantly to refute the challenge. He noted that the team had conducted a highly serious study and captured exactly the reality of their village. He added that he would be happy to take the bureaucrat or any others who doubted the results back home with him to show them that not only was this the reality in their village but that it was common practice throughout the zone. I don't think the bureaucrat took him up on his offer, but neither did he cause us any further problems during the workshop.

Confronting complexity

While the implicit assumption behind all this is that the results of RRA studies will help policymakers in their decisionmaking, I will end these reflections by noting that in fact the result is exactly the opposite. It is much easier for policymakers to make decisions without information from RRAs. Good RRAs expose competing interests, challenge orthodox assumptions and reveal complexities that make decisionmaking extremely difficult. One can only hope, however, that policymakers who have access to greater information will be willing to struggle through the challenge of using RRA to improve their decisions. A further, and perhaps even more quixotic, hope is that they will use this information to become more responsive to poorer rural peoples whose concerns have been consistently either ignored or misunderstood in policy deliberations.

9

Scottish Forestry-policy U-turn: was PRA behind it?

ANDY INGLIS AND SUSAN GUY

In 1994, one local PRA event was conducted in the Highland village of Laggan to assist local people to assess what forestry could offer their area if they had the opportunity to acquire or manage the local woodland. In 1996, the British government announced the launching of a new policy to enable just such local ownership and management of woodland throughout Scotland by offering local people first refusal to purchase government-owned forest being sold prior to going to the open market. Chapter 9 documents a return visit to Laggan two years after the PRA event. The objective of this visit was to understand better, using a PRA approach, to what extent the original PRA activities may have influenced this fundamental reversal of forest policy in Scotland. The authors remain totally uncertain as to the nature and degree of influence of the earlier PRA events. There is some evidence to suggest, however, that changes did result from people understanding each other better, with the PRA process helping to create the 'conducive environment' for change; in addition, the PRA products (i.e. the outcome of the PRA process) seem to have played an indirect role in influencing policy. They were useful for the purpose of providing the media with the Laggan story; in turn, it was the media that were perceived to have made the most impact on the policymakers. Perhaps most importantly, the media, politicians and civil servants may have been influenced by the increased confidence of Laggan residents. Despite such conclusions, PRA practitioners must avoid falling into the trap of explaining essentially fuzzy, complex processes in terms of simple linear causality, nor should such reductionism be used to try and convince sceptics of the value of PRA.

Overview

In April 1996, the then-Scottish Office Forestry Minister, Lord Lindsay, announced a plan 'to bring forestry back to the people'. The British government was to launch an initiative to encourage local ownership and management of woodland through the selling of government-owned forest to local communities. This move has been hailed as the biggest reversal of forest policy in a generation.[1] Previously, the Forestry Commission, the biggest landowner in Scotland (owning 1.5 million acres) had refused to sell land to local people, preferring bids from large commercial companies.[2] The shift in attitude of the government has prompted the Forestry Commission to develop a discussion document on the future use of its land and how this land can be used to benefit local communities.

It took many factors and events to get Lord Lindsay and Michael Forsyth, the then-Scottish Secretary, to take notice of public opinion and make changes to forest policy. The people of Laggan, a Highland village, had spent five years trying to buy a forest, and have been catalysts for this policy change.

PRA in Laggan

Prior to any change in forest policy, a PRA event had been held in Laggan in April 1994.

(1) The PRA event was designed for the Laggan Community Association. The objective was to assist people to share and record their own analysis of their situation and the land around them, and assess what forestry could offer their area.

An evening meeting was held in the Laggan Village Hall. The people who turned up for the event worked in randomly formed groups. The outcome was: the start of a more general positive attitude to acquiring an area of state-owned forest; and a report documenting the villagers' analysis of their situation.

PRA and policy change: a return to Laggan

To what extent did the PRA event in Laggan influenced recent forest policy change in Scotland? As PRA practitioners, we are aware that we could not draw a straight line through factors and events leading to policy change. We were completely uncertain how or if PRA had had any influence.

How could anyone attempt to unravel a web of factors and events which may have influenced policy change? Yet who would want to hear a non-linear story? Who, indeed, would dare write a chapter that declared: 'We are 100 per cent uncertain to what extent, if any, PRA may have influenced the policy change.'

In a case such as this, one cannot rely solely on the point of view of the PRA practitioner. It is but one faithful representation of what someone has experienced. We need to take a different approach in order to understand the complexities of causality. The dilemma is not that one cannot prove causality, it is that it is very difficult to disprove the assumption that PRA events influenced policy change. The very nature of PRA processes means that they can very quickly become invisible. The answer lies somewhere between 'yes' and 'no'.[3]

With the tacit knowledge that the causes of policy change are 're-lentlessly non-linear' a PA practitioner not previously involved before went back to Laggan two years after the PRA events to try to enable people interviewed to describe and record their own opinions regarding factors and events they felt influenced policy change. A facilitator met with as many people as possible who were involved in the process leading to change. Semi-structured interviews were conducted over the telephone and a PA practitioner spent three days and nights in the village meeting with people individually or in small groups. PRA tools were used, such as mapping, time lines and Venn diagrams to get a better understanding of the different factors and events leading to policy change. A map of Laggan

(Figure 1.12) was drawn by the first person met in the village. Information was added to the map by different people. This map enabled people to guide the interviewer to others they thought should be interviewed.

Time lines and Venn diagrams which were produced (see figures 1.13 and 1.14 for examples) enabled people to identify the events they thought were important in leading to policy change, and the sequence of these events. The villagers assessed the importance of events, individuals and organizations involved in policy change, as well as their relationship to one another.

Conclusion: what did we learn?

We remain completely uncertain as to how far PRA in Laggan in 1994 may have influenced forest policy change in April 1996. Based upon what different people have told us, however, we learned the following:

○ the 1994 PRA event in the village enabled more people to become involved in the forestry initiative and start thinking about their situation in a different way;

○ the PRA process and products (outcomes) helped to strengthen local people's confidence;

○ the media, politicians and civil servants were informed by the PRA report;

○ finally, and perhaps most importantly, the media, politicians and civil servants may have been influenced by the increased confidence level of the people of Laggan.

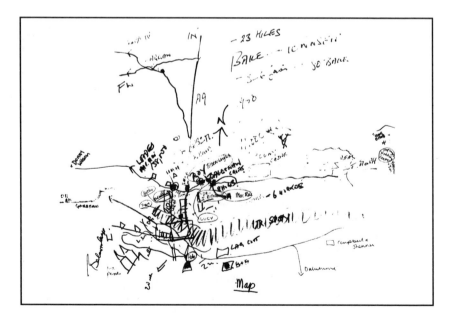

Figure 1.12   *Map of Laggan*

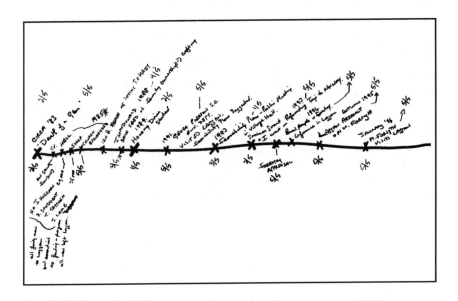

Figure 1.13 *Time line, produced by two crofters in Laggan*

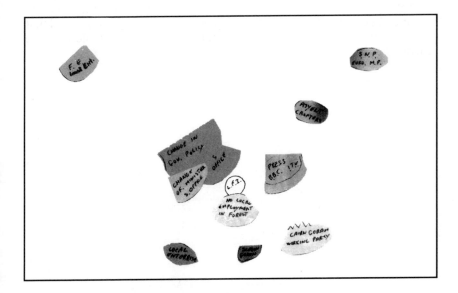

Figure 1.14 *Venn diagram, produced by a forester in Laggan*

As PRA practitioners we are learning not to take ourselves too seriously. We do not want to be a part of mythmaking related to any claims of PRA influencing policy change. What we have learned suggests that although not everyone in Laggan remembered the PRA events unless we reminded them, there is some evidence that allows us to think that it is 'possible' that changes did result from people better understanding each other and that the PRA events may have enabled the right environment for change. The products generated by the events were very useful for the purpose of providing the media with the Laggan story. It has been suggested by several people in the village and elsewhere that it was the media, and in particular the story which appeared in *Daily Telegraph* on 30 October 1995, which made the most impact on influencing policy change. The *Daily Telegraph* journalist used the Laggan PRA report to prepare for an interview with the Scottish Secretary and to write the story.

The call for PRA practitioners to demonstrate how PRA has influenced policy can encourage linear descriptions in order to simplify and describe causality for policy change. The hope is that nobody will notice when the answers are not entirely realistic. So seductive are linear descriptions of causality that researchers may even be willing to compromise their PRA beliefs to promote them. Linearity is a trap; if one believes that only linear descriptions of causality are worth noting, self-censorship sets in.[4]

Attempting to fit PRA into a linear-type equation has the uncanny tendency to shunt people into a 'hall of mirrors'. Accounts of the influence of PRA on phenomena such as policy change are challenged constantly with linear types of analysis. This can bury the complexity of PRA so deep that the 'graves go unmarked and the existence of these graves may go unremarked'.[5] The effects of PRA can be invisible, tacit, fuzzy. We cannot triumph by convincing sceptics of its value, we cannot make them see the potential, but we can trust that PRA's opponents eventually retire, and that a new generation is growing up that is familiar and comfortable with the practice.[6]

10

IDS Workshop: reflections on thematic and sectoral studies

What influence have thematic and sectoral studies had?

The range of case studies presented in Part 1 does not collectively persuade us that there is an easy or formulaic solution to the challenge of amplifying local voices in the policy process. Indeed, some of the contributors deliberately distance themselves from any notion of simple cause and effect when talking about participatory studies within a complex course of events that has policy change as an outcome. While it is difficult to talk about impact and causality, in particular where policy change is concerned, it can be stated with confidence that these participatory studies contributed to change, that they did play a part.

Realities revealed and explained

Realities were revealed by the studies. Local analysis not only filled information gaps but also explained them. Social analysis by local people produced local interpretations of social reality that could not always be knowable in advance, and that often surprised policymakers. For example, PRA methods applied in the Tarai region of Nepal revealed that the ongoing introduction of irrigation and new crop varieties increased yields but masked long-term declines in soil fertility. Similar research in urban Jamaica revealed that forms of interpersonal violence were the most common types of violence cited by local people, when much media and policy attention was centred on higher-profile gang war and political violence. Furthermore, area stigma was widely perceived to be a major factor behind a lack of access to jobs by young and old, women and men in poor urban areas. In Guinea, contrary to officials' views, indigenous land-tenure systems persisted, and were complex and diverse. In The Gambia, one-quarter of school-age girls were overlooked at village level because they were pregnant, married or about to be married; yet girls generally felt strongly about being denied education. In India, local analysts showed that their understanding of national-park ecology was better than that of the professionals: excluding buffaloes in the name of conservation both damaged their livelihoods and reduced bird populations in the park.

So what? Did anything change?

It is difficult for policymakers to challenge the views of the poor. They may disagree, but it is more difficult to disagree when the poor are reflecting directly, and profoundly, on their own reality. It is easier for policymakers not to listen to participatory outputs because these so often contradict and challenge their preconceptions of what interventions are needed for the poor. When done well, participatory studies enable the poorest and most marginalized groups in society and in communities to conduct their own analysis of their lives and conditions, and come to their own conclusions. The thematic and sectoral chapters in Part 1 have proved that realities were revealed. But did this mean anything? Did it engender any meaningful change for the good?

There *was* change and it was change in two directions:

(1) *Policymakers, and in some instances their policies, were influenced* to varying degrees, at various levels, and in a range of policy contexts. Gambian education policymakers were convinced by the power of policy analysis emerging from the PRAs in local communities. The effects of the PRA policy recommendations were reflected in the subsequent policy changes detailed in Chapter 5. These took account of the need to make schools geographically, academically, financially and culturally accessible to girls. The eventual design of the Jamaican Social Investment Fund was clearly influenced by local analysis; again, specific policy changes were made as a direct outcome of PRA recommendations. For example, policy priorities emerging from the study, and feeding directly into the Jamaican Social Investment Funds' subproject menu, reflected an emphasis on social cohesion-building projects not traditionally associated with social fund schemes.

(2) *Local people themselves in some instances changed and acted*, mobilizing at least in part through the experience of participatory analysis of their social realities. PRA in villages in conservation areas in Punjab and Rajastan did not subsequently demonstrate policy change as an outcome, yet was highly successful in facilitating local articulation of opposition to policies for accessing important resources. PRA reports from Laggan and other villages in Scotland provided the basis for working groups to 'tackle barriers to community forestry', one component of a complex process that led to forestry-policy change in Scotland.

How can the thematic approach be improved?

Be strategic

Gerard Gill (Chapter 3) argued that the demands placed upon product-focused research make it less participatory, but that 'the approach may be extractive but it is not exploitative'. His comment reflects the fact that for much policy-focused research the focus is on influencing policy through the power of its product rather than investing in the process as an agent of change in itself. Researchers who make this choice shift away from an organic approach and towards a strategic approach to participation and policy. This choice means that researchers and other intermediaries make themselves instruments for policy change. They must not abuse this power but must use it tactically to amplify local voices by representing them faithfully in the policy process. The role of researcher as actor is discussed further in Part 3.

Norton (Chapter 24) suggests that effective policy-focused research should 'think the process backwards'. Amongst other considerations, this means involving policymakers early. In certain case studies, the research process is demand driven and therefore more likely to find open ears. The case studies in The Gambia (Chapter 5) and Jamaica (Chapter 6) were characterized by their 'demand-driven' origins. The Girls' Education Programme in The Gambia was driven by the Ministry of Education's recognition that 'even the best strategies will achieve only modest results unless local communities, community-based groups and the people as individuals play increasingly assertive roles in defining, managing, implementing and monitoring the development efforts that affect their lives'. The study of violence and poverty in Jamaica was driven in part by the Jamaican Social Investment Fund's desire to respond more sensitively to local needs and priorities.

Being strategic also means:

o considering ways in which policymakers are most likely to sit up and take notice;
o getting focused on research questions early;
o assessing which clientele group is important for policy analysis;
o tailoring research methods to facilitate policy analysis by local participants most effectively, and thus strengthen policy messages; and
o being flexible about modes of investigation. Booth (Chapter 4) calls for a strategic embracing of different research traditions and methods, arguing that policy research should not be denuded by a blinkered attachment to a single methodology.

Be inclusive

Strategies must be qualified by the need to be inclusive. Participatory policy-focused research can be a fundamental learning experience for policymakers. If included in the process, policymakers can learn directly in face-to-face interaction with poor people. This was shown to be an important aspect of influencing the policy process for girls' education in The Gambia, as well as in land-tenure issues in Guinea and Madagascar (Chapter 8). An alternative scenario is to empower people as consultants to provincial headquarters or capital cities to present their visualizations and priorities. This emerges, for example, out of the discussion of the effect of videoed PRA workshops with local fishermen in Tanzania (Johansson, Box 3.1). The potential of such face-to-face interaction and the implications for attitudes and behaviour are discussed further in Part 3.

Ensuring inclusion also requires enhancing communication between researchers and stakeholders throughout the research process. The effectiveness of workshops at various levels for planning and familiarization, discussing findings and exploring practicalities for policy change was clearly demonstrated through the research process in Guinea and Madagascar.

Alongside such considerations as inclusion of secondary or 'institutional' stakeholders, researchers must reflect more critically on inclusion of the complex aggregation of interest groups they often label 'the poor' or 'local people'. Criticism of participatory research methodologies often centres on the seeming arbitrariness of the consulting procedure. Critics go even further when they suggest that the participatory investigative process lays itself open to appropriation by the more powerful interest groups in society and in communities, with the voices of women, ethnic groups and other interest groups potentially muted by this appropriation (Hanmer *et al.*, 1996; Kabeer, 1997). There is a clear need to ensure that all voices in the community are heard and that the priorities emerging are not those of the more vocal or powerful. In The Gambia case study, the strength of intra-community interest groups was critical to prioritizing the process. In particular, women's voices were not even heard in the final session.

This is not a weakness of the methodology in itself but of the researcher. Issues of inclusion underpin the participatory research ethic, so it cannot be a weakness of principle. The research process when implemented with thoroughness and integrity has, moreover, been shown to be inclusive, to amplify rather than mute the voices of the marginalized within 'the community'.

Successful inclusion relies on a the recognition of conflicts of interest and inequities of power within communities; in other words on 'problematizing' the community (see Norton, Chapter 24). It then requires that researchers are sensitive to partisan traits and tensions in the research process so that the study does not get hijacked along with its integrity. In this way, ensuring space for all groups becomes a central plank of the research process itself.

In the long run, rigorous research requires rigorous training (see Chapter 23). The quality of training of research teams is essential to the success of a research methodology that does not so obviously have the crutch of objectivity, measured by statistical significance, to fall back on in the face of sceptical policymakers and others. Ultimately, training is also important in instilling 'best practice' in the research process. There is a danger that researchers are missing the epistemological wood for the technique trees. To be successful, priority must be placed on attitudes and behaviour rather than on a blind and often self-defeating adherence to a set of tools.

PART 2

PARTICIPATORY POVERTY ASSESSMENTS

11

Introduction

Disillusionment with existing poverty-line measurements, allied to a belief that the poor should be involved in the development of poverty-reduction strategies, has created space for participatory methods to be adopted alongside more conventional quantitative methodologies in cross-cutting poverty research. The purpose of a participatory poverty assessment (PPA) is to create space for the voice for the poor[1] in providing a deeper understanding of the dynamics of poverty and its regional contextual characteristics, of the coping mechanisms adopted by the poor, and of local perceptions of problems and priority interventions.[2] To this end, PPAs use a variety of participatory methods and represent a groundbreaking new departure in policy-based poverty research.

The use of PPAs in the preparation of poverty assessments (PAs) and other poverty-related work is a new and very promising approach to generating policy-relevant conclusions in a manner which can complement, test and inform the results of more conventional economic and social analysis. The methodologies of PPAs are still evolving, but it is already clear that the results can have important policy relevance and impact (Norton and Stephens, 1995: 2).

These research processes were pioneered within the World Bank, which has been involved with PPAs worldwide in 30 countries, but mainly and most successfully within Africa.

The context

In 1992, the World Bank indicated that it would be carrying out PAs as a key piece of analytical work in all borrower countries in an effort to strengthen the link between the Bank's assistance strategy and the countries own efforts to reduce poverty (World Bank, 1991). The analytical approach which was outlined for undertaking these assessments was based on a conception of poverty dominated by household-level income and consumption data, collected through survey-questionnaire methods.[3] The centrepiece of the analysis was a poverty line constructed on the basis of household-level consumption data.

At this time, various participants in the Bank-wide Participatory Development Learning Group were interested in exploring ideas for scaling-up participatory approaches from the project level to the country level, analytical work which informs the development of the Bank's own programme and policy dialogue with borrower governments. Poverty assessments were identified as a new form of analytical work which might be particularly appropriate for introducing a participatory approach. Following discussion papers by two members of the learning group (see Clarke and Salmen, 1993), a climate was created in which it was possible to interest operational managers in incorporating participatory approaches into country PAs. PPAs started to be implemented alongside PAs, supported by bilateral-donor trust funds, particularly from the UK Overseas Development Administration (ODA), the Netherlands Ministry of Development Cooperation and Sida.

The number of PPAs gradually increased, with one-quarter of the PAs completed in the financial year 1994 including a PPA, rising to one-half in 1995. Out of the 29 PPAs completed by June 1996, 21 were in Africa, 6 in Latin America, 1 in Eastern Europe and 1 in South Asia. Box 2.1 details the distribution by region and by the various participatory methodologies employed.

In seeking to introduce a participatory element into the more conventional poverty analysis, the PPA is not conducted as a discrete research process, but is designed to produce results 'that can help to complement, inform or validate conclusions drawn from other kinds of more traditional Bank analysis' (Norton and Stephens, 1995: 5). Increasingly, debates within

---

Box 2.1 PPAs: location and methodology, 1993–6

AFRICA		AFRICA (cont.)		EASTERN EUROPE		SOUTH ASIA		LATIN AMERICA	
Benin	RRA	Mali	RRA/BA	Armenia	Various	Pakistan	PRA/Various	Argentina	BA
Burkina Faso	PRA	Mozambique	PRA					Brazil	BA
Cameroon	BA	Nigeria	PRA					Costa Rica	BA
Central African Republic	RRA	Swaziland	PRA					Ecuador	PRA
Equatorial Guinea	RRA	South Africa	PRA					Guatemala	BA
Eritrea	RRA	Togo	RRA					Mexico	BA
Ghana	PRA	Tanzania	PRA/SARAR						
Guinea	RRA	Uganda	RRA						
Kenya	PRA/SARAR	Zambia	PRA						
Lesotho	PRA								
Madagascar	BA								

Notes: RRA = rapid rural appraisal; PRA = participatory rural appraisal; BA = beneficiary assessment; SARAR = self-esteem, associative strength, resourcefulness, action planning, and responsibility for follow-through (builds on local knowledge and strengthens local capacity through a variety of participatory methods); 'various' includes open-ended interviews, focus groups, and semi-structured interviews.

Source: Caroline Robb.

the World Bank are centred on how best to integrate participatory and conventional methods, distinguished as 'qualitative' and 'quantitative' respectively in Bank discourse.[4]

Process

There is no one single formula for conducting PPAs. Indeed, PPAs are characterized by the variety of approaches adopted in their design and implementation. In the World Bank experience, however, the task manager responsible for organizing a PPA usually locates a senior social scientist (whether within the World Bank or outside) to take responsibility for following the process through to completion. Objectives, methodology and research agenda are established by the task manager with the social scientist, and institutions and researchers within the country are identified for potential collaboration. A training input is set up, and provision made for support and supervision during the fieldwork implementation phase. Analysis and synthesis of the research material is conducted at least in part in the field, but tend to involve analytical input from individuals with experience of policy formulation at the level of development agencies such as the World Bank (Norton and Stephens, 1995: 17).

Issues addressed

Where implemented, the PPA has become one component of a range of procedures that complement and inform country PAs, which in turn influence the design of 'country assistance strategies' and subsequent lending programmes and non-lending outputs (see World Bank, 1996a, for details). The PPA rapidly came to be seen as a framework for addressing a range of issues of substance and process which would otherwise have been overlooked. These include:

o The *multi-dimensional character of poverty*, and local conceptions of the dimensions of deprivation not easily captured through questionnaire methods, including the seasonal aspects of poverty. Among these concepts are: vulnerability, powerlessness, isolation, survival, security and self-respect, familiar from social-development literature on poverty (Chambers, 1983; *IDS Bulletin*, 1989).[5] These concepts raise the critical importance of broader aspects of livelihoods than those dealt with by income and consumption measures,[6] especially in rural areas, e.g. access to water and fuelwood.

o Aspects of poverty applying to levels of *social organization*, within and beyond the household (the dominant unit of analysis for questionnaire-survey methods). These include: intra-household issues of distribution; separation of incomes and livelihoods; and dimensions of poverty which apply at the community level (such as access to common-property resources, some kinds of services and infrastructure and community-level social capital).

o Access to, relevance and utilization of *basic social services*: user's view and provider's view. The experiences that the poor have in dealing with government services; their perspectives on the specific constraints they experience in trying to gain access; and of the quality and relevance of those services.

○ Local views from poor urban and rural communities on the *priority actions* for poverty reduction which could be taken by government agencies, NGOs and communities themselves.

With respect to the above, the great strength of the PPA is that, through use of PRA and associated methods, it is able to elicit surprises, information not knowable in advance that would be unlikely to emerge through conventional inquiry based on a preconceived set of questions. In Ghana, for example, infrastructure was found to be a higher priority amongst rural people than had been recognized. In Zambia, seasonality analysis revealed that payment of school fees coincided with a season of high stress, the result of high incidence of sickness and hard work combined with shortages of money and food. In South Africa also, seasonal deprivation was revealed to be more significant than previously assumed.

The potential

There is a growing consensus that conventional poverty analysis, based on narrow consumption- or income-based definitions of poverty, is unsatisfactory at best and ineffective at worst. At the same time, there is a growing conviction that participatory methodologies, when implemented well, provide the conceptual and methodological weight necessary to create alternative frameworks[7] for understanding. Hanmer *et al.* (1996: 8.1), reviewing the World Bank's achievements with PAs to date, conclude that 'social assessments and participatory processes should play a growing role in helping to understand poverty and in refining the design and implementation of poverty interventions'. There is a tremendous potential for PPAs to become more central to poverty analysis, both within the World Bank and within other institutions. This potential stems from three characteristics of PPAs: they are flexible instruments; they lend themselves to institutional collaboration; and they can be (and have been) used in any institutional context.

The flexibility of PPAs is demonstrated by the wide range of contrasting approaches adopted by various World Bank-initiated assessments, both within Africa and in other continents. The Ghana, Zambia and Mozambique PPAs, for example, were open-ended, encouraging participatory analysis through the broad and cross-cutting entry point of 'poverty'. The South Africa PPA involved the commissioning of a collection of studies on a variety of poverty-related themes, including catchment management, access to land and services, farming systems for small-scale farmers and child homelessness. The Kenya and Tanzania PPAs emphasized a more statistical approach to data analysis, introducing categories of analysis across populations and regions in order to aggregate findings and recommendations.

PPAs typically involve a wide range of institutions. The PPA-type study is not and should not be limited to the World Bank or even to multilateral development agencies. The most successful PPAs have been those which have involved collaboration with national and international stakeholders. As Robb points out (Chapter 16), these have on occasion led to sustained in-country promotion and adoption of participatory methodologies. In Ecuador, for instance, UNICEF later employed the PPA approach to evaluate programme impacts. The United Nations Development Programme (UNDP) was involved in the PPA in Togo and is now promoting participatory analysis in-country from its resident mission.

Although most commonly associated with World Bank initiatives, PPAs have been and continue to be instigated and conducted in different institutional contexts, increasingly independent of the Bank. For example, dialogue between the Government of Gambia and the UNDP in 1990 led to the formulation of a national Strategy for Poverty Alleviation (SPA) (see Robb, nd). This provided the institutional framework within which the poor could express their views and through which organizations could respond to these views. Action Aid assisted the government in organizing focus-group discussions using participatory methods within local communities in which local people analysed poverty and its causes. Subsequent cross-sectoral government dialogue considered, in the light of this participatory poverty analysis, how existing sectoral policy could achieve a poverty focus. Through the SPA, in other words, space was created within the established policy framework for the views of a wider range of stakeholders to be expressed, including those of the poor themselves.

Other examples of 'non-Bank' PPAs include a Livelihood Analysis conducted by Action Aid Nepal, a PPA conducted for DANIDA in Nepal by a local NGO, New ERA, to evaluate the performance of Danish bilateral development assistance for poverty alleviation (New ERA, 1995), and a recent national participatory poverty study sponsored by UNDP in Bangladesh (UNDP, 1996). The study was conducted using a participatory rapid rural appraisal (PRRA) approach and provides another striking illustration of the power and potential of this open-ended method. As with the PPAs discussed in chapters 12–17, the study elicited surprises in problem identification and policy recommendations by local people. It emerged that a major difficulty for both poor men and women was the dowry. Demands for dowry have escalated in recent years, forcing parents with grown-up daughters to take out loans at high interest rates from moneylenders. Daughters become a burden to their parents, and wives are divorced, or abused if the dowry is not paid or if the payment is compromised. Daughters are sometimes denied education because this might increase the dowry (if they do not subsequently find a job). Across the country, poor people whose lives were affected by the dowry stressed the need to enforce existing anti-dowry laws.

The case studies

The case studies in Part 2 convey the views of individuals involved with several African PPAs on different aspects of this participatory research process. Dogbe (Chapter 12) describes the experience of his organization, CEDEP, in conducting the Ghana PPA. He stresses the importance of local ownership of the research process and of evoking the views of the poor on what it means to be poor and how poverty can be tackled. Milimo *et al.* in Chapter 13 demonstrate how the Zambia PPA helped influence specific sectoral policies of government ministries as well as contribute to a shift in the sectoral balance of resource allocation within the World Bank-lending programme to Zambia. Reflecting on the Mozambique PPA, Owen (Chapter 14) argues for a process-based approach to PPAs, designed to bridge the gap between primary and institutional stakeholders. This, he argues, would increase the likelihood that policymakers take ownership of decisions arising out of the research process while ensuring that local voices are heard. Attwood and May (Chapter 15) describe a PPA in South Africa in which participation was built into every stage of the research process – design, methodology, management, facilitation and synthesis – with multiple-stakeholder inclusion from the outset.[8] Their chapter also provides a brief overview of the process of moving from research results to policy analysis, and addresses the question of translating complex realities into a usable policy framework without losing the voice of the poor.

Robb (Chapter 16) provides a synthesis of the World Bank's experience to date with PPAs. She highlights key issues of management of the assessment process at community, country and institutional levels, and suggests a threefold classification of PPAs, based upon the varying objectives and outcomes of each PPA experience. Finally, Norton (Chapter 17) reflects on the influence that PPAs have exerted to date. From his experience of instigating PPAs within the World Bank, and drawing on additional comments made during the IDS workshop, he proposes a series of guidelines for improving the PPA process.

The case studies in Part 2 are loosely linked under the organizational umbrella of the World Bank, yet PPAs themselves are not, as we have seen, institutionally grounded in one development agency, to be judged as such. They represent, rather, a genus from which people operating in different institutions and in different regions can invent their own experiences. By presenting the experiences of several African PPAs we are encouraging continuing debate as to how such an approach can be improved, modified and adapted to suit different contexts.

12

'The One Who Rides the Donkey Does Not Know the Ground is Hot': CEDEP's involvement in the Ghana PPA

TONY DOGBE

Chapter 12 discusses a series of participatory poverty assessment (PPAs) exercises conducted in Ghana by the Centre for Development of People (CEDEP) in three phases between May 1993 and November 1994. The aims of the PPAs were: (i) to gain insights into the poor's living experiences and conceptions of wealth, poverty and well-being; (ii) to elicit local perceptions of needs and priorities to be considered in the formulation of any policies and programmes to reduce poverty; and (iii) to examine access to and utilization of basic social services by the poor. The PPA series in Ghana provided a space for the interaction of practitioners and institutions in the South, building capacity through skills sharing and networking. Moreover, during the research process itself, ownership and responsibility for the PPA series was progressively transferred to CEDEP, so that by the third phase of the PPA it was responsible for every aspect of the research process.

Chapter 12 argues that the PPA series, although essentially extractive, gave the poor a voice by conveying to policymakers their perceptions of poverty and their priorities for poverty reduction. It identifies subsequent World Bank-policy priorities for Ghana that are likely to have been influenced by this information, notably a long-term focus on rural infrastructure through the development of a rural infrastructure project, and increased attention on basic education through joint-donor support for a government initiative to provide free compulsory education. From a methodological perspective the PPA series has been instrumental in raising the credibility of participatory research in Ghana, with an increased demand from policymakers and officials for timely information conducted through participatory studies.

Rich man, poor man

During a focus-group discussion on members' perception of poverty, a group of men in Komaka, a village in the Upper-East Region of Ghana, stated that 'the one who rides the donkey does not know the ground is hot'. In other words, the rich man cannot know or feel the poor man's problems unless he gets off the donkey and walks on the ground or unless he asks the poor man.

I have chosen this proverb as the title for this Chapter because it captures the essence of the PPA exercises that the Centre for Development of People (CEDEP) played a major role in organizing in 1993 and 1994. One of the reasons for our PPAs was to 'hand over the stick' to the poor to lead the discussion on poverty and on the strategies which should be adopted to mitigate it. It is the poor who can best give us insight into what poverty means and how it can be tackled. PRA methods were used during the PPA exercises to evoke these insights, but have also been adopted subsequently to get the policymakers and others removed from the ground to listen to the voices of the poor.

The PPA studies in Ghana

The Ghana PPA series was initiated by the World Bank as part of a series of research initiatives under the Extended Poverty Study, eventually published as a World Bank document (World Bank, 1995a), the rationale for which is discussed by Norton and Francis (1992). Sponsored by ODA, GTZ and UNICEF, the assessment was conducted in three phases. Each phase lasted around two to three months, including training, but spread over a period of more than two years, between May 1993 and November 1994. Phases 1 and 2 focused on gaining insights into the poor's living experiences and conceptions of wealth, poverty and well-being, and the needs and priorities which they considered essential in the formulation of any poverty-reduction policies and programmes. Phase 3 of the series concentrated specifically on access to and utilization of basic social services by the poor.

South–South skills share and networking

Up until 1993, we were not aware of anybody in-country who utilized PRA methods widely, and there was a need to bring in trainers from outside, in this case two IDS trainers from India. This was in itself significant. Coming from another Third World country, with conditions similar to those in Ghana, it was easy for the trainers to carry their experiences, conviction and enthusiasm across to us, the trainees. In addition, the training materials (slides, videos and handouts) reflected Indian experiences. As such we saw many parallels with our own circumstances which convinced us that these methods were applicable in Ghana.

By the second phase, CEDEP took responsibility for training as well as logistics. I doubt very much if two trainers from the North could have made the impact so forcefully. For this reason, as much as possible, more of such South–South skills, transfers should be encouraged.

IDS facilitated this skills, transfer not by sending its own staff when contacted for help, but by recommending the two Indian trainers. I would like to see many more institutions of the North, especially the bilateral agencies, shifting towards this approach. For me, as a citizen of a poor country, it gives me pride and dignity to see someone from a similar background share their experiences and knowledge with us.

I am aware that team composition and selection for the PPAs differed for each country. I would, however, like to mention that the idea of drawing people from academia, NGOs and government institutions has worked well in our PPAs. For us in CEDEP, it has fostered strong ties with the institutions of some of the participants which have spilled over into other areas of collaboration.

Handing over the stick

In the first two phases of the PPA studies, CEDEP was contracted to carry out the logistical arrangements, such as finding a training venue, contacting communities to be visited, and assisting with the recruitment of the research team. This was a very important learning process for us as an organization that had not had any previous experience in managing a research process of any kind, let alone one of such magnitude.

By the third phase, the research supervisor was able to hand over every aspect of this process to us. We had to meet and negotiate fees with UNICEF, the funding institution, recruit and contact the lead and support researchers, undertake the training, in addition to all the other tasks of the previous phases. The research supervisor's inputs were restricted by this stage to participating in the debriefing workshop and minor editing of the draft report. By entrusting this last stage to us he had completed the formal process of building our capacity to undertake studies of this kind. Since November 1994, we have overseen seven studies of varied scales and related to different themes or sectors.

Unfortunately, this approach of combining capacity building with accomplishing a task was the initiative of an individual but not of the institution for which he was working; you can imagine the impact were the bilateral- and multilateral-aid agencies to adopt this approach as a mode of operation.

The RRA–PRA spectrum

Since CEDEP was introduced to PRA methods, we have used them in undertaking a number of policy-oriented studies with communities, in identifying project activities and in planning the execution of these activities. My observation is that when used for research, the approach is more in the nature of RRA because, most often, the research teams: come for a short period; do not live in the community; raise a lot of expectations which are not fulfilled; and in most of the studies have been unable to provide feedback to the community, making the process extractive. When used for project activities, however, the participation of the community is increased, the process is not extractive and any expectations raised are met through the activities. Irrespective of these differences in process and outcomes, we have labelled everything we have done as PRA. At various fora, especially when doing PRA training, I have said that our PRA activities must be placed on a spectrum, with RRA at one end and PRA at the other, and admit to ourselves where our work falls on that spectrum. Awareness of this would enable us to accept the limitations of what we can or cannot do with any community.

Face-to-face interaction

An important aspect of PRA is its ability, within a short period, to influence the attitude of the educated and urban élite towards the poor, illiterate and rural people. During PRA training, more often than not, trainees are sceptical as to the capacity of the poor to carry out intelligent assessments. A couple of hours in the community and their attitude becomes one of respect and admiration. After one PRA exercise with top Ministry of Health officials, a district official who had originally been opposed to the PRA team entering a community confessed his greatest lesson to have been never to describe a community as 'difficult', and to recognize that the problem lies with officials' attitude towards communities and its influence on district teams' strategies. From this experience, the participating officials requested that training be repeated for the benefit of those working in other districts so that they could learn to listen and to learn from the villagers they currently looked down on.

Presenting the findings of PRA-style studies

The report of Phase 3 of the PPA study was distributed widely by UNICEF, and it was arranged for CEDEP to make a presentation. During this, and other, presentations, I realized that what impacted most forcefully on those who read the report were the excerpts or quotations from what the poor themselves had to say. Officials and staff, far removed from grassroots' contact, were surprised at the insight and depth of analysis of people on whose behalf they had until now been speaking. They had clearly underrated the ability of the poor to speak for themselves. In one workshop, the staff who worked within the communities agreed with almost everything said, including criticisms of their own performance. It is important, therefore, that reports of PRA-style studies should strive to capture not just the letter, but also the spirit of what people are saying.

Policy influence

It is too early for us to say whether our PPA and other PRA-related studies have had any direct and appreciable influence on the policies of government, non-government, bilateral and multilateral organizations. As part of a number of studies on poverty in Ghana, it would be difficult to attribute any policy changes specifically to the PPAs.

Norton *et al.* (1995) reflect that the PPA process contributed to the World Bank's Extended Poverty Study in several ways:

o it provided an extensive representation of alternative views of poverty to the consumption-based poverty-line analysis, including discussions of vulnerability and seasonal dimensions of poverty;
o it conveyed the views of poor communities on priorities for poverty reduction and strategies for moving out of poverty; and
o it contributed extensive material on access, quality and relevance of social services from the perspective of PPA participants.

In addition, the following policy priorities within the World Bank study can be identified as reflecting the PPA contributions:

(1) An emphasis deriving from priority-ranking exercises was placed on the need for a long-term focus on rural infrastructure, including

improved water supply and rural roads, resulting in the development of a World Bank Rural Infrastructure Project, which will attempt to deliver resources for this kind of initiative to the community level.

(2) The PPAs' thorough and extensive analysis of priority issues in education for poor rural and urban communities revealed an urgent need to improve the quality of basic education. The World Bank country department is developing a major scheme, with other donors, to support a recent initiative of the Government of Ghana, designed to provide free compulsory basic education.

(3) The PPA emphasis on the barriers to access to public health services experienced by the poor was reflected in the Extended Poverty Study, and contributed to the instigation of a multi-donor initiative to support a Sector Investment Programme in health.

(4) The PPAs contributed to the study's call for the need to develop mechanisms for improved targeting of poverty-focused interventions, with measures proposed in relation to a possible social-fund type programme.

(5) In relation to poverty monitoring, the World Bank study acknowledges the need for pluralist approaches, including qualitative, participatory analysis as a well as questionnaire-based methods.

At the national level, CEDEP has not evolved a mechanism for following up on the use to which the studies have been put. This is an area we hope to turn our attention to in the future. There are, however, recent government initiatives that reflect areas of emphasis in the PPA output. The Ministry of Education, for example, has now directed that all communities should form school management committees, with grants available to match funds raised locally to implement their plans. CEDEP has been asked to assist these committees in drawing up ways to improve the quality of schooling in 60 pilot communities.

When it comes to planning programmes, an area of frustration for many government officials and those of bilateral, multilateral and non-governmental organizations is a lack of basic information. The last population census in Ghana was in 1983. For this reason, we can say confidently that as a result of the PPAs, PRA has come to be seen by many of these officials as a worthwhile approach for collecting data, within a short time, to provide an overview of the situation on the ground and to take some interim decisions or actions. This is evident from the kind of studies we have been called to undertake. As I write, CEDEP has been asked to assist the Department of Social Welfare to come up with poverty profiles of five districts in the Ashanti Region under a project being funded by Save the Children Fund, UK.

A great strength of PRA studies in the eyes of officials is that there is often very little room for dispute because it is the people's voices that are speaking, whether they are in agreement with those voices or not. If ordinary people have the 'wrong' impression or perception, then, as many concluded, it could be that the government or agency involved is not explaining itself well enough or failing to supply the necessary information. It could also be that a policy or programme is not having the intended impact. In the same vein, because PRA brings to the fore the views and perceptions of the people, it is easier to write a project proposal based on PRA findings and get it accepted.

Conclusion

Compared to countries in Asia, PRA is relatively new in Ghana. My organization, CEDEP, was introduced to it only three years ago but it has become an integral part of our activities, whether gathering information or working with communities. Judging from the increasing number of requests we receive from various bodies to undertake PRA studies and training for them, it is evident that it is gaining popularity as a tool for eliciting the views of the grassroots and channelling those into programmes for policy formulation. For PRA to continue to meet the needs of both the grassroots and policymakers/programme designers in a country like Ghana, however, where the views of the grassroots are hardly heard, PRA practitioners must seek to represent not just the letter, but the spirit of what the people are saying. With time, as we gain more experience, we should be moving towards a situation where ordinary people can present their own findings. Remember, 'The one who rides the donkey does not know the ground is hot'. Making the voices of the poor heard is one of the major strengths of PRA. It should not be lost. To minimize this danger, there is a need for PRA practitioners to network and share ideas and experiences.

13

The Impact of PRA Approaches and Methods on Policy and Practice: the Zambia PPA

JOHN MILIMO, ANDREW NORTON AND DANIEL OWEN

It is becoming increasingly widely recognized that participatory approaches to policy research hold a clear comparative advantage over more traditional methods of enquiry. Chapter 13 describes the methodological approach adopted by the Zambia Participatory Poverty Assessment (PPA), illustrating how different participatory methods can produce highly specific policy-relevant information. The Zambia PPA, one component of a series of studies conducted in the preparation of a World Bank poverty assessment for Zambia, was conducted by a local NGO, the Participatory Assessment Group (PAG). It aimed to explore, at the local level, conceptions of poverty and perceptions of major trends and their impacts, to understand coping strategies, and to elicit priorities and policy recommendations for poverty reduction. The PPA prompted a shift of sectoral emphasis within the World Bank-lending programme by highlighting the importance of rural infrastructure and environmental issues to the poor and by emphasizing continuing problems with the delivery of education services. In addition, the ministries of health and education both made use of the PPA results in subsequent policy development, in particular with respect to user-charge exemption and timing. Finally, the very positive feedback of the PPA on the emergency safety-net implemented during the southern Africa drought of 1992 influenced policy recommendations on continuing provision for vulnerability in the poverty assessment. Chapter 13 also discusses issues of training and methodology, with the importance of close teamwork, strong analysis and focused use of PRA techniques stressed. Assumptions to be challenged when applying this rural-research tradition to urban sites are considered. The authors reflect, finally, on the strengths of the PPA process and discuss some key lessons learned. The Zambia experience demonstrated that PRA methods can deliver useful and timely policy messages, particularly when the research process is of high quality, policymakers are committed and results are triangulated with other sources. At the same time, in-country capacity was built, with a number of follow-up research projects commissioned. The PPA was able to produce a type of analysis distinct from that of conventional research, while giving voice to the poor, albeit in a necessarily imperfect, rapid and restricted fashion.

Rationale and objectives

The Zambia Participatory Poverty Assessment (PPA) was carried out in late 1993 as a component part of a series of studies leading up to the preparation of a poverty assessment for Zambia (World Bank, 1994). The overall objectives of the assessment were to establish a poverty profile for Zambia and to identify appropriate actions for poverty alleviation. This in turn would help guide Bank strategy and provide input for revisions to the Bank's work programme, on the basis of a poverty-alleviation action plan, which would also seek to identify appropriate actions for other agencies including government, NGOs and other donors. The primary rationale of the PPA was to contribute to this process by including within the analysis the views, perceptions, experience and preferences of the poor themselves. The specific objectives of the PPA were:

○ to explore local conceptions of poverty, vulnerability and relative well-being in poor urban and rural communities in Zambia;
○ to explore what the poor themselves see as the most effective actions for poverty reduction which can be taken by: (i) individuals or families; (ii) communities; (iii) government agencies; and (iv) other institutions;
○ to investigate what people in poor urban and rural communities see as the main concerns and problems in their lives at present and how these have changed over the last 5–10 years; and
○ to investigate local perceptions of key policy changes related to economic liberalization.

The role of the Participatory Assessment Group (PAG)

The use of PRA approaches and methods is becoming increasingly popular in Zambia, mainly amongst NGOs and some government ministries, with several donor agencies also now increasingly promoting these methods and approaches. The PAG is a recently registered NGO whose prime goal is to assist in the improvement of the quality of life of the rural and urban poor, with emphasis on empowering local communities to participate and take a leading role in decisionmaking, activities and programmes affecting their livelihoods.

In terms of both the existence of in-country capacity to carry out qualitative field research on development issues, and the adoption of the practice of consultative approaches with intended beneficiaries, the Zambia PPA was building on an existing base. Members of the present PAG had worked together on beneficiary-assessment exercises in relation to the World Bank's Social Recovery Project's (SRP) activities. These exercises used qualitative research methods, such as focus-group discussions and semi-structured interviewing, in order to consult with beneficiaries of the various community-level micro-projects which the SRP was sponsoring about aspects of implementing the projects. The value of consultation with intended beneficiaries in policy formulation was thus already to some extent recognized, and a team existed with experience in the field.

Methodology

The fieldwork was carried out by two teams of Zambian researchers, with support from two World Bank researchers and Dr Milimo.[1] The teams were balanced in terms of gender, and contained a range of linguistic skills

Table 2.1: Zambia PPA: issues and methods in a rural context

Issues	*Methods*
Perceptions and indicators of wealth, well-being, poverty, vulnerability, powerlessness. Local terminologies and their correspondence with such concepts. Differences in perception by gender.	Wealth/well-being grouping, for criteria and indicators. Social mapping Semi-structured interviews.
Perceptions of change over time in welfare indicators, terms of trade.	Time line (for migration, rural terms of trade, environment etc.). Trend analysis.
Access to services (and usage of services) such as health, education, credit. Preferences, especially where choice between options is possible. Perceptions of services, including views (or awareness) of recent change. Again, differing perceptions and values for men and women.	Institutional diagramming. Semi-structured interviews. Trend analysis of services – e.g. health, education, agricultural extension, marketing.
Seasonal stress: food security, health, general livelihoods.	Seasonal calendar (health, food security, food intake, access to fuel, water etc.). Comparative seasonal calendars: good years, bad years, average years.
Assets of rural communities (access to services, common-property resources, other natural resources).	Resource mapping. Focus group. Institutional diagramming (Venn).
Assets of rural households.	Wealth-ranking/grouping. Livelihood analysis.
Coping strategies in times of crisis.	Livelihood analysis. Semi-structured interviews. Ranking exercises.
Perceptions of consumption levels in terms of food, clothing, and in relation to well-being.	Well-being grouping/ranking, social mapping. Semi-structured interviews.
Community-based support mechanisms for the rural poor (community safety nets).	Institutional mapping. Semi-structured interviews.
Role of community institutions in service/infrastructure provision.	Institutional mapping. Semi-structured interviews.
Long-term environmental trends, e.g. declining soil fertility, declining rainfall.	Historical transects. Community time lines. Resource mapping at different points in time. Trend analysis.

Table 2.2: Zambia PPA: issues and methods in a urban context

Issues	*Methods*
Perceptions and indicators of wealth, well-being, poverty, vulnerability, power-lessness. Local terminologies and their correspondence with such concepts. Differences in perception by gender.	Well-being/wealth ranking, for criteria and indicators. Semi-structured interviews.
Perceptions of change over time in welfare, indicators, terms of trade, access to employment/income.	Time line. Matrix scoring over time for changes in the labour-market.
Access to services (and usage of services) such as health, education, credit. Perceptions of services, including views (or awareness) of recent change. Again, differing perceptions and values for men and women.	Institutional diagramming. Semi-structured interviews. Time lines of health and education services.
Seasonal stress: food security, health, income, expenditure, activity (by selected occupational groups).	Seasonal calendar – by occupational/residential group – activity, income, expenditure, health.
Assets of urban households.	Wealth-ranking/grouping. Livelihood analysis.
Fall-back strategies in times of crisis.	Livelihood analysis. Semi-structured interviews. Ranking exercises.
Perceptions of consumption levels in terms of food, clothing, and in relation to well-being.	Well-being grouping/ranking, social mapping. Semi-structured interviews.
Local institutions of self-help and support for the urban poor (e.g. market-traders' associations, trade associations, churches etc.).	Institutional mapping. Semi-structured interviews.
Role of community institutions in service/infrastructure provision.	Institutional mapping. Semi-structured interviews.
Responsibilities, obligations within households (support to children, provision of food, payment of school fees etc. by gender).	Semi-structured interviews. Decisionmaking matrix.

appropriate to the geographical coverage of the two areas. They were encouraged to prepare site reports following each period of fieldwork, which were used at a final synthesis workshop to help to bring together policy insights and information from the exercise.

The methodology for the PPA included a mix of methods and techniques known to the teams under the labels 'beneficiary assessment' and 'participatory rural appraisal'. All of these methods were either covered or 're-capped' in the training workshop, which was led by an experienced Indian trainer, Meera Shah, building on the experience of working with the Ghana Poverty Assessment.

A semi-structured interview (SSI) guide was prepared, and research teams encouraged to use it flexibly, with researchers probing and seeking to follow relevant and interesting leads as they came up. The teams were also urged to develop thematic SSI interview guides on specific topics they wished to probe as the research progressed; for example access to, and perceptions of, key social services.

In addition, the teams faced the challenge of using methods from the PRA family to access not only the knowledge and information possessed by the rural and urban poor, but also their own analysis of their situation. They were encouraged:

o to think for themselves concerning how to investigate topics using sequences of methods, and mixing the visual methods with the semi-structured interviewing;
o to use wealth ranking to attempt to generate samples of different community strata with which to follow up in particular instances; and
o to record the verbal interactions between the members of the group carrying out the analysis, the process of interpretation and the criteria which local people were applying, and (generally after completion of the diagram and a preliminary explanation by the analysts) to probe key issues which emerged.[2]

Tables 2.1 and 2.2 were prepared to outline correspondence between some key issues in poverty assessment and some of the PRA methods for the research teams.[3] This was intended as a suggested guide, and does not give indications of sequencing. Team members were urged to use their initiative and judgement, and build on their own experience, to determine the best means of exploring those issues, in line with the objectives of the PPA.

Sampling and representativeness

The ten research sites were selected in order to represent a variety of communities differentiated by:

o rural/urban characteristics;
o mode of livelihood;
o cultural/ethnic group;
o agro-ecological zone;
o level of access to infrastructure and services; and
o level of integration with markets.

The selection of participants was achieved largely through identifying poor urban and rural communities; selections were based in part on the field teams' prior knowledge (some of the communities had been visited before in the course of other exercises)[4] and in part on the advice of key informants. Within those communities, a range of people was usually interviewed. Many of these would not necessarily consider themselves poor in local terms, being full and active members of their own societies, yet the great majority would fall below a national poverty line, however this was defined. Even the wealthier members of these communities were suffering, as was evident from the range of problems which affect everyone within a given community: poor roads and infrastructure, lack of access to safe water supply, lack of social infrastructure and services, and lack of access to markets.

Policy impact

Evaluating the policy impact of PPAs presents a number of difficulties: the PPA is only one of a number of influences on the recommendations of a poverty assessment; in turn, the poverty assessment itself influences policy, but in many cases is only one of a number of factors that influence any specific instance of policy change.

In order to assess the policy impact of the Zambia PPA, the World Bank Task Manager for the Zambia Poverty Assessment was interviewed and the initial experience with PPAs evaluated. The following comments are drawn largely from that assessment.[5]

The impact of the PPA on the PA document was clearly strong, especially on the action plan. Specific elements which influenced the plan included stress on rural infrastructure investments (roads and water) and on urban services (mainly water supply). Other parts of the PA, which drew heavily on the findings of the PPA, included the poverty profile (especially for community-level identification of the 'very poor') and the chapter dealing with survival strategies and poverty-focused interventions.

The task manager for the PA gave the following assessment of the overall impact of the Zambia PPA on the policy formulation in the country:

o ongoing discussions on the sectoral emphasis of the Bank-lending programme with the government were influenced by the priorities expressed in poor communities in ranking exercises in the PPA (through reinforcing the current emphasis on agriculture and health, stressing the importance of rural infrastructure and environmental issues to the poor, and emphasizing ongoing problems with the delivery of education services);
o the Ministry of Health used the results of the PPA and the PA as a whole extensively in policy development (Dr Milimo participated in a policy committee looking into issues of exemption from user charges for the poor; a problem, identified in the PPA, of hostile attitudes and behaviour of health staff towards clients from the poor rural communities has been addressed through a programme of training);
o observations from the PPA related to the timing of school-fee payments (which coincide with the period of maximum stress for most rural communities) have contributed to ongoing work in the education ministry on school fees; and
o the very positive feedback from communities in the PPA on the functioning of the emergency safety net during the Southern Africa drought of 1992 influenced policy recommendations on continuing provision for vulnerability in the poverty assessment.

Issues of training and methodology

Two points are worth noting with respect to the training of the field teams. As with experience elsewhere, it is difficult to over-stress the importance of training in recording, reporting and analysis of PRA and qualitative research material. This issue is examined in more depth by Norton (Chapter 24). A second point to emerge very clearly was the critical importance of the quality of teamwork. In the first PPA one of the field teams held regular meetings to check on recording and reporting, to discuss findings and strategies and to plan the next day's work, while the other field team functioned with less cohesion. The difference in the quality and coherence of the outputs and policy insights was striking. As in the general experience with PRA/PLA methods, the critical importance of team building as a component of training is clear.

Several issues of methodology were highlighted by the overall manager for the poverty assessment in Zambia wherein the PPA provided inputs of high value in policy formulation:

○ priority-ranking exercises with the poor provided valuable insights when addressing issues of cross-sectoral balance (particularly in the action plan); consistent messages were generated by these exercises which created a convincing composite picture of the priorities of the rural and urban poor in relation to public policy;
○ information on seasonal dimensions of poverty generated by seasonality-diagramming exercises provided valuable insights on dynamic dimensions of poverty which covered issues such as income and expenditure, health status and food security;
○ information on the survival strategies of the poor from semi-structured interviews and ranking exercises provided a valuable basis for generating appropriate policies for provision for vulnerable households and communities; while
○ wealth-ranking exercises produced strong and consistent messages on the characteristics by which communities identified the ultra poor (including gender, age, disability and lack of adult children). In policy terms, the lesson which emerged was that while care of the ultra poor was generally regarded as an issue for community-based action, large-scale vulnerability (such as seasonal stress due to drought) was seen as a sphere where policy response and planning was essential.

In hindsight, however, the use of some methods could have been sharpened to improve policy relevance. Investigating local perception of trends on specific issues, such as food marketing, for instance, would have improved the analysis of trends in livelihoods within the PPA.

Emerging strengths of the Zambia PPA process

Reflection on the process of conducting the Zambia PPA highlights several particularly strong characteristics, with implications for future good practice:

○ the Zambia PPA was critical in demonstrating that PRA/PLA methods can deliver useful policy messages in a timely fashion; in other words, that under the right conditions a national-scale cross-sectoral exercise can begin to produce important policy inputs within a few months;

o in achieving this it was extremely helpful that the group of researchers already knew each other and had some comparable experience, as was the fact that the Country Department within the World Bank had been using methods for consulting beneficiaries for some time and therefore had a prior sense of commitment to the exercise and the results it was to produce;

o triangulating key findings from the PPA with the results of other sources was important in encouraging policymakers to act with confidence on the basis of recommendations derived from participatory research;

o the decision to focus the policy messages of the PA as a whole through preparation of an action plan meant that addressing the balance of sectoral priorities for investment was critical: the kinds of information the PPA provided on the priorities of poor rural and urban communities were a valuable source of input for these judgements.

Institutional impact

As in the Ghana case, one of the strongest aspects of the long-term policy impact of the process has been the creation of an in-country capacity to carry out participatory research into policy issues. A number of follow-up research projects were commissioned, including the 'repeat' of the PPA which was carried out a year later, and focused on monitoring of trends in livelihoods for the poor, and in delivery of social services to poor urban and rural communities.[6] This exercise has allowed for the results of the first PPA, and the poverty assessment as a whole, to be fed back to communities and district-level government staff for dissemination, discussion and dialogue. Another is the Sida-sponsored study on the impact of cost recovery in basic services on the poor (see Chapter 4). Ultimately, the network of largely freelance researchers who were the core group for these studies was able to form an institution to carry participatory policy research further within Zambia, including participatory poverty studies which are integrated into a national poverty-monitoring system.

Emerging lessons from the Zambia PPA process

A number of areas can also be highlighted where with hindsight the process of the PPA could have been improved:

o the PPA was much more effective at eliciting priorities at the local level than in outlining the institutional mechanisms by which identified needs and problems could be resolved; a stronger focus on institutional issues would have increased policy impact;

o work on the PPA was carried out in parallel with other inputs to the poverty assessment; if the PPA had been completed before the main mission then institutional issues in service delivery could have been followed up for the precise areas which the PPA suggested were priorities;

o given more preparatory time, efforts could have been made to draw governmental policymakers into the process of carrying out the PPA; having government staff from key agencies for poverty issues on the teams would have helped with policy impact.

Conclusion

Although clearly part of a wider research process, it emerged that the PPA played a relatively important role in addressing existing policy priorities of the government and donors, particularly in challenging sectoral allocations of resources. Through its ability to combine qualitative in-depth research with a package of flexible participatory research tools, the exercise produced a type of analysis that could not be produced by conventional poverty-assessment methods.

Various authors have argued that the participatory character of PRA derives from the extent to which the information generated is 'owned and used' by the participants themselves, for example to develop action plans at the community level. It should be acknowledged that this was not the primary objective of this exercise, which was to give voice to the poor, albeit in a necessarily imperfect, rapid and restricted fashion, within a process of policy formulation.

It should also be recognized that there are necessary limits to an activity of this kind, with around only six weeks fieldwork by each of two teams. The agenda of a poverty assessment is by definition broad and cross-sectoral. This kind of rapid appraisal exercise can indicate what people see as the main trends in their lives, and can establish how they themselves perceive issues such as stress points in the annual cycle in terms of household expenditures, vulnerability to disease, food security etc. It cannot, however, quantify these in any detail. It presents an agenda in terms of poverty and poverty reduction that reflects concerns in poor rural and urban communities. To situate the significance of this agenda in terms of poverty reduction as a whole requires, inevitably, a broader process of policy formulation.

14

Whose PPA is this? Lessons learned from the Mozambique PPA

DANIEL OWEN

Recent experience of participatory poverty assessments (PPAs) reveals that process is as much, if not more significant than product in determining their quality and effectiveness. Chapter 14 reflects on the process of conducting a PPA in Mozambique, and draws out important lessons for future PPAs. Local ownership of the PPA process was ensured right from the start through purposeful collaboration between stakeholders and by widespread dissemination of PPA information. Furthermore, for the PPA to contribute constructively to a national discussion on poverty, it was deemed important to distance the exercise from a World Bank initiative and the attendant suspicion with which this is often viewed. Not only did local ownership emerge as critical to its local acceptability, it also encouraged the participation of an array of local stakeholders and ensured that the process was successfully internalized in the continuing strategic work on poverty and policy of the government Poverty Alleviation Unit, line ministries and local NGOs. In attempting to promote local ownership, however, a trade-off between the quality-control demands of the World Bank and the imperative of in-country ownership was identified. Throughout the PPA process, from recruitment and preparation of the research team, coordination with other institutions, fieldwork approach and supervision, through to analysis and writing up, contradictions emerged between the expectations of the Bank and the reality of local ownership.

The extended work programme of the Mozambique PPA perhaps resulted in missed opportunities for policy influence within institutions working to their own deadlines. Yet the trade-off from such lost opportunities is the greater likelihood that this new approach to poverty monitoring will be sustained beyond the life of the World Bank-supported PPA. Ultimately this tension raises the question: 'Whose PPA is this?' Different stakeholders expect different types of information from the PPA, with implications for the ownership of the process. In Mozambique, the World Bank's objective was to promote local ownership, yet the demands of the Bank raised doubts as to its commitment to divesting Bank control over the PPA process and outcomes.

Introduction

The quality and effectiveness of recent PPAs has as much, if not more to do with process as with product, a process which combines attitudinal change with policy-influencing and policy-delivery frameworks. This process involves establishing a dialogue with communities, creating bridges between those communities and the state and with development organizations, and facilitating reliable, timely and systematic information feedback for poverty analysis and action. In the countries where a process-oriented approach to the PPA has been adopted, PRA methods have been drawn upon as the primary consultative mechanism.

The PPAs are oriented towards three sets of intended beneficiaries, incorporating two families of institutions: (i) the poor, for whom service provision and pro-poor policy frameworks, guided by relevant findings from a PPA, could be more closely attuned; (ii) the borrower – the host government – and the government's policy-alleviation programme; and (iii) the World Bank and its attendant country programme.

This Chapter reflects on the experience with the ongoing work in Mozambique. The intention is to bring to light some of the potential barriers encountered in setting up an effective policy-oriented PPA rather than to discuss the specific impact of the project in policy terms.[1]

Objectives and planning

The objectives of the Mozambique PPA were:

○ to contribute to government policy formation in the Poverty Alleviation Unit (PAU) in the Ministry of Planning and serve as one component amongst several leading to the preparation of a poverty assessment for Mozambique;
○ to sharpen the focus on poverty alleviation within the World Bank's country programme and serve as a conduit for feedback of operationally relevant material for project preparation and monitoring;
○ to contribute more broadly to an understanding of livelihood trends and changes in the country; and
○ to enhance the capacity of the Universidade Eduardo Mondlane (UEM), the PAU, the social welfare ministry and collaborating agencies to carry out participatory research.

The design of the Mozambique PPA provided for three phases of fieldwork:

Phase I,   a preparatory phase organized around a relatively flexible and wide-ranging research agenda, based on extensive consultation with other aid agencies, institutions and researchers;
Phase II,   focused on a narrower research agenda, to be determined through Phase I findings;
Phase III, designed to capture aspects of seasonality change.

Both Phase I and Phase II were to involve PRA methods as the primary research tools, although their comprehensive use was to be geared more to the second phase of the work. For the purposes of Phase I, wealth and preference/problem ranking were to be used extensively with the objective of establishing an indicative poverty profile and priority-needs assessment.

The idea for the exercise originated at the World Bank, in light of the positive outcome of the Zambia PPA. The proposal was well-received by UEM in Maputo, with which a contract to coordinate the work was established and to whom responsibility for the work and day-to-day coordination, including financial management, of the exercise was to be assigned, with overall task management located in the local field office of the World

Bank. The PPA received an initial lukewarm response from the PAU in the Ministry of Planning because it had been conceived in Washington and carried to the field. Enthusiasm increased, however, as the UEM became increasingly responsible as facilitators of the process.

Trade-offs in the PPA process: ownership vs. quality

Enabling the UEM to own the PPA locally was crucial to its acceptability, especially given its inception in Washington. For the assessment to contribute constructively to a national policy discussion on poverty, it was also deemed important to distance the exercise from a World Bank initiative and the attendant suspicion with which this is often viewed.

It emerged, however, that 'handing over the stick' has also carried costs, with trade-offs between ownership and quality control:

(1) The *recruitment and preparation of the research team* was problematic in a way hitherto unanticipated. The selection of the team and the design of a core training module were to be the responsibility of the UEM coordinating institute. For the initial phase of the work, researchers known to the institute were included in the team at the expense of key resource people elsewhere. Furthermore, coordination with other institutions initially translated more into coordinating and less cooperating, an issue of existing management practice rather than of manipulation. Coupling such sovereignty to an exercise based on PRA principles has resulted in an occasionally uncomfortable marriage of organizational structure and a PRA 'social contract'. Since the core PRA exercise and the formal PRA training were planned as a Phase II activity, the organization of Phase I induction and training was left to UEM, but was overall poorly focused on the research agenda, with too weak a 'link to poverty analysis and the PPA. The descriptive field manual produced as a result of the workshop has proved useful for other institutions seeking a Portuguese-language training reference, but is overall too cumbersome and too diffuse for the purpose of the PPA. The lesson is one of relevance and of careful matching of research issues to methods of investigation. As became clear during the fieldwork, the teams were not comfortable with either the range of methods or of how to sequence their use in the field.

(2) The Phase I rural *fieldwork* was planned around a relatively open research agenda, but lacked the necessary supervision to ensure systematization of both investigating and reporting. This resulted, in many instances, in the breakdown of a teamwork approach, with researchers often acting independently, a geographical bias towards administrative centres in the provinces and districts, methods slipping into semi-structured interviewing, and the inappropriate use of visualization exercises. In all, during the fieldwork, too little time was spent in the field and the teams were too unfamiliar with the communities to develop trust and, apparently, 'too unfamiliar with the participatory research methods to apply them effectively'.[2]

The Phase I urban fieldwork was accelerated so as to enable a World Bank-infrastructure operation, at an advanced stage of preparation, to benefit from the preliminary findings. A contract was also established with an experienced external consultant to lead the urban work. Although successfully completed and widely drawn upon by the World Bank and other agencies, the report was treated somewhat dismissively by the PPA team, which resented divesting control over this part of the exercise, as well as remaining unconvinced that the urban agenda required any methodological adaptation, despite evidence to the contrary from other PPAs.[3]

(3) The third issue related to the quality of *writing up*. A combination of an extravagant writing style and the colossal output of the UEM was inappropriate to the needs of the PAU, the Bank and the PPA itself for concise, economical, relevant and easy-to-read reports. Policy change cannot be induced by sheer weight and volume of documentation, though fortunately the final summary reports and thematic extracts have been more concise and effective at a policy level. For an institution accustomed to punctilious documentation, asking for a change to a rapid turnaround of information and analysis is akin to asking for a considerable shift in internal culture and a new type of procedural process.

(4) The decentralization of control of the PPA to the local coordinating institution has introduced one further order of complexity to the project: the potential conflict between the *multiple roles of the technical advisor* or '*outsider*'. From the UEM perspective, the technical advisor has been expected to play the role of colleague and team member. At the World Bank, two roles were assumed: those of advisor/trainer and of task manager (a quality-control role). From the PAU perspective, the role assumption was somewhere between the two, involving both task management and technical guidance. Ultimately, the technical-advisory role is one of ensuring that the PPA meets its objectives, the prime one being to improve the knowledge base that supports policymaking. Role misperceptions can inhibit this process, as opportunities for discussion of findings and policy implications can fast become derailed by endless attention to forms and functions of coordination.

Trade-offs in policy outcomes: rapid information feedback vs. policy-level acceptability

Local ownership of the PPA process has encouraged the participation of, and made policy contributions to, an array of local institutions and stakeholders (see Table 2.3):

o the PPA has successfully become internalized in the strategic work on poverty undertaken by the PAU, and therefore intimately linked to policy;
o NGOs have used field-site data for improved targeting and poverty-mapping data for longer-term planning;
o working groups in sectoral ministries have utilized information on specific sectoral issues (such as health, water and livestock);
o the design options of a World Bank-financed project were also influenced by the PPA; and
o the Ministry of Social Action has contributed provincial-level staff to the PPA training and as members of the field teams.

Table 2.3: The Mozambique PPA process, with policy outcomes

Phase	Output	Beneficiary	Policy outcomes
Preparatory work	(i) Discussion paper (ii) Site-selection document (iii) Field manual	PAU, provincial planning units, NGOs UEM, NGOs	Mapping contributed to PAU poverty profile; provincial- and district-level social-welfare targeting; NGO policy planning.
Phase I	(i) Urban Phase I preliminary report, May/June 1995 (ii) Rural field-site draft reports, December 1995 (iii) Summary report, April 1996	PAU, World Bank, donors, NGOs PAU, NGOs, sectoral ministries	WB Urban Infrastructure Project design input (problem ranking and institutional analysis); urban NGOs and UN agency use as basis for project planning. Input to PAU rural-poverty profile; input to sectoral working groups – synthesis extracts on water and livestock prepared.
Phase II	Phase II fieldwork and report: June–September 1996	PAU, World Bank, NGOs	Expected policy outcome: continued feedback to PAU poverty assessment preparation; input to WB-country portfolio discussions; support to local NGOs active in field-site areas.

As yet, the PPA has not presented an overall poverty assessment or a summary of policy implications. But what it has achieved is purposeful collaboration, through alliances with NGOs and government and through widespread dissemination of PPA material right from the start. This is the kind of collaboration that paves the way for more likely acceptance of policy suggestions as they emerge. The question arises, however: what is the trade-off between rapid information feedback and policy-level acceptability?

From the work done to date on the PPA, two types of policy-relevant information are apparent:

(1) On the one hand, outputs from wealth-ranking and problem-ranking exercises address two predominant questions in poverty assessments: who are the poor? and what are their priority needs? These outputs are immediately impressive, are amenable to direct policy use, and even in rough form, with little analysis, can have considerable influence on the policy agenda.

(2) As important, but of increasing complexity, are findings derived from aggregation of livelihood analyses, which are multi-sectoral, requiring

116

more thorough analysis and some persuasiveness in presentation. In general, PPAs have a good record of contributing to poverty profiles by lending a sense of the poor's own perceptions and ideas of stratification at the community level, and of providing a skeleton of major issues of importance to their well-being. But perhaps the most important contribution of PPAs over a longer term is their illumination of the collective and multi-dimensional causes and consequences of deprivation. Exposing this multi-dimensionality can suggest readily implementable donor and government actions to combat poverty.

In the case of the Mozambique PPA, the extended work programme has resulted, perhaps, in several missed opportunities for policy influence, both in the PAU, working to deadlines in the preparation of the overall poverty assessment, and in the Bank, facing similar deadlines in the project cycle of various operational tasks.[4] The perhaps-unintended effect of a more drawn-out preparation phase is, however, greater institutional credibility and greater chances for sustainability of a new approach to poverty monitoring after the Bank-supported PPA is completed.

'Whose PPA is this?'

Three compelling reasons for setting up a PPA in Mozambique were apparent in late 1994: (i) the timetable of the government's preparation of a poverty assessment and the relative paucity of available primary qualitative data at the household and community level; (ii) debate within the World Bank over the nature and composition of the project portfolio and country assistance strategy; and (iii) pressing community consultation needs of World Bank-financed projects under implementation.

Expectations were that the PPA would effect changes in each of these areas at both their implementation and institutional levels; in other words, that the PPA would both motivate attitudinal changes in the higher-level institutions of government and the World Bank and also influence project implementation directly at the community level. In practice, this has involved going to scale in different directions at the same time; PPA has been expected to deliver different types of information on different fronts, for different stakeholders at both the local and external (institutional) levels.[5] Prioritizing the demands of the various stakeholders and producing policy-relevant information at prescribed times for them has exposed stress points in coordination of the exercise, raising the same question repeatedly. 'Whose PPA is this?'.

Identifying stakeholders in a PPA is relatively straightforward: communities, government, NGOs, the university, the donors, the World Bank etc. Situating ownership is, however, more complicated. At the World Bank, the opinion was that the PPA should be locally owned. In reality, however, the relative degrees of control of the World Bank, the PAU and UEM were constantly tested. What has become clear during the course of Phase I is that every stakeholder expecting a policy outcome from the PPA feels entitled to an ownership claim over aspects of the work they identify with. Multiple stakeholders (and multiple stakeholders within institutions) create multiple policy demands.

117

A very apparent danger in this situation is that of the PPA beginning to deliver so as to satisfy primarily institutional or management goals for those bodies that invest in the process (interim reports, extracts of findings, premature summaries and syntheses of poorly analysed material churned out to keep up appearances of work on-track) rather than concentrating on the substantive aspects of fieldwork. The (il)logical conclusion of this is the demotion of fieldwork, the presentation of some form of output as an end in itself with scant question made of the validity of the results. This is precisely why it is vital that a PPA, which, with Bank support, automatically has some measure of policy credibility, bases itself on thorough, principled and systematic fieldwork.

15

Kicking Down Doors and Lighting Fires: the South African PPA

HEIDI ATTWOOD AND JULIAN MAY

Chapter 15 documents the process of conducting a participatory povery assessment (PPA) in South Africa in 1995/6. The project followed a national quantitative poverty assessment, and was based on a qualitative and participatory investigation into poverty. Although the primary aim of the PPA was to improve policy analysis, it was characterized by a concerted effort to build participation and stakeholder inclusion into every stage of the research process, from research design and methodology to management, facilitation and synthesis. In essence, the approach entailed a partnership, albeit unequal, between community participants, NGOs, professional researchers, the national government and the donor agencies. Adhering as closely as possible to participatory principles, a balance was sought between the generalizable results and broad policy-directive outcomes of policy research and the localized results and project-implementation outcomes of the PRA process. In this way, the research formed part of continuing development initiatives and was not simply an extractive exercise for a purpose remote from the needs of the participants.

Chapter 15 reflects on the challenges thrown up by the process of moving from research results to policy analysis, addressing the question of translating, or 'filtering', complex realities into a usable policy framework without losing the voice of the poor. The chapter concludes by summarizing the strengths and weaknesses of the SA–PPA process, arguing that the process did not allow for continued support of on-the-ground action and development by the main institutions involved. An additional challenge remains: to propel policy recommendations into implementation. This requires a continuous process of 'strategic activism' on the part of intermediary institutions, centred on a recognition of the abstractions required in policy formulation.

A means to an end

PRA embodies different things for different people. For the purposes of this chapter, our understanding of PRA is that it is an approach that, if used as part of a development process, can lead to control over that process by the people for whom development and local delivery/action is supposed to be happening.[1] Research, using only PRA methods, is not PRA. Hence, when considering the relationship between PRA and policy, the concern is not how we can use PRA to influence policy but rather how, through the use of PRA (participatory techniques and process), the poor can influence the policy that affects their lives while at the same time furthering their own development. We are concerned with finding or improving ways in which people can determine or have a voice in policymaking. Control over their own lives is critical if the poor and poor communities are to be able to improve their positions. PRA, as part of a policy or development process, is a means to an end. The end is the principle and practice of participation; In policy terms, the end is people's voices being heard and reflected in policy, so that policy supports them in attempts to improve their day-to-day situations.

The poor, on the whole, do not currently have a policy voice, as in South Africa they are largely unorganized and the policymaking process has not been addressed from the principle and practice that those affected by policy should have a voice in its determination. Policymaking is, rather, in the hands of organized groupings, 'experts' and government. The culture, attitudes, behaviour and beliefs of those in power towards policymaking need, therefore, to be addressed.

The South African Participatory Poverty Assessment (SA-PPA) was undertaken in 1995/6. It followed a national quantitative poverty assessment, and was based on a qualitative and participatory investigation into poverty. Commissioned by the World Bank on behalf of the South African Reconstruction and Development Programme (RDP) office,[2] the study was to form a part of the South African government's and World Bank's research agenda directed towards the completion of a Poverty Assessment Report.

This chapter reflects on the process of compiling an input document on poverty-alleviation policy, and the nature of participation and of the poor in the process, in order to share insights and learnings with others and hopefully to enhance similar projects in the future. The chapter summarizes the design of the PPA, emphasizing how participatory principles were built in to it at every stage; it provides a brief overview of the process of moving from research results to policy analysis, and addresses the question of translating complex realities into a usable policy framework without losing the voice of the poor. Key findings and their policy implications are presented in Annexe 3.

Table 2.4: Policy research vs PRA

Policy research	PRA
Generalized results	Localized results
Indirect linkages	Direct linkages
'Corridors-of-power' abstraction	On-the-ground complexity
Broad-policy directives	Project implementation
'The purpose of the SA-PPA is to provide a fuller and more integrated understanding of poverty from the perspective of the poor and to fill the gaps which an earlier quantitative study could not readily explain.'	*'The Nlhangwini Development Committee's (NDC) work is on-going and broad-based, currently focusing on sanitation. The research work took place in the context of the development work of the NDC. It provided a chance to assess the extent to which development activities target poor women and how this could be improved in future development work.'*

Designing the South African PPA process

The South African PPA was primarily a research project directed at improving policy analysis. The implication of this is that the exercise could easily have been undertaken using the tools of participatory research, without necessarily adhering to the principles which have underpinned the development of these tools. The alternative, which was followed, was to seek a balance between the requirements of policy research and those of a PRA-based process (see Table 2.4).

The PPA was conducted by Data Research Africa (DRA), a consultancy development research organization, from February 1995 until April 1996.[3] Figure 2.1 summarizes the SA-PPA process. Dates given are approximate.

After the World Bank had selected an organization to conduct the PPA, DRA was given limited funding to produce a proposal. The first step was to call a national meeting to consult and begin the involvement of the broader South African research and development-work community in the design and implementation of the SA-PPA. The workshop was attended by over 50 individuals from over 40 South African government and non-government organizations, and representatives from the World Bank.

Key sessions during the workshop were group discussions on *who* (control of research process), *how* (methodology), and *what* (research or poverty issues) in relation to the proposed study. Participants in these three group discussions, conducted simultaneously, were self-selecting. A fourth proposed discussion on *where* did not materialize, the three other issues proved far too interesting and contentious.

Who should control and take part in the study?

Through the discussion at the initial design workshop on who should control the research process, DRA's intention to facilitate the PPA in a participative, transparent and accountable way was not only accepted, but demanded. Other key principles suggested were gender sensitivity and equality, and equal geographical representation. The issue of who controlled the study was more concerned with who in relative power controlled the process, rather than control by local people. Strong racial, and to a lesser extent, gender dimensions emerged and were addressed in the formation of a management committee (MC) to direct the study. The MC of 6 people consisted of 2 women and 4 men, 2 black people and 4 white. It had representation from the World Bank, DRA, academia and NGOs.

Over 150 organizations and individuals (including community-based associations, NGOs, academics and other researchers) were invited to submit proposals to take part in the SA-PPA. The project allowed for assistance to be provided to those interested in submitting proposals. This proved critical in getting the only CBO research team involved in the project. After two rounds of proposal selection, 12 organizations were selected to undertake research for the SA-PPA. After additional funding was secured from the Overseas Development Administration (ODA), additional projects were included, bringing the total number of research

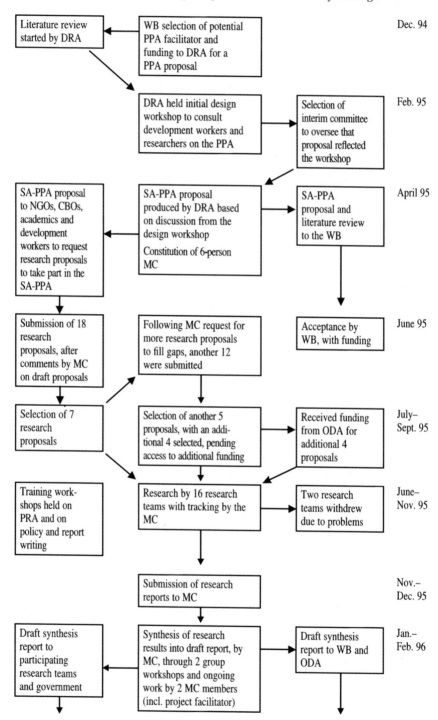

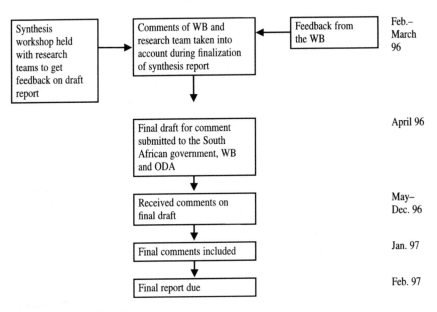

MC = Management Committee
WB = World Bank
ODA = Overseas Development Administration
DRA = Data Research Africa

Figure 2.1   *Flow diagram of the SA-PPA process*

bodies to sixteen. These consisted 6 NGOs, 4 academics, 2 consultants, 1 NGO/ CBO research grouping, and 1 academic/ NGO research group, with 2 selected research teams withdrawing.[4]

Throughout the study, the principles of transparency and accountability were pursued through open access to any documentation or information regarding the study. Of course, in practice, use of this principle depended on knowledge of the study and the ability to request information and to comment on it, thus these principles were not realized for the poor.

Proactive information dissemination took the form of a SA-PPA newsletter, distributed to over 150 South African organizations, which: listed participants of the study; outlined the process to date; listed those who had sent proposals to take part and who was selected; the research issues of selected researchers; and the SA-PPA budget.

From the outset of the project, South Africans insisted on a direct link with government regarding the process and outcome. This meant that the results would be fed directly to the government RDP office to allow South Africans to start working with the results of the SA-PPA as soon as possible, thus not having to wait for acceptance of the study by the World Bank. Ownership was in South African hands.

How should the research be undertaken?

In South Africa, tensions surrounding research conducted on communities by research professionals for their own gain (having racial dimensions) are rife. During a training workshop introducing PRA to South Africa in 1993, this issue was raised as a concern in relation to the possible use and abuse of PRA for research as opposed to development. Subsequent events have proven this concern to be warranted, as PRA methods have been used for extractive research purposes by outsiders and passed off as PRA. This is still happening and is, therefore, currently still of concern to development practitioners using PRA. In light of this, the suggested use of PRA for the SA-PPA was a contentious one.

Nevertheless, the promotion of PRA as a possible methodology for the SA-PPA was clear in that DRA invited Robert Chambers to talk on PRA at the initial design workshop. Discussion on methodology (how the research should be undertaken) raised issues around the ethics of the use of PRA for the SA-PPA research. From this forum (which included PRA practitioners), it was agreed that PRA principles, methods and process could be used as a methodology for the SA-PPA as long as work undertaken through PRA was by an organization which had a relationship with the community(ies) to be worked with and that the PRA work was part of on-going programmes of the researchers.

The proposal emerging from the workshop reflected this view. Researchers who wished to take part could select any qualitative methodology or PRA for their study, as long as it was appropriate and they demonstrated an understanding of it. A further selection criterion was that any proposed work was to form part of an ongoing programme, regardless of whether PRA was used or not.

While research proposals which did not propose PRA were in no way negatively biased during the selection process, the MC continued to suggest PRA training for research teams, including a policy- and report-writing workshop,[5] as part of a capacity-building component of the study. Of the fourteen eventual participating research teams, eight used PRA, with the others using mainly in-depth interviewing.

What issues should be researched?

The group at the initial design workshop came up with shopping list of what should be researched, which was grouped for the proposal to the World Bank. This listing of research issues was intended only as a guideline to researchers, although all studies had to have a gender focus. Potential researchers indicated in their proposals the work with which they were presently involved and the link to their proposed research issues, which may or may not have been on the SA-PPA proposal listing. Considering all suggestions together, the best ideas covering collectively the widest range of issues initially identified, as well as others, were chosen. In this way, the overall research agenda emerged ultimately from an interaction between researchers and those at the initial design workshop.

A criticism is that people in poverty did not have a direct input into the agenda. The extent to which CBO and NGO researchers were proposing studies that were part of their ongoing work with poor communities, which the communities had directed, would reflect one remote and indirect manner in which poor people could have had an effect; the other possible impact would be the degree to which agendas were changed in the field, by poor people. While researchers were contractually bound to investigate certain topics, the MC worked on an understanding of PRA and qualitative research that researchers might need to change their agendas in field, in the best interests, and on direction, of the poor.

From research results to policy recommendations

Given the policy-purpose of the study, the audience of the policy outcome and the number of input studies, the 'voices of the poor' needed to go through a structuring and filtering process. After direction from the research agenda: (i) the information was recorded, which can be less of a filter if it is recorded by all who have access to it; (ii) the research team analysed[6] and wrote up the information; (iii) the team drew out policy suggestions and implications; and (iv) the MC interpreted and re-analysed the research reports as inputs to the synthesis report.[7] The objectives of the MC in this entire process were:

1. *To structure the synthesis report in a manner which complies with the participatory process. This would allow the complex realities of poor people's lives to be reflected and analysed via their voice, and would respect their knowledge.*

The management team held two synthesis workshops which made use of many PRA tools including the visual sharing of information, an awareness of group dynamics and an emphasis on lateral thinking. Recognizing themselves to be the last filter, the MC steered away from discussing its own perception of poverty to guide the synthesis report, starting the synthesis process by referring directly to the input-research reports. Using cards, the MC brainstormed key points that emerged from the reports. These were noted separately on cards for all nine reports. The cards were then arranged on the floor into broad groupings which ultimately formed the structure of the synthesis report. Each grouping of cards was again considered for cohesiveness, and subgroups were formed. The research reports were then revisited in detail, to find more information to fit into each of the various groups, again using cards. The result was a series of flow diagrams, noting the essential points from the various reports. The cards in these flow diagrams guided the detailed writing of the synthesis report.

It was felt that this participative approach to synthesis-report writing had the greatest potential for limiting the influence of the MC's views on poverty and allowed the voices of the poor to be reflected in the final document as much as possible, given the research process. In some ways, a familiarity with the methods, results and shortfalls of more conventional research methodologies proved to be invaluable, both as a point of reference and as an indication of the usefulness of those methodologies utilizing participatory techniques.

2. To interpret this reality into a usable framework for policy formulation without losing the voice of the poor.

It was originally envisaged that the pivotal role of the policy-orientated team of researchers who made up the MC would be to inform and direct the individual research projects. During the course of the SA-PPA it became apparent that this MC had to deal with the far more complex task of translating the richness of the findings of the various projects into some form of analytical framework, without losing local voices, and spend less time on directing individual studies. In this process, a central principle which emerged was a recognition that while poverty is complex, multi-dimensional, and cross-sectoral, policy is simplifying, one-dimensional and sectoral. This results in a tension in the formulation and design of intervention. In recognizing this, it was also acknowledged that a policy analysis has to deal with a structural constraint imposed by the very organization of government itself. In the majority of countries, and certainly in South Africa, governments are structured into sectorally defined departments, budgets and responsibilities.[8] At this stage, therefore, much of the policy analysis of the SA-PPA remains sectorally defined and a source of dissatisfaction for the authors of the study.

3. To propel this effort forward in order to have an impact on the alleviation of poverty through the facilitation and translation of these findings into appropriate and useful policy.

A summary of the key messages and suggested policy interpretations of the SA-PPA is presented in Annexe 3. A research exercise which attempts, however, to move from synthesis into policy recommendations also has to consider the ways in which such recommendations can be implemented. This is probably the most challenging component of a study such as the SA-PPA, which tries to reconcile the experience of on-the-ground development practitioners with the broad requirements of policy-makers concerned with generalizable issues which are implemented through macro policy.

Broadly, the approach has been one of 'strategic activism', which tries to recognize the abstractions which are required in policy formulation. In the case of the SA-PPA, this stage necessitated an additional unplanned workshop. At this point also, the experience of the researchers on the MC required increasing self-management as 'expertise' began to filter and supplant the results of the various studies.

4. To give feedback to the researchers as to the outcome of the synthesis process and subsequent recommendations for policy, thereby allowing them to comment on this process.

As researchers had a responsibility to provide feedback and continue working with the communities which had collaborated with them on the research, so the DRA and MC had a responsibility to researchers, to show them what was done with their input-research reports. A workshop was held to discuss the draft synthesis report, during which researchers expressed general satisfaction but made specific suggestions for improvement, which together with comments from the World Bank, were considered when finalizing the synthesis report.

Strengths and weaknesses

Chapter 15 has attempted to share with others the experience of the South African Participatory Poverty Assessment so that future countries which attempt to improve or develop poverty-alleviation policies can learn from a process which attempted to develop policy suggestions informed by the voices and lives of the poor.[9] The MC attempted to conduct the PPA in a participative way in terms of design, research, methodology, management, facilitation and synthesis. On reflection, several strengths and weaknesses of the process emerge.

Strengths

In essence, the SA-PPA has been a broadly empowering experience. After some fairly blunt discussion, and the production of acceptable interim products,[10] the South African management team succeeded in winning the strategic and daily management responsibility of the PPA. Project management was, in turn, delegated to the individual NGOs, although support was available at all times throughout the study. An open World Bank and DRA agenda enabled development workers and academics to provide input and allowed participating researchers to select their own agenda.

Convening a stakeholder workshop at the beginning of the process, though time consuming, brought advantages which became apparent as the process evolved. The workshop identified the most appropriate approach for undertaking the PPA, and the methodology for the fieldwork. As a result, the implementation of the PPA was both rapid and efficient. Good quality reports were submitted by the teams in the field. The management of the process by the local consulting firm was transparent and effective. Overall, early stakeholder involvement engendered a high level of ownership and commitment. Documentation on the budget, participants and the process were open to any interested party.

PRA was not enforced as a methodology, rather any qualitative research methodology could be used, given appropriateness and ability, yet because the majority of organizations was committed to the use of PRA as their means of operation, the central role to be played by research participants in generating analyses and directions for action was emphasized. Some associations were already skilled in the use of PRA tools, with additional training provided by experienced South African PRA trainers, thereby ensuring that participatory research methods were fully understood and, more importantly, that experimentation could take place.

Different types of organizations and individuals conducted the research. The bulk was undertaken by NGOs as part of their own project planning and evaluation process or by academics working with them. This ensured that the research formed a part of on-going development initiatives and was not simply an extractive exercise for a remote purpose. Selecting projects linked to ongoing or past research-and-development work also represented an attempt to account for expectation-raising through the participative research process. A recent workshop with the participating researchers confirmed that the majority of the research activities had moved into an implementation phase and that the research had contributed towards better project design. There was obviously a varying degree of success between the projects. Examples included one scheme being able to obtain funding for a relatively large-scale nutrition-awareness training programme, with another project using the results to assist the representation of women on a local water-management committee.

The continued application of the principles and the methods of PRA enhanced greatly the interpretation and further analysis of the individual studies. Many of the results of the individual research projects could be triangulated across the different schemes, and against other qualitative, quantitative and participatory research work, allowing the analysis to move into generalizable findings. Where this was impossible, the information still acted as useful case-study material which could be used to support the feasibility of particular arguments. Finally, the texture and depth of the information served as a motivating force, pushing organizations and researchers into new directions and opening up new debates.

Synthesis-report writing was based on key points of the research studies, keeping as far away as possible from the MC's preconceived and academic views on poverty and policy. The linkage established to the South African government via the RDP office proved to a be a useful way of communicating the study to senior civil servants and politicians. The involvement of an advisor with wide experience in PPAs elsewhere in Africa ensured that a skills transfer took place, at least to the project leaders and perhaps to some of the individual researchers.

Finally, utilizing a team approach to management, which consisted of established policy researchers, the messages of the SA-PPA have the potential to be introduced into the policy debate through a wide range of fora. Between them, the researchers contributed to task-team reviews of South Africa's child-welfare and pensions systems, the statistical service, land reform and land restitution, urban- and rural-development strategies, agricultural extension and training, regional economic policy, farmworker rights and access to services and rural finance. The individual researchers and NGOs are also active in the policy-formulation process, including: AIDS/HIV assistance, nutritional training and surveillance, natural-resource conservation, domestic-energy provision; and local government.

Weaknesses

Through the course of the PPA exercise, several weaknesses became apparent. Communities had a limited voice in conceptualizing the study, determining research agenda, and commenting on the synthesis report; CBOs as research teams, arguably the most linked into communities, were under-represented. Accountability, transparency and access to information were, in practice, not realized for the poor.

Despite local management of the process, the timing of the overall project (initially just under one year but extended to 15 months) was still guided by the World Bank. Given the participative design, selection and synthesis processes, this meant that most researchers had between 3 and 4 months to produce a policy document, resulting in rushed qualitative and participative research. This timing was recognized by the MC, whose efficiency was critical to the success of the project, and commented on continually by researchers as being restrictive.

The principle of research being part of ongoing work was not applied strictly enough. It was also beyond the scope of the SA-PPA, given financial and time constraints, to follow up on feedback.

Potential researchers were contacted through a snowballing process, building on DRA and MC links. This was not systematic, and on reflection a wider grouping could have been consulted, although those that were invited were encouraged themselves to invite or suggest others that should be approached.

The SA-PPA was, finally, affected by an unexpected change in government policy – the recent closure of the RDP office, and the transfer of many of its civil servants to the Ministry of Finance or to the deputy president's office – which exposed the weakness of concentrating policy advocacy on one policymaker or department. Great care had been taken to draw senior officials in the RDP office into the SA-PPA. As the flagship policy of the new government, it was felt that direct access to the minister responsible for the RDP would ensure that the results of the SA-PPA would be absorbed rapidly into the policy debate. Insufficient effort was given to drawing in other government departments which might have been relevant, such as the departments of welfare, health, land affairs, agriculture and housing. With the closure of the RDP office, the crucial link to policymakers was undermined. The efforts of the individual members of the research team did ensure, however, that some of the results of the SA-PPA were fed into a number of important commissions of inquiry, such as those established to investigate child welfare, rural finance and the formulation of a provincial-development strategy.

From empowerment to meeting policy objectives: kicking down doors and lighting fires

Since the closure of the RDP office, events have again overtaken the SA-PPA, but this time in a positive manner. In October 1995, the South African cabinet approved the preparation of a report on poverty and inequality for South Africa. This was a response to proposals from the World Bank to complete a poverty assessment report for South Africa, and from the UNDP to prepare a country Human Development Report. After a tender process, a group of researchers was appointed to compile the document. The group included some of the research team from the SA-PPA; as a result, the knowledge which was gained by the latter has directly affected in manner in which the Poverty and Inequality Report has been conceived. Importantly, the report has been managed directly by the Office of Deputy President Thabo Mbeki, assisted by an inter-ministerial committee comprising the cabinet ministers of 10 government departments. As the Poverty and Inequality Report is focused on integrating the many policies affecting poverty in South Africa, and on recommending ways in which their impact on poverty and inequality can be improved, it is hoped that the SA-PPA is finally positioned to ensure that the voices of the poor will indeed be heard by policymakers.

A key lesson to emerge from the SA-PPA relates to the need for assertiveness on the part of the participants at all levels, and the importance of sustaining this. Comparison with the results of the PPA and other forms of research clearly demonstrates that neither an apologetic nor evangelistic attitude towards the methodology is either called for, or beneficial. The methodology has an internal rigour which can be sustained throughout all stages of collection and interpretation, and results in an analysis which both deepens and adds to more conventional research methodologies. The approach, if sustained, has in particular the potential to empower not only the community but also researchers in their engagement with different levels of government or other development agencies.

Despite the risk to the sustainability of the SA-PPA posed by recent political events in South Africa, it would seem that policy objectives have, to date, been met. Yet the present stage, that of moving policy recommendations into implementation, remains the most perilous of any research project, whether quantitative, qualitative or participatory, and with the most likely outcome being the 'report on the shelf'.

As one member of the SA-PPA team pointed out, moving information into useful policy requires a continuous process of strategic activism, identifying the appropriate institution, person or forum, and the appropriate way in which different issues can be placed on the policy agenda, in other words, identifying the most appropriate doors to kick down, the desks on which to light fires and the best way of lighting the fires.

16

PPAs: a review of the World Bank's experience

CAROLINE ROBB

Chapter 16 summarizes the results of a study which investigated the World Bank's experience in developing participatory methods for policy-focused research in the form of participatory poverty assessments (PPAs). The chapter focuses on the issues of management of the PPA research process at the community, country and institutional levels, highlighting key variables and possible outcomes. At the community level, the quality, credibility and effectiveness of the PPA relates to the nature of its sequencing with the quantitative World Bank-poverty analysis, the length of time allocated for fieldwork, the skill levels of research coordinators and their teams, and to the degree of institutional linkage established through the fieldwork process. At the country level, the potential influence of PPAs on policy change is influenced by the degree of government support for the exercise, and more generally the level of ownership and commitment of in-country stakeholders. At the level of the World Bank, policy impact again relates to ownership, with a team approach emerging as particularly important.

Although simple linear causality cannot be established, Chapter 16 gives examples of cases where PPAs have been seen to exert an influence on policy at the country level and within the World Bank itself. A threefold classification of the PPAs is proposed, based upon the varying objectives and outcomes of the PPA exercises: (i) information gathering; (ii) attitudinal change towards policy; and (iii) the strengthening of the policy-delivery framework. Chapter 16 concludes that to date most PPAs have focused on the first and/ or second objective, and calls for a shift towards addressing the wide objective of strengthening the policy-delivery framework through encouraging stakeholder dialogue and building capacity for policy delivery.

Introduction

Chapter 16 is a summary of the World Bank's experiences in developing participatory methods for policy-focused research in the form of participatory poverty assessments (PPAs).[1] The focus is on the diversity of experiences in both the approach and the outcome of the PPAs. This is illustrated in Annexes 1 and 2,[2] which analyse the methodologies and the impacts on a country-specific basis. The chapter draws upon the information contained in these annexes to explain the diversity and the wider processes affecting policy change.

The results of PPAs to date have been mixed, but lessons are emerging. Table 2.5 highlights the management issue, which is sometimes overlooked, within the context of the key variables of policy change. The table is

Table 2.5: Management of the PPA process

Management at the community level	Management in-country	Management in the Bank
Key variables	Key variables	Key variables
o Sequencing o Skill of the facilitators o Techniques selected o Community composition o Sampling/representation o 'Optimal ignorance' o Timing o Processing	o Bureaucratic structures o Political stability/support o Technical advice o International actors o Historical and institutional contexts o Power relations with the Bank o Perceived credibility of PPA and PA	o Ownership within the Bank – team approach, planning and preparation o Management support and follow-up o Interpretation of information o Role of resident missions o Time and sequencing
Outcome/impact	Outcome/impact	Outcome/impact
o Facilitation of the process at the community level weak => information does not represent the views of the communities but is biased by poor facilitation => value of qualitative information undermined o Participatory methods are used as information gathering tools => limited changes of perception by the poor, researchers and officials o Participatory methodologies are linked to work of in-country NGOs and government line ministries => potential for moving from information sharing to wider process of change and building time sequence data o Short-term one-off methodologies will inevitably exclude the more vulnerable (i.e. women and certain ethnic groups) => misrepresentation of the problem => vulnerable groups further marginalised o Urban groups fragmented => limited scope of promoting horizontal communications re issues such as poverty => participation limited	o Key policymakers excluded from the beginning because lack of political support for the PPA => lack of policy space to include controversial issues such as poverty on the political agenda => results of PPA have limited impact o Top-down approach adopted by Bank => lack of commitment and ownership of borrower => short-term changes in policy but no attitudinal shift o Policymakers feel threatened by the process => institutional survival remains the overall objective to the exclusion of poverty issues	o Technical advisor leads and manages the PPA with limited consultation in-house => lack of ownership of both the process and the information in other departments => limited impact on other documents o PPA information perceived as not credible => limited impact upon other documents o Bank documents reflect differing priorities => limited coordination at the country level => governments responding to the 'credible' documents which they are familiar with => poverty issues marginalised o Promote participatory, process management as opposed to data gathering exercises => Bank country teams and management participate in the facilitation of the methodologies at the community level in borrower countries => increased awareness of the problem and understanding of the value of the methodology o Team approach and management support => PPAs viewed as the first step in a process of building dialogue with key stakeholders within the Bank and borrower countries and not an end in

divided into three levels of analysis: community, in-country and the World Bank. It is recognized that all three are inter-linked but for ease of analysis they have been separated. Key issues of management at the community, country and institutional levels as seen from the PPA experiences of the World Bank are examined in the text and, using case examples, lessons learned from these experiences are discussed. The concluding section of the chapter proposes a threefold classification of the PPAs based upon the varying objectives and outcomes.

Community-level issues

(1) *The sequencing of the PPA* in relation to the quantitative poverty analysis. In some cases the PPA has been conducted before the quantitative survey. In Ecuador, the facilitator of the assessment suggested that the qualitative study should precede the quantitative one in order that the former influence the focus of the latter. The results of the Ecuador PPA fed directly into the type of questions analysed using the quantitative survey. There are, however, also advantages in conducting the PPA last: the quantitative results can be used to identify the poorest geographical areas for the qualitative survey to focus on; in addition, the qualitative studies may be used to explain perceived data anomalies from the quantitative assessment. In Mali, the quantitative survey showed what was thought to be a disproportionate amount of money spent on clothing. The qualitative research explained that clothing was an investment.

(2) *Length of fieldwork.* In Uganda, Togo, Benin and Mali short and rapid qualitative surveys were undertaken for three to four weeks.[3] Methods were based upon RRAs so feedback to communities was limited. In Togo, time constraints were placed on the fieldworkers by the World Bank's internal deadlines. Some results were consequently not disaggregated by gender and the final report was not written in a way which was easily understood by policymakers. In some more recent PPAs such as that in Cameroon, the lack of time for community-level analysis has meant that the results have been too generic. In Ecuador, the PPA was renamed the Qualitative Survey because it was felt that the limited feedback to the communities made the study non-participatory. In contrast, the Zambia PPA took 16 months to prepare and communities are now being consulted on an ongoing basis. A baseline has been developed for yearly community-participatory monitoring of poverty.

(3) *Achieving credibility of PPA data* (credibility of PPAs has been questioned for different reasons). The skill and role of facilitators becomes increasingly important to achieving credibility as participatory exercises are scaled-up for large assessments. In Mexico, for example, it was difficult to find a suitable national consultant who was not politically affiliated to coordinate the PPA. Controlling the process of gathering qualitative information proved problematic as the teams would attempt to follow their own agenda. In Togo, the teams within the field had limited analytical skills, whereas in Mozambique it was

concluded that teams were too unfamiliar with the communities to develop trust, and in addition were often not able to apply the methods effectively (see Chapter 14).[4]

The lessons that are emerging are that more time should be spent in training teams who undertake the fieldwork, with a focus on recording, reporting and analysis of the results. Time should also be spent in building up teams. In order to increase the credibility of collecting qualitative information it may be appropriate in some countries to use the existing NGO networks, where there is often a wealth of knowledge and skills. The advantages of this approach as opposed to training new teams, are as follows:

○ many NGOs have already-established trust with communities they are working with and have undertaken extensive qualitative research;
○ to ensure that research is not purely extractive, the surveys could be undertaken by NGOs which are already working with a community. The results could be followed up by the NGOs;
○ the capacity of existing NGO networks could be strengthened by undertaking country-wide PPA research; and
○ to bridge the gap between the quantitative and qualitative data, time-sequencing data could be collected by NGOs, and links established between NGOs, policymakers and statistical departments.

(4) PPAs should try and achieve '*optimal ignorance*' (Chambers, 1993a), and collect only that information which is of use to the policymaker. Careful selection of relevant methods which link to the identified research issues is, therefore, required. In Mozambique, the PPA presented too much information to the policymaker. This was the result of the lack of coordination between the research agenda/methods applied in the field and the internal reporting style of the coordinating institution.

(5) *Linking fieldwork with the work of other institutions*, such as country NGOs and government line ministries, as, for example, in the PPAs of Argentina and Brazil. As a result, potential now exists for moving from information sharing to continuous dialogue with various stakeholders, including those at the community level. The Cameroon manager of the PPA states that working with NGOs in preparing the PA and PPA provided a highly cost-effective means of tapping into the expertise and capacity of the NGOs.

Country-level issues

The links between policy change and the PPAs are difficult to determine. Policy change is part of a wider process of complex social and economic interaction involving many actors and played out in an historical and institutional context (Wuyts *et al.*, 1992). In order to appreciate the dynamics of policy change, it is important to understand the complexities of this process, addressing issues such as patronage, ethnic alliances, political parties, decentralization, and the strength of NGOs and CBOs (Grindle and Thomas, 1991).

In some of the countries where PPAs have been undertaken, poverty has not always been high on the political agenda, with implications for the *degree of government support* for the exercise. Issues surrounding poverty are highly political. Limited political support, or a lack of trust between the government and the World Bank, has led to a lack of support in-country for some PPAs. In Mali, due to the sensitivity of the issues surrounding poverty, the PPA had to be renamed the Living Conditions Survey. In Cameroon there was a perceived lack of support for the PPA from the government, some key government policymakers felt excluded from the PPA dialogue from the beginning. Although the fieldwork was considered of good quality and the results relevant, the environment was not conducive to embrace the outcome of the PPA. Thus there was a lack of policy space to include controversial issues coming from the PPAs on the political agenda.

In contrast, in Argentina the government requested assistance from the World Bank to undertake a qualitative analysis. As a result, a strong level of commitment and coordination exists between government ministries in the preparation of the PA and the PPA. Clearly, where there is not a climate of acceptance the value of conducting PPAs should be questioned. If there is a lack of room, dialogue should be established in order to create a general climate of acceptance. Generating a more open atmosphere may lead to the results of the PPA having more impact with governments less threatened by the resulting data.

More generally, the level of *ownership and commitment of stakeholders* in-country has varied amongst the PPAs. In many cases, ownership has depended on the degree to which the various stakeholders were involved. There is no blueprint for this; the inclusion of the various stakeholders should be attuned to the political, social and economic environment. The World Bank's experience has shown, however, that the involvement from the beginning of key policymakers enhances eventual ownership and commitment. In Togo, for instance, key policymakers were not included early on in the process, and therefore the impact has been limited, as in Lesotho, where the government was initially excluded and there was thus limited ownership. Local ownership was created only after the drafting of the action plan which was formulated by the government with a cross-section of the stakeholders. In Pakistan key stakeholders were involved and workshops convened. However, some government officials and NGOs felt the final report was not representative of the poverty situation in the country; others felt that their views had not been considered. Ownership of the final PA was, consequently, limited.

In contrast, in Argentina, key government officials were involved from the beginning and often led the process. As other stakeholders were gradually included, room for dialogue increased. This led to a greater understanding between the Argentinean government and the NGOs. In South Africa, stakeholder involvement from the outset was a time-consuming but important step in a complex process of dialogue, with a high level of ownership and commitment evident (see Chapter 15).

The degree to which governments feel able *to negotiate with the World Bank* has an impact upon the ownership. Generally, if donors adopt a top-down approach to assisting in policy formulation, there will be limited ownership of, and commitment to, the policy within governments. Several government officials in Guatemala felt excluded from the decisionmaking process, and relations between the World Bank and the university which undertook the PPA were not strong. Ownership and commitment was limited. While the qualitative information from the PPAs may be relevant and result in short-term changes to policy documents, without ownership there may be no long-term shifts in attitude.

The policy implementation process often becomes a filter that may alter intended policies. Thus, it is important *to identify and include those who influence policy* by understanding the linkages between the policy intention and the implementation outcome. It is also important to involve those with a quantitative perspective from government line ministries, in order to combine the qualitative- and the quantitative-data analysis. In Kenya, the Central Bureau of Statistics assisted in coordinating the PPA. An outcome was that the analysis of poverty combined both the quantitative and qualitative survey results.

Other international actors also have the power to influence policy. An emerging lesson is that the PPAs which have worked with other donors have a greater long-term impact. In Togo, the PPA exercise was undertaken with the UNDP which has continued to promote qualitative analysis in-country from its own resident mission. In Ecuador, UNICEF used the same methodologies employed by the PPAs to evaluate the impact of their programme. In Nigeria, the PPA process has assisted in coordinating the donors' interventions in the area of poverty alleviation.

World Bank issues

As at the country level, *ownership within the World Bank* emerges as a key issue when considering the impact of PPA exercises on World Bank policy. In Pakistan and Cameroon, for example, one person led the PPA, and there was limited ownership and understanding of the process. The results were consequently not reflected in other World Bank documents. In Cameroon, changes in the team managing the country programme occurred during the preparation of the PA; in addition, the country economist was not involved in the PPA. Keeping poverty issues on the agenda in the Cameroon country work was therefore difficult. When the CFA was devalued, the country team shifted its emphasis back to macro-economic issues. The qualitative information was viewed as having limited credibility by those who were excluded from the PPA process.

For greater policy relevance and broader ownership, a team approach is required. In Ghana, the information from the PPA was relatively complex and extensive, making incorporation into other World Bank reports time consuming and unclear. In contrast, in the Argentina Country Department, the PA was planned and prepared through the adoption of an inclusive, consultative approach.

A limited team approach in the World Bank may lead to Bank documents reflecting differing priorities. The governments will respond to those with which they are familiar and which they perceive to be the most credible. In Ghana, for example, key policymakers in-country were reluctant to accept the PA and PPA as credible documents until the Country

Economic Memorandum (an influential World Bank instrument) reflected their results. To influence policymakers, it may be appropriate to understand which documents and mechanisms have more credibility. This requires continual coordination between World Bank reports and priorities in country.

Many of the PPAs have emphasized the difficulty of coordinating the PPA process from Washington HQ, which makes the *role of World Bank resident missions* an important issue. The manager of the Tanzania PPA, for example, suggested that more time and resources were required to strengthen the mission in Tanzania to undertake frequent PPAs and contribute towards a broader poverty assessment. Teams could be located in the field, and skilled people in the analysis of poverty could be located within the mission. To increase the capacity of the resident mission, training in the best practice of qualitative research could be conducted and tool kits provided. This would require some decentralization of resources. In the future, the NGO/participation officers, recently recruited in some of the resident missions, will be able to assist in such poverty-focused work.

Where *management support and follow-up* within the World Bank has been limited, many opportunities have been lost. In Madagascar, there was a high degree of back-up in-country since key policymakers were included from the beginning. There was, however, a delay for over a year and a half within the World Bank. The commitment and interest of the Government of Madagascar weakened as a consequence. In Equatorial Guinea, the information was accurate but the institutional frameworks of both the borrower and the World Bank were unable to embrace the results. The impact has, therefore, been limited.

An emerging lesson is that dissemination to various stakeholders should be part of the design of PPAs and key stakeholders should be involved in the development of suitable strategies. In many PPAs, information has not been fed back to local people, there has been limited follow-up at the community level as a result. Sharing results with local people is important for many reasons:

○ validating information which has been gathered, thereby increasing its credibility;
○ encouraging action at the community level;
○ showing respect to communities from which information has been gained; and
○ building up partnerships with communities through contained dialogue and feedback.

At the country level, clearer communications on dissemination strategies need to be established. In Costa Rica, the government was eager to disseminate the results of the PPA, but there was a delay for over nine months while it sought permission to publish from the World Bank. The Costa Rican experience is in contrast to that of Cameroon where the results of the assessment were published without full government support. In both cases, the impact of the PPA has been reduced due to lack of government ownership.

PPAs and country policy

Again it must be stressed that it is not possible to establish causality between the PPA and policy since policymaking is part of a wider inter-related social process. Below, however, are some outcomes which may have been influenced by the information and the process of the PPAs.

(1) *In Lesotho*, three key themes emerged from the PPA which were not identified in the quantitative surveys: alcoholism, political factors such as injustice and corruption, and a hatred of witchcraft. Through the government's action plan these issues were fed into the policy level. As government ownership increased, such issues as corruption and the role of local government began to appear in speeches and documents.

(2) *In Nigeria*, the PPA has initiated an ongoing debate in government about poverty and gender issues, such as the relationship between polygamy and poverty.

(3) *In Tanzania*, the government was initially cautious but became more receptive as it appreciated the value of the approach. The PPA high-lighted the capacity of local people to analyse their own problems. As such, policymakers began to understand the value of including the poor.

(4) *In Zambia*, the government was influenced by the priorities expressed by the poor in the ranking exercises. The Ministry of Health has been using the results of the PPA and the PA in developing policy. In the Ministry of Education, a new policy is in preparation with reference to the timing of school fees.

(5) *In Mexico*, the quality of the information from the PPA was mixed. Although the information was not ranked adequately, it added value because it was gender-specific. For example, the PPA found that the women of Mexico City were unwilling to leave their houses and go to work. Since they did not have clear tenancy rights they were afraid that their homes might become occupied in their absence or disappear. In the northern areas it was easier for women to obtain jobs than men. This was challenging traditional gender roles as many men found them-selves out of work. Conflict within the household had become a major issue. This information highlighted the gender differences and influ-enced the poverty assessment.

(6) *In Armenia*, the PPA highlighted the existence of a great variety of coping strategies, as it did the prevailing lack of trust in local govern-ment and the lack of respect for the private sector. This explained why many were reluctant to become involved in private-sector activities.

PPAs and World Bank policy

One of the outcomes of the PPA process has been to challenge the policies not only of the countries concerned but also of the World Bank. It is difficult, however, to evaluate the impact of the PPAs on specific World Bank policies. It could be argued that the PPA often remains an add-on to the poverty assessment and that its impact is thereby limited. There is a growing realization, however, of the value of integrating quantitative and qualitative data in the analysis of poverty in order to produce better measurement, better analysis, and, through more appropriate policy recommendations, better action (Carvalho and White, 1997).

The issues arising from the PPAs are contributing also towards broader debates within the World Bank. These debates include the effective measuring and monitoring of poverty, the integration of social dimensions into policy and project work, and increasing the impact of the Bank's operations by adopting participatory development.

Early observations show that the impact of the PPA on specific country documents has been mixed. In certain instances, PPAs contributed successfully to a shift of policy emphasis. In Nigeria, for example, the World Bank had been focusing on health and education, yet the PPA highlighted that the poor viewed water and roads as their priorities. There is now a greater focus on these. Similarly, in Ecuador, the PPA highlighted that off-farm enterprises were viewed by the poor as a major escape route from poverty. The country programme in Ecuador now places greater emphasis on these off-farm enterprises.

In other cases impact has been less evident and especially limited if other members of the country team are not included in the process. The Kenyan Poverty Assessment reflected the major findings of the PPA, yet some in the country department felt that the results of the PA and PPA could be more extensively incorporated into the country reports. In Costa Rica, delays in the analysis and dissemination of the findings have meant that impact has been limited to date.

Objectives

The original objective of the PPAs was to collect qualitative information on the poor's perceptions of poverty. Most PPAs have achieved this objective but the effectiveness and the impact of the exercise have varied: some PPAs have had limited impact whereas others have moved beyond the original objective. As such, the PPAs can be classified into three broad categories as detailed below and in Table 2.6. The differing objectives determine the approach and methodology of the PPAs and the consequent impact. As understanding and acceptance of the first objective grows, it becomes possible to include wider and more complex considerations. As such, the following objectives have been identified:

Narrow

Information gathering: The PPA highlights the importance of including qualitative information in the analysis of poverty. The approach concentrates on information gathering and is quick. The inclusion of stakeholders and the follow-up at all levels (within the World Bank, with policymakers and with the poor) is consequently limited. The information may be contained in policy documents but there is limited commitment, ownership, attitudinal shift and institutional capacity building. Policy is viewed as a static document.

Table 2.6: Participatory poverty assessments: widening the objectives

PPA objective	Required shift in approach	Strategy	Outcome
1. *Narrow objective:* Information gathering – to incorporate qualitative information in the analysis of poverty	o poverty is a multi-dimensional phenomenon, not just an economic problem o necessitates the appreciation of the value of qualitative analysis *Policy is viewed as a static document*	o rapid appraisals in the field (e.g. 3 weeks); information extraction; limited feedback and action at the community level o policymakers not necessarily included in the process; prescriptive and often top-down in nature o one-off isolated exercises with limited impact upon the wider development process o monitoring and evaluation is limited and external	o changes in policy documents reflecting some of the qualitative findings o the information may be accurate and interesting but there is limited room for change and government ownership o the poor are given a voice but limited commitment from the top to ensure that the poor's concerns remain on the agenda o issues such as power, decentralization and gender are considered but limited room to include them in an ongoing debate. Policymakers may feel threatened
2. *Broader objective:* Attitudinal change – to realign polices towards poverty on a long-term basis through focusing on changing attitudes (combines 1 and 2)	o policymakers seen as partners who should be included from the beginning o World Bank is one of many stakeholders *Policy change is viewed as a social process*	o feedback and follow-up to field appraisals (e.g. poor validate information); ownership of the information at the community level: development of action plans and follow-up; longer process (e.g. 1 year) o government takes the lead in analytical and policy work o redefinition of the relationships between stakeholders; emphasis on building partnerships and trust; increasing coordination and conflict resolution through consensus building o institutional flexibility required o PPA is a means of initiating dialogue among stakeholders and not an end in itself o participatory monitoring and	o attitudinal shifts of key stakeholders are reflected in policy changes; Policies aligned towards a poverty focus o administrators and those who implement policy are included in the debate o power, decentralization and gender are put on the agenda for continuous negotiation o government ownership and commitment are high

| 3. *Wide objective:* To strengthening the policy-delivery framework (combines 1, 2 and 3) | ○ policy agenda setting, decisionmaking and implementation are inter-related processes; looks beyond the mainstream policy model which assumes a linear approach from decisionmaking to implementation
○ participation is seen as more than an add-on or even a component (unlike gender or environment); it is viewed as an approach within which an overall framework is created for more effective policy formulation and implementation
○ this requires new ways of thinking; a paradigm shift from prescription to process and from linear to adaptive

The process of policy change is part of a wider process of establishing linkages between the poor and those in power. | ○ long, slow, process (e.g. continuous)
○ identification of credible institutions for strengthening; strengthen the relationships between formal and informal institutions; awareness of traditional management practices
○ organizational development and institutional change
○ participatory monitoring and evaluation | ○ strengthening the policy-delivery framework by building the capacity of the appropriate institutions both formal and traditional
○ those who implement policy are not only included in the debate but their capacity is also increased
○ cross-stakeholder ownership and commitment
○ increased transparency and accountability
○ building institutions from the micro level contributes towards a slow process of decentralization
○ challenging the existing power relations |

Note: Cannot widen the objective unless institutional support and flexibility exists. If the process evolves too quickly there is potential for undermining the whole approach.

141

Broader

Attitudinal change: At this stage, policy change is viewed as a social process. The way in which this information is gathered, i.e. the process, will determine the extent to which policy is influenced. The PPA influences the way in which policymakers approach the problem of poverty and, therefore, policy is influenced on a more long-term basis.

Wide

Strengthening the policy-delivery framework: A third step or objective of the PPA could be to consider the implementation of the policies in an attempt to ensure that action reflects stated aims. The gap between rhetoric and reality may be explained by weak implementation, poor follow-up and a lack of focus upon the policy-delivery framework. Whilst conducting PPAs, it may be possible to build dialogue and the capacity of credible institutions, and to create linkages between traditional and formal institutions. This would create room for a more coordinated approach between the cross-section of stakeholders (including the donors). The approach has the potential of contributing towards the development of an effective policy-delivery framework where there is an increased and ongoing interaction between policy change and stakeholder dialogue. This is a long, slow, continuous process and requires the redefinition of stakeholder relationships, including that of the World Bank. The governments would lead the process and their development partners would offer support and advice. This process of policy change and institutional strengthening, at all levels, is viewed as part of a wider process of establishing linkages between the poor and those in power.

To date, most of the PPAs have focused on information gathering and attitudinal change to influence policy. To have a greater long-term impact more PPAs should move towards the wider objective of strengthening the policy-delivery framework. The PPA would then contribute towards the collection of qualitative information, continuous stakeholder dialogue and capacity building for policy delivery.

17

Some Reflections on the PPA Process and Lessons Learned

ANDREW NORTON[1]

The policy influence of participatory research is difficult to evaluate. It seems clear that some PPAs at least have had relatively direct policy outcomes. As important as these, however, has been the development of the capacity in-country to carry out participatory research on key policy issues, and along with that the familiarisation of key policymakers in government and donor agencies with the benefits of using participatory research and planning methods. The outcomes of PPAs can be considerably strengthened over the early examples by paying more attention to the following features: negotiation of clear objectives early in the process; training of research teams, especially in policy analysis using participatory research material; better integration in national policy processes; more attention to integrating PPA results with other forms of policy research; more attention to verifying final results through cross-checking with community-level participants.

What influence have PPAs had?

While it is still too early to say exactly how much influence the PPAs have had and in what areas, two key questions are posed here in trying to evaluate their impact:

(1) *How successful is the PPA in influencing policy in its own right?* Is it simply an add-on, embellishing and providing some qualitative anecdotal colour to an otherwise conventional analysis based on consumption-income? While those involved in the PPAs acknowledge that often they ran parallel to, rather than iteratively with, the larger poverty assessment itself, they also demonstrate that PPAs were successful at different levels. By targeting and emphasizing particular issues emerging from the research, they were able to promote specific policy changes within sectors. For example:
   o In Zambia, the Ministry of Health used the PPA results extensively in policy development, and observations from the PPA relating to the timing of school-fee payments (which coincide with the period of maximum stress for most rural communities) have contributed to ongoing work in the Ministry of Education on school fees.
   o In Mozambique, urban participatory research provided inputs to the project planning of urban NGOs and a UN agency, as well as to the World Bank Urban Infrastructure project design. By providing a cross-sectoral analysis through the lens of 'poverty', the PPAs were able in certain instances to address sectoral imbalance in policy.

○ The Ghana PPA influenced a shift of emphasis within the World Bank towards rural infrastructure and the quality and accessibility of education and health.[2]

(2) *How successful have PPAs been in making the policy process more participatory?* In most cases, the promotion of participation by primary stakeholders in policymaking through 'giving the poor a voice' seems to have been achieved. Indeed, Dogbe (Chapter 12) comments that retaining the voice of the poor in synthesis documents is the most effective way of getting policymakers to sit up and take notice. Yet is the PPA intrinsically participatory? As a product-focused rather than process-oriented activity, its function is mainly limited to information sharing, with no built-in component for the community to take part in action. Milimo, Norton and Owen (Chapter 13) acknowledge that the primary objective of the PPA in Zambia was to give voice to the poor in a process of policy formulation rather than to enable the community to 'own and use' information to develop action plans at the community level. This underlines the tension that exists between the requirements of policy-focused research and those of a PRA-based process.

In some cases the single most important outcome of the process of conducting PPAs was the development of capacity in the country to carry out participatory research on key policy issues. This is not only a question of competence in PRA methods but also of confidence in dealing with policymakers, and experience in producing policy analysis based on this kind of process.

Capacity building, however, extends beyond the research process itself to the knowledge and attitudes of policymakers towards that process. Another critical element here is the familiarization of key policymakers in government and donor agencies with the benefits of using participatory research and planning methods. As a result of the PPA in Ghana, for instance, there is now a generalized recognition of the value of this within the Country Department of the World Bank, reflected in a continuing interest in participatory research for policy development.

With these two elements in place, the conditions exist for a long-term learning process. which can both influence policy and practice, and provide the context for continual learning with a view to improving the methods for this kind of research.

How can the PPA process be improved?

A broad cross-sectoral approach to policy research underpins the PPA approach and distinguishes it from the thematic one outlined in the first part of this book. The entry point of poverty, a cross-sectoral and dynamic concept, has been shown to bring with it particular advantages: (i) it enables policymakers to reflect on the existing allocation of resources between sectors and redress any sectoral imbalances that emerge; and (ii) it does not predetermine the agenda of the community, enabling participants to set their own research priorities.

For the same reason, however, the approach can be more prone to ineffectiveness in influencing policy. The analysis, synthesis and 'packaging' of the research becomes critical (Chapter 24). Yet it is clear that such an approach complicates the research process itself, particularly when moving from the broad to the specific. In the first phase of the Ghanaian research, specification of objectives was not sufficiently well-defined (although this improved substantially by the third phase). Without a clear initial focus, research teams have less guidance in tailoring participatory methods to particular issues or trends, with the result that potentially powerful methods may be used less effectively. Similarly, the sequencing of methods may lack direction in the exploration of an emerging theme.

A successful shift from the broad to the specific requires a minimum quality standard for training, subsequent fieldwork and analysis, an issue raised with respect to the Mozambique PPA, and emerging elsewhere in this book (Chapter 23). It also demands that there is continuing evaluation between team members of emerging issues and priorities to be pursued, and of how methods can be used most effectively to analyse these issues.

From the perspective of national governments, PPAs need to be better integrated into national-policy frameworks in order to be consistently effective in influencing policy. Existing PPAs have often been ad hoc events, left hanging on their own, unable to influence policy by design. An important reason for this lack of integration is the emphasis of existing processes on the in-house policy framework of the donors, with research geared to influencing a particular piece of analytical work.

While relatively successful in this goal, with hindsight a more independent line could have been taken in terms of in-country processes. This would involve creating conditions for inter-institutional collaboration early in the process, in particular engaging senior local policymakers in the research at an earlier stage, involving local organizations, such as NGOs, to ensure follow-up in the communities where studies were done, and involving government and universities to ensure follow-up at macro level. In general, there should be a greater emphasis on building inter-organizational links between constituencies, through triangulation of policy, research and local action. This means looking beyond the PPA, ensuring that it precipitates a process of continuous learning through feedback, follow-up, monitoring and evaluation.

Similarly, within donor agencies there is a need to integrate PPAs more convincingly into conventional analysis for poverty alleviation, with the challenge of mainstreaming 'participatory data' remaining. Policymakers need to be convinced as to the representativeness and robustness of results (see Chapter 23). Many participatory methods are quantitatively robust, yet are not promoted as such; they are all too quickly labelled qualitative and dismissed as anecdotal. Ultimately, PPAs are most likely to be influential where they are triangulated with other methodologies and data sources.

Understanding the importance of triangulation means recognizing that the PPA needs to be sequenced within the broader research process. Conducting the PPA before the poverty analysis itself creates a space for the results of the participatory research to inform the emphasis given to the follow-up research. Reflecting on the Zambia PA, Norton and Stephens (1995: 15) argue that if the PPA had been completed before the main analysis, 'then institutional issues in service delivery could have been followed up for the precise areas which the PPA suggested were priorities'. However, as Robb points out in Chapter 16, there are also case studies where conducting the PPA after the quantitative survey proved advantageous, particularly in identifying the poorest geographical areas. Whatever the order of events, sequencing should be recognized as valuable to the effectiveness and influence of the PPA.

The emerging consensus amongst those involved is that the PPA creates a sounding-board for the poor in the policy debate, but that it is essentially an extractive process. This conceptualization of the role of the PPA is often reflected in the relative emphasis given to product over process during the PPA. Inbuilt constraints, often temporal and financial, mitigate against a more participatory approach, with implications for feedback into the community and continuing change at local level. In Zambia, the need to produce material and policy insights which could contribute to the overall poverty analysis resulted in severe time constraints. The entire PPA process, from research design, through training of the field teams, fieldwork, analysis and developing preliminary policy conclusions, had to be completed in four months. Following up on feedback and involvement of research in ongoing programmes was beyond the financial and time scope of the South Africa PPA, weakening the principle of research being part of ongoing work. In Ghana, no financial or other allowance was made for revisiting the communities involved in the PPA.

To some extent, this all reflects a lack of confidence; applying participatory research methods on a national scale to macro- and sector-policy issues was new, with uncertainty as to the outcome. As confidence in the process grows, however, efforts should be made to ensure a minimum level of engagement of both primary and institutional stakeholders in the ongoing dialogue, whatever the constraints.

But constraints can themselves reveal a fundamental tension over ownership. Local ownership of the research process emerges as a key determinant of the success of a PPA process. The South Africa PPA was characterized by strong local ownership from a very early stage, while the Mozambique exercise was conceived and imposed from Washington, gaining local acceptability only through efforts to 'hand over the (ownership) stick'.

Even if local ownership is ensured, however, conflicting demands on the output of a research exercise will inevitably place limits on the research process itself. As Owen points out (Chapter 14), 'multiple stakeholders create multiple policy demands', bringing the danger that the PPA becomes compromised by the demands of investing institutions wanting to keep work 'on track'. If PPAs are to take on and maintain a significant role in participatory policy research, they should not driven by such demands but should instead be sited within a wider participatory policy process.

PART 3

WHOSE VOICE? REFLECTIONS FROM THE IDS WORKSHOP

18

Introduction

Policy is about what to do, the process of social and political decision-making about how to allocate resources for the needs and interests of society (Moser, 1993b; Conyers, 1982). Most policies exist as strategic statements, regulations or laws, underpinned by conceptual norms, formulated to address predefined problems, and implemented usually in the form of projects or programmes (Cusworth and Franks, 1993; Rondinelli, 1983).[1]

Policy change occurs as the result of political interaction between different interest groups (Wildavsky, 1979).[2] Advocacy, whether born of participatory research or otherwise, is therefore integral to this political process. In order to increase the effectiveness with which participatory research can engender policy change, certain aspects of the policy process itself need to be addressed.

o Policymaking is chaotic and complex: 'a tangled web of constitutional decrees, legislative acts, instructions, rules, guidelines and orders that can be issued by officials at different levels, and in accordance with strongly rooted traditions and practices' (Blackburn, Chapter 20). Failure to understand the legal and bureaucratic complexities of policy formulation leaves non-governmental advocates powerless in their ignorance. Policy-change advocates should know precisely which element of this policy environment needs change in order to facilitate development (Anil Shah, Chapter 21).

o Context influences policy change. Policy advocates need to consider the socio-economic, historical and institutional circumstances in which policy change occurs. Policy formulation and policy change are contingent upon such issues as patronage, ethnic alliances, the role of political parties, decentralization, and the relative strength of NGOs and CBOs (Robb, Chapter 16). Only by considering such contextual variables can advocates make informed decisions about how to engage policymakers and change policy.

o Changes in policy do not necessarily lead to changes in outcome. Policy can exist as intention, or as a symbol, but may never be put into practice (Walt, 1994; Moser, 1993b: 149). Lots of good policy exists which is not implemented properly if at all, reflecting a gap between policymaking (the setting of objectives) and policy implementation (the strategies to achieve those goals). Booth (Chapter 4) relates that the poorest in Zambia were not benefiting from health-sector exemptions targeted at the destitute and those with infectious or chronic diseases. Inglis and Guy (Chapter 9) describe how a Scottish Office policy initiative to encourage local ownership and management of woodland had little influence on the thinking and practice of officials in the Forestry Commission.

Alternatively, implementation itself may change when policy does not. In many cases, 'beneficiaries' will do what they want regardless of existing or changing policy. Advocates must be aware that, more than whether a policy exists, their concern must be about whether it has been implemented. Impact depends on what actually happens, and it is impact that people care about.

Part 3 discusses key issues arising during the IDS workshop. Chapter 19 explores the channels through which local voices are projected to policymakers. Workshop participants suggested that there are two distinct scenarios in which the worlds of local people and officialdom can be linked:

(1) Intermediary structures can be created by third-party organizations. They mediate between local people and policymakers, projecting local voices and seeking to ensure that the policy priorities of local people are listened to and acted upon. This scenario heightens the policy-analysis role of such 'participatory intermediary structures', on the premise that there is often a need to filter and translate complex local messages into a language and a format that policymakers will respond to. Intermediaries must act faithfully yet strategically on behalf of local people by seeking to influence the policy process without distorting the messages they are carrying from the world of the local to that of the official.

(2) Bringing policymakers and local people face to face, thus reducing the emphasis on intermediaries. In reality, this approach is often more difficult to effect, yet its strength lies in challenging the inbuilt attitudes and behaviour of both local people and policymakers and in creating a space for policy analysis more powerful than most second-hand reports.

The discussion then turns to take a closer look at the role of advocacy in the policy process. The flow of information from the local to the official cannot be viewed as a discrete, linear activity, as Inglis and Guy's study of Scottish forest policy change (Chapter 9) demonstrated. Appreciating the 'fuzzy' nature of such change means recognizing that there are multiple gateways into the policy process and thus multiple strategies for influencing the outcome. Chapters 20, 21 and 22 by Blackburn, Anil Shah and Osuga respectively present case studies of the strategies adopted by policy advocates in pursuing policy change for participatory development. Drawing on Anil Shah's experience of facilitating Participatory Irrigation Management in Gujarat and more broadly in India, Blackburn reflects that the success of participatory approaches often requires a challenge to existing policy praxis through public advocacy. Anil Shah himself provides practical guidance on how to set about influencing public policy, whether to promote issues for the public agenda, to follow up policy announcements or to improve the implementation of public policy. Finally, Osuga, discussing his experience of influencing the Uganda National Health Plan, demonstrates that reaching policymakers requires a flexible and multi-pronged approach which includes personal–informal as well as institutional–formal processes.[3]

Policy advocates can learn from lessons emerging throughout this book. Targeting entry points too precisely, for instance, is an inherently weak strategy, because the target is liable to move as officials are transferred or promoted. The reorganization of the ministerial structure in Guinea part way through the research year meant that those ministers carefully selected for the research teams were moved from key departments and their ability to influence land and resource policy consequently weakened (Chapter 8). The unexpected closure of the South African Reconstruction and Development Programme office exposed the weakness inherent in the PPA's initial strategy of concentrating advocacy on one particular department (Chapter 15).

Doors are different, dynamic and two-way. They need not necessarily be kicked down against reluctant or hostile keyholders, but can instead be opened by receptive policymakers. For example, where there is an interest expressed by government in a community-based approach then opportunities should be taken to get PRA adopted by key people, as Kane *et al.* illustrate (Chapter 5). In this instance, informal networking and sharing had more impact than formal or systematized procedures for influencing policy. On the other hand, some doors will not open, and efforts need to be harnessed to find alternative entry points. Different people have, furthermore, differing potential to pass through doors, with strategic choices to be made as a result.

Adopting a range of strategies is itself based on the key participatory principle of inclusion: promoting communications at all levels and building consensus through networks and alliances against all stakeholders; involving primary stakeholders in collective action for policy change; and understanding and utilizing the strengths of different stakeholders. Timing – linking the right events and stakeholders at the right time – is a critical factor here. Early involvement of policymakers can be very important, more so if the research process is demand-led, because this creates a space for policy change.

Such alliances also bring the resource of understanding what policy instruments exist and how these might be changed. In other words, the process of integrating the voice of the poor into the policymaking process, however achieved, needs to be reconciled with the complex nature of policy itself. Promoting the principles of inclusion and consensus building can often understate the political nature of the policy process. Gaining access to the process also involves understanding, working with and fighting off vested interests. Influencing policy is, above all, a long-term and continuous process of nitty-gritty changes.

Following on from the chapters on policy advocacy, Chapter 23 summarizes discussions that arose during the IDS workshop on the nature of the research process itself and its relationship with the policy process. A critical distinction is made between 'methodologies', which describe research traditions such as PRA, and 'methods', which describe individual tools or techniques that can be applied within a particular methodology. The respective strengths and weaknesses of 'positivist' and 'postpositivist' methodologies are discussed, attempts to integrate the two traditions evaluated, and arguments for an ecumenical approach to treating different methodologies (and their respective methods) as 'independent yet interchangeable', in order to strengthen policy impact, are put forward.

The training process emerged as a critical aspect of quality control and maximizing impact; this is also discussed in Chapter 23. The workshop debate about introducing and sustaining good practice in training was a lively one. Various aspects of PRA were specified as needing a training component in order to build capacity and sustain quality. In particular, there is a need to instil in trainees key PRA principles concerning learning reversal, and attitudes and behaviour, while also transferring the more specific mechanistic skills of PRA techniques. The tension in training process between the need to 'make ourselves (as trainers) redundant' and the need to ensure sustained quality in participatory research is also examined.

Norton's experiences of working on several of the African PPAs informs his chapter on the role of analysis in policy-focused research (Chapter 24). Qualifying his discussion with a reminder that policy-oriented research, however participatory, should not make exaggerated claims about outcomes in terms of participation or empowerment, Norton provides some concrete guidance on how best to design, prepare, conduct, record and analyse such a process. He argues that the policy focus is less likely to be blurred if the researcher 'thinks the process backwards' from the anticipated desired result. He concludes by calling for an 'inclusive language and approach' to the kinds of social analysis he describes, reflecting earlier calls for epistemological pluralism.

Part 3 reflects, finally, on participation, policy change and empowerment. Despite an apparent tension between the requirements of policy-focused research and the empowering principles of PRA, workshop participants produced a list of minimum standards/procedures that can enhance participation in the research process while preventing the best from becoming the enemy of the good.

19

How Are Local Voices Heard by Policymakers?

IDS WORKSHOP

Moving successfully into the policy process involves bridging the gap between local issues and voices, and increasingly abstract policy directives.

Bridging discourses: participatory intermediary structures and the role of the researcher

One way to achieve this is to put into place 'participatory intermediary structures', individuals or agencies that feed the results of participatory research into the policy process. Boundaries between academic research and the 'third sector' (of non-profitmaking, non-party political organizations) have become increasingly blurred (Hulme, 1994: 251). Where once researchers distinguished knowledge from action and were accountable only to their traditional peer reference group, many are now re-examining and redefining their role in relation to new bodies, notably within the third sector and 'the community', often in the face of academic hostility to the principles underlying such a process.

This changing role is illustrated by Attwood and May's reflections on the South African PPA process (Chapter 15), in which researchers are defined as 'strategic activists', sequencing and strategizing interventions. Skilled at translating discourse from the local to the official, they become filters in the flow of information from the field to the policy process, categorizing, identifying causal relationships, systematizing and disseminating results, while drawing out the implications for policymakers. Researchers cannot abdicate their responsibility to create knowledge and generate debate. They must decide on a specific focus and target policy issues to be challenged or changed, with the analysis and packaging of research output critical to that end (see Norton, Chapter 24).

According to this conceptualization, participatory intermediary structures are characterized by researchers with agency, in other words with power. Accepting this premise means asking how and to what extent this power is shared, and to what end.

Merging discourses: bringing policymakers and local people together

Perhaps the most difficult aspect of raising local voices in the policy process is challenging the inbuilt attitudes and assumptions of the policymakers themselves. An alternative approach to putting participation into policy change is to minimize intermediary structures by bringing officials and local people together, to facilitate the merging of official discourse with that of the local.

The distinction between face-to-face interaction and 'strategic activist' mediation is well illustrated by Schoonmaker Freudenberger's comparison of the processes by which participatory research influenced national land or resource-management laws in Madagascar and Guinea (Chapter 8). In the Madagascar case, a team of outside researchers (albeit the majority being nationals) tried to 'sell' their results to policymakers. In contrast, the research process in Guinea took place from within. Government officials, drawn into the process from the beginning and brought face to face with local people, were provided with an opportunity to discover their own solutions to tenure- and land-reform challenges. Throughout the training and research process in Guinea, the participating officials were encouraged to question their behaviour and attitudes and learn through their own experiences as part of a study team. This, argues Schoonmaker Freudenberger, is ultimately a more profound and more lasting experience than that of being persuaded through second-hand reports.

Bringing policymakers to local people

In this scenario, policymakers are brought to the field and a process of face-to-face interaction with local participants is set in motion. The Participation in Action Network, India, for example, reports on training exercises organized and conducted by villagers in Uttar Pradesh and Karnataka. On both occasions, local farmers were first trained in PRA, then invited outsiders from various NGOs and the UNDP to attend a training programme in their villages. These programmes are described as 'Win-Win Trainings'. Outsiders gained through their close interaction with local people and their participation in village life, while village trainers were paid for their service, with profits invested in public assets, such as hand pumps, community halls and temples: 'Village people and outsiders had a relationship of both interdependency and exchange. Everybody in this situation came away a winner' (*Participation in Action*, nd).

A similar approach was adopted by the Institute of Resource Assessment (IRA) at the University of Dar Es Salaam as part of the Government of Tanzania's Forest Resources Management project (Johansson and Hoben, 1995). In order to support ministerial efforts to formulate more effective land policy, it was arranged that mid-level government officials would first attend a seminar to identify and discuss land issues, and then participate in a series of RRAs conducted in selected villages. This enabled the officials to gather information about how recent land-use planning (LUP) exercises had been carried out[1] and to determine their effectiveness. Through face-to-face interaction, these policymakers came to question their behaviour and attitudes towards local people, concluding that 'Tanzanian laws, policies and procedures have rested on a top-down and patronizing attitude towards small-scale rural producers'. They were also forced to challenge key assumptions they had held, such as that current grazing practices were haphazard and unplanned, and that grazing caused deforestation. As a consequence, it became clear that many of the government's 'implementation programmes', based on the principle of 'modernizing' existing practices, were simply not practical. Most importantly, they

Box 3.1 Fishermen, videos, empowerment . . . and policy change?

I was back to Tanzania last month for a follow-up. A similar week-long workshop was arranged in another village, Msimbati. Most of the participants from Sudi turned up again together with 50+ others including local politicians, three MPs, police officers etc. This workshop was also recorded on video. I discovered that both good and bad things happened after the tours with the video. It is a long, complicated and fascinating story that keeps unfolding.

After the first workshop, dynamite fishing suddenly became an issue. It was evident that high-government officers were indirectly involved in financing it, police were involved in dynamite trade etc., and it was not easy to sweep these allegations under the carpet when it appeared on video. New but somewhat misdirected amendments to the fisheries legislation were made but these changes must have been prepared before the video reached Dar Es Salaam. Possibly the video speeded up the process. People started voicing new demands for legislative change to provide territorial rights for village fishing waters.

For a few months, while the video was being toured, the police started patrols and the 'sea was silent' as they put it. But then when the apprehended people were not convicted it started all over again. Last year was worse than ever; 446 blasts were registered in three months from one site on a beach in Mnazi bay. Important fishing grounds were totally devastated. Sub-committees were organized in most fishing villages following the video campaign. But as donors got involved in financing patrols and credit schemes for youth etc., the fisheries officers in the districts coopted the plans that had been made in Sudi, and local committees were marginalized for lack of information and communication. There was an agreement that the taxation from a fish market that villagers had helped construct should in part go to finance protection, but the district cheated and kept all the money. These things were not fully revealed until now, when everyone got together again; it will be interesting to see how the government system reacts.

People have risked their lives to deliver to the police dynamiters, their dynamite, boats, catch and even the corpses of people blasted to death, and the next day these people have been released for lack of evidence and the dynamite re-sold by the police. When this situation was revealed in area after area in this workshop by participants the total failure of the authorities to actually do something was almost overwhelming. Encouraged by the politicians they finally agreed to registering an NGO in which only people who directly depend on the sea can be members, and to work on their own from now on. They made statutes, elected a board which now has had its first meeting in Kilwa in which they have agreed on some action plan. The chairman and secretary have gone to Dar Es Salaam again and will be showing the old video and new material recorded in the December workshop to the parliament's environment committee during this week. Their aim is to get a statement from the prime minister and to change the legislation. It is a new government now, and they have great expectations of change.

It is not easy to say what the video actually accomplished. It did not stop dynamite fishing, it was not that simple after all. But it helped fishermen to get organised over a vast stretch of coast and across ethnic boundaries, even if it took three years. It gave them a voice but it also created local organisation by forcing villagers to take sides. I have seen people cry during video shows in villages. Everywhere it is shown some kind of local committee seems to have been formed the day after. It is a source of confidence, inspires to action. Fishermen feel in touch with projects and ministries; it is quite remarkable to hear them talking about whom they should see next. New groups emerge and ask to be heard; in Msimbati a number of local village youth took us aside and asked to be recorded when they did not agree to what elder people were saying. Their views and suggestions were provocative but constructive and stirred up a lot of discussion when we showed the tape in the evening. The next day they were invited to sit in among the invited participants.

The video really did make policymakers listen to villagers, even when they seemed unable to act. It created awareness among politicians and officials who had not realised what was going on, many of whom come from the mainland and are actually scared of the sea and have no idea what a reef is (they thought it was just rocks). Fishermen showed them blasted and intact reef from a boat through a mask. They came back full of stories of how the corals grow like a forest, that it's a fragile structure, home of the fish. We have an amazing video statement of an almost shocked MP who makes analogies with burning a forest and bombing a village. The experience has convinced at least me that there is tremendous potential in using video like this. I will go back soon to continue evaluating the impact and to make a video for international distribution.

Source: Lars Johansson, pers. comm.

gained a new perspective on the whole concept of the LUP exercise, criticizing it for not involving local people, with their knowledge of the environment and experience of sustainable land-use systems. Village leaders, it emerged, had simply been presented with the plan as a package and asked to approve it.

Bringing local people to policymakers

A merging of discourses can be achieved equally by bringing local people, or at least their voices, to policymakers.[2] Johansson (1994) describes a process of communicating with policymakers by video in Tanzania. At a conference in Sudi in 1994, Tanzanian fishermen, who came from a vast stretch of coast, were informed that the authorities typically blamed environmental destruction on the local fishermen's ignorance. During the next six days, both fishermen and fisherwomen were filmed explaining their perceptions of the true situation to fellow villagers and 'to an establishment of anonymous decision makers' (ibid: 3).

Participants were able to exert control over the production of the video by watching and approving the results of the day's shooting every evening. The process allowed for people's voices to be heard, undistorted and unappropriated, by creating space for communication: 'People . . . want to speak loud and clear. Many of those who never have had access to modern, public fora seem to love the concept of being seen saying something for the records' (ibid: 4). The participants revealed the dynamiting of fish and destruction of the local marine environment, even giving names of corrupt police and dynamite dealers, demanding 'to make such statements to the camera under their own names and in front of participating police officers' (ibid: 5).

Johansson returned to Tanzania in December 1996 to attend a second video workshop in a nearby village (pers. comm., see Box 3.1). He discovered that the original video had had an extraordinary impact. It had not produced a miracle policy shift protecting future fishing grounds and coral reefs, but it had engendered community mobilization on a massive scale, bridging regional and ethnic divisions between villagers and instilling confidence and inspiring action, only for them to be let down time and time again by corrupt local police and fisheries officers. Policymakers did listen and learn, some were shocked, and their awareness was raised, even when they themselves seemed unable to act. A fishermen's NGO was formed and was sending representatives that week to show the video to parliament's environment committee in Dar Es Salaam. The use of PRA and video had empowered and inspired local people to challenge policy and push for legislative change.

There are often difficulties with the approach of bringing policymakers and local people into direct contact. The cost of a prolonged process of interaction can be prohibitive, or can leave the process dependent on the continued good will of external donors. Policymakers going to the field must be willing and available to commit themselves to the research process and must sustain their new way of thinking once back in their world rather than slipping back into existing dogmas. Yet the potential power and effectiveness of the strategy make it a compelling option. Repeated exposure creates a cumulative and reinforcing process of change on both sides of the divide. Local people and policymakers learn to respect and listen to each other. Voices are heard, preconceptions are challenged and attitudes changed.

20

Getting Policymakers to Move the Bricks Around: advocacy and participatory irrigation management in India[1]

JAMES BLACKBURN[2]

The development literature on the benefits of participation (involving local people to conduct their own research, and design, monitor, evaluate, and manage their own projects) is now extensive. There has been, however, very little writing on how NGOs and/or popular organizations can influence government officials to effect those specific policy changes which are often indispensable for the effective scaling-up of participatory processes/projects. Indeed, the enormous enthusiasm generated by local-level participatory success stories has tended to overlook the great number of participatory initiatives which have been frustrated by unfriendly policy environments. The fact is that existing policies often impede rather than facilitate participation. Drawing on Anil Shah's experience of facilitating participatory irrigation management (PIM) in Gujarat (see Box 3.2), and more broadly in India, the question posed here is not so much 'How can PRA be used (or how has it been used) to influence policy?' (which appears to be the central question in the PRA and policy research agenda), but rather 'How can policy be influenced to facilitate the spread of participatory approaches?'

Inspiration from the Philippines

In 1992, Anil Shah obtained a Ford Foundation grant to study the Philippines' PIM programme in which 50 per cent of the country's irrigation schemes have been handed over to be managed by some 3500 farmer organizations. With some variations, this programme has since been replicated in Thailand and Indonesia, as well as in Gujarat and other Indian states.

Fundamental to the success of PIM in the Philippines is the communication, one might say triangulation, that has been facilitated between a range of different actors: government officials from different departments and at different levels, NGO staff, representatives of farmers' organizations, villagers, academics and media professionals. Anil Shah was quick to see this coming together of different participants as one of the keys to PIM's success in the Philippines, and it was to become a central element of PIM's replication in Gujarat.

Too often, projects are hatched by one set of actors, and then presented to others who are, not surprisingly, less enthusiastic than if they had been involved in designing a project from the beginning. Just as village-level development projects tend not to work unless the villagers concerned are involved in the exercise from its inception, so larger-scale undertakings that require the green light from a much wider variety of actors are unlikely to work unless those same actors are asked to knock heads together from the start.

Working groups

In replicating the Philippines experience in Gujarat, Anil Shah pressed for the setting up of working groups, at both state and district levels, composed of key senior officers of the relevant government departments, NGO staff with an intimate understanding and knowledge of participatory processes, representatives of farmer organizations, and academics with a social-science background who could provide the groups with feedback on pilot projects. The working groups are now considered a model, and are being recommended by the Ministry of Water Resources of the Government of India to other state governments. A national working group on PIM is about to be set up, mirroring the national working group on Participatory Forest Management which is already in operation.

Unlike government committees, in which official and non-official members tend to regard each other with suspicion, a working group has a relaxed atmosphere which encourages the exchange of information, experience and innovative ideas. It could be said that in this case the philosophy of PRA has percolated up from the village to higher-government echelons. People from different organizational cultures are making the effort to listen and learn from each other.

Process Documentation Research (PDR)

Better communication between participants with different perspectives is, however, not enough. For working groups to function well and play an important role in influencing policy formulation (or changing existing policies), it is essential that they have access to information about grassroots developments. 'Good' data from the field is a prerequisite for informed discussion and analysis. In the PIM working group in Gujarat, and indeed in the Philippines beforehand and elsewhere since, it was PDR that ensured the timely delivery of good useful information. PDR was and remains a key component in the strategy of bridging communication gaps between the many participants involved in field implementation, and deserves some attention here.

PDR provides a window through which working-group members can see directly the how and why of uncensored field experience as the PIM programme proceeds. PDR is not preoccupied with monitoring or evaluating the projects against set objectives and targets. Based on disciplined observation, accurate recording and commonsense analysis, it focuses on documenting in detail vital aspects of the interactions between different sets of actors in the field, relating the dynamics of field situations, their successes and failures, and identifying the processes that lead to the kind of local capacity building so essential to successful participatory management. The kind of information made available to working groups through PDR is the

Box 3.2   More or Less

The Aga Khan Rural Support Programme (India) (AKRSP-I) was persuaded by the Irrigation Department of the Government of Gujarat, India, that its experience of promoting co-operative lift-irrigation societies might be used for organizing farmers to take over the management of Government Canals. The Irrigation Department ordered on May 9, 1989 that the water management function of the PINGOT Irrigation Project (command area 1400 hectares), be handed over to the AKRSP, which would organize farmers' societies within three years to take over the management of the canal. The order laid down the following conditions for the pricing of water:

> AKRSP shall pay water rates to the Government on a volumetric basis, according to the rates decided by the Government from time to time. AKRSP shall not charge from the farmers any rates higher than the Government would usually have charged, in the flow irrigation projects operated directly by the Government.

This was the standard condition applied in all previous cases. However, the AKRSP calculated that it would be incurring a loss if it had to supply water to the farmers at Government rates for flow water schemes, with irrigation societies eventually going bankrupt. The Government refused, however, to change the condition about the pricing of water on the grounds that it might lead to similar demands from other societies.

The AKRSP pressed for a reversal of the basic condition of water pricing. A committee of four chief engineers was appointed to examine the matter, but recommended only a reduction of the volumetric rate. AKRSP was not satisfied. With the knowledge of the Secretary of the department, AKRSP approached the Minister of Irrigation. After giving the background of the issue, the Chief Executive asked the Minister:

Chief Executive: Sir, would you like the irrigation society to be self reliant in the management of its affairs, or to be perpetually dependent on Government/AKRSP subsidy?

Minister: Of course a good co-operative should manage its affairs without subsidy.

Chief Executive: I have a request for a small change in the Government order, that the Government should supply water to the AKRSP/ Society not on high volumetric rates, but the usual rates the department charges in its flow irrigation schemes. It is true that the present Government rates are low and AKRSP would support the Government if it decides to raise the water rates. But attempts to fully recover the Government's operations and management (O&M) costs only from the farmers irrigation societies, is not fair! Secondly, the AKRSP/Society should not be bound down to charge no more than

Government rates when it supplies water to the farmers. The Government loses nothing if it permits AKRSP/Society to charge higher rates to the farmers, which would make the society self reliant.
Minister: I agree in principle. Now what do you want me to do?
Chief Executive: In place of the limit that AKRSP/Society cannot charge MORE than the Government rates, the condition may specify that the AKRSP/Society shall not charge LESS than the Government rates.
Minister: This is sensible. I agree.

The government issue a revised order on June 19, 1990 that the 'AKRSP shall not charge the farmers a water rate lower than what the Government usually charges in its flow irrigation schemes.' Farmers co-operatives now decide every year the water rates that would cover its O&M costs, these rates exceeding the Government rates by 50 to 500 per cent. The societies are self-reliant and none incurs a loss. In contrast, most of the earlier societies are bankrupt and defunct. A Government order of November 22, 1995 extended the water pricing formula applied to the AKRSP to all future societies, with retrospective application potentially reviving some of the defunct societies.

The government of Gujarat has invested 40 Billion Rupees (US$130 million) in the irrigation sector. Its annual loss on O&M is 300 Million Rupees (US$1 million) or 0.75 per cent. In India as a whole, investment in the irrigation sector is 600 Billion Rupees (US$2000 million). The annual loss on O&M is 30 Billion Rupees (US$100 million) or 5 per cent.

Source: Anil C. Shah, pers. comm.

next best thing to 'being right there where the action is'; another benefit of PDR is the awareness it instils in key government officers of the changes demanded in departmental cultures by participatory development.

A call for NGOs to learn

Information and knowledge must flow both ways for lasting change to occur. Getting policymakers to 'hit the ground' must be complemented by those in the field gaining greater knowledge of the world of policymaking. This is perhaps even more essential in persuading senior government officials to 'move the bricks around'.

The usual strategy adopted by NGOs when confronted with unfriendly policy environments is to invite government officials to seminars and workshops in the hope of convincing them of the worth of innovative approaches, and of the necessity of opening up policy spaces to enable such approaches to spread. While this, and other kinds of advocacy work, is important and should continue, NGOs also have a responsibility, sadly often overlooked, to understand how government works. Anil Shah believes there is a glaring knowledge gap on the part of NGOs in this regard and, more specifically, in the way policies are formulated. NGOs must make an effort to bridge that gap.

This may require some soul searching. NGOs have, by tradition, tended to be highly suspicious of government officials, and in some cases appear rather arrogant, taking the view that 'government people don't know anything about what really goes on; they just sit around in offices'. While this undoubtedly holds some truth, it is an attitude that has tended to limit NGOs' understanding of government and the policy world in general.

Anil Shah is struck, for example, by how certain NGOs, and some academics, tend to see policy as a single block, whereas policy is, in fact, made up of a rather tangled web: of constitutional decrees, legislative acts, instructions, rules, guidelines and orders that can be issued by officials at different levels, and in accordance with strongly rooted traditions and practices. Bureaucracies themselves are complex and multi-layered, with a high staff turnover. It is usually difficult to know who is responsible for which policies. Why certain policies, and not others, are formulated has usually more to do with internal bureaucratic dynamics (for example: power struggles, career moves, reshuffles, budget modifications) than a response to external reality (the cost efficiency of participatory management, for example).

Who should be approached in government, how and what for, are fundamental questions that require more time and effort than most NGOs are at present willing to recognize if government officials are to be convinced of introducing new policies, or modifying existing ones. It took Anil Shah three years to get the Indian government officially to sanction the National Participatory Forest Management Working Group, and that is only one of the many examples of the kind of patience that is required.

21

Challenges in Influencing Public Policy: an NGO perspective

ANIL C. SHAH

*Participatory development aims at enabling individuals, groups and commu-
nities to plan, execute and manage development that improves their living
conditions; technical, administrative, organizational, financial and legal support is often required. Some of this support exists in the public domain, yet
may be cumbersome or obstructive of development processes, and therefore
need change. Grassroots experiences demonstrate the need for public-policy
advocacy, with PRA often throwing up important issues that can be resolved
only through policy changes. Such advocacy has already been shown to suc-
ceed. On 1 June 1990, for example, an order of the Government of India on
Participatory Forest Management was issued, the culmination of three years'
effort invested by an NGO to remove policy bottlenecks in its fieldwork.*

Contexts for policy influencing

In addition to the need for advocacy that arises from work in the field,
NGOs may also be in a position to engage in influencing policy in other
situations:

o *To improve implementation of a government programme that has essential components of a participatory approach.* NGOs may work for appropriate further action by public agencies in terms of mechanisms and
procedures. The Watershed Development Programme of the Ministry of
Rural Development in India, for instance, has all the features essential to
a participatory programme, yet NGOs can still contribute to its more
satisfactory implementation.
o *To follow up a policy announcement when a government department is
engaged in formulation of a programme.* An NGO may try to associate
itself with this process in order to ensure that essential participatory
features are incorporated into the programme. Participatory Irrigation
Management (PIM) in India, for example, is now moving from policy to
programme.
o *To persuade public agencies to take on their agenda issues, such as gender,
that are important from a participatory approach perspective.*

Since influencing public agencies is an arduous and daunting task,
NGOs should be ready to expend considerable time and effort when they
take up the challenge. They may prefer to continue their work with the
hope and confidence that its soundness will eventually attract the attention of public agencies, who will appreciate the need for providing supportive policy changes.

What needs to change?

Public policy is embodied in a country's constitution: legislative acts, rules, administrative instructions, issued through manuals, guidelines and orders by government bodies/officers at different levels. It works also through established decisionmaking practices and their implemention. Policy-change advocates should know precisely which of these need change in order to facilitate development.

The bus is crowded

Those who decide policy changes are usually preoccupied in implementing already existing courses of action, and considering and sifting a plethora of proposals for change. Such proposals are made by: influential political parties/leaders, interest groups, committee recommendations, research findings, public-spirited experts, and in letters to the editors of newspapers/ magazines. Policymakers are bombarded daily with proposals for change; they are not waiting for good ideas. Their basket is full, the bus is crowded.

Selecting ideas

Development agencies will do well to select a few advocacy ideas out of the many that emerge in the course of their work. These should have the potential for a large impact in furthering the cause of development, par-ticularly for deprived areas, communities, groups and families. Even if convinced, the decisionmaker will take months to change administrative orders, years to modify legislating provisions and decades to amend a country's constitution. Development agencies should, therefore, give pri-ority to ideas that require a change in practice, administrative orders, man-uals, rules, acts and a country's constitution – in that order.

Plan of action

After carefully selecting ideas for policy change, an agency will need to develop a plan of action by which to influence the decisionmaker to know, appreciate, accept and act upon the proposal. The following steps are useful:

- o build up a strong case for proposed change: why it is necessary, import-ant, urgent, whom it will benefit and by how much;
- o find out precise policy that requires change, who is authorized to decide on the proposal, and the process that will be followed;
- o contact like-minded organizations and individuals likely to support and join in presenting the proposal;
- o formulate the proposal which should, as far as possible, incorporate:
  - (i) information about the proposing organization(s): what is the motive?
  - (ii) the problems in the field that are blocking development;
  - (iii) the precise policy that needs change; and
  - (iv) a request for a personal meeting to explain the details.

A copy of the proposal may be sent to those interested in the issues, or whose support may prove valuable.

Strategy for drawing attention

Since this proposal will be one of many, the agency will need to work out a strategy for gaining early attention. This may include:

o locating the officer whose acceptance of the proposal is crucial and those whose opinion s/he values;
o locating a key officer who is sympathetic to the development programme promoted by the development agency. Take his/her advice on how to go about promoting the proposal;
o contacting influential people and taking their advice and help in influencing decisionmakers;
o requesting influential officers to view the NGOs work for better appreciation of the proposal; during such visits presentation by the people incorporating PRA exercises would strengthen the case; if necessary, a meeting with the decisionmakers should be arranged; and
o using the media to create a climate favourable for the acceptance of the proposal.

In the event of rejection

If the crucial officer is not impressed by the proposal, if s/he rejects or is likely to reject it, work out a strategy to overcome the obstacle. The agency may approach higher levels in government to direct the officer to reconsider the proposal sympathetically and expeditiously. The agency may have to wait until the unsympathetic officer is transferred or a more favourable situation develops.

In the event of a favourable response

If and when the response of the decisionmaker is favourable, the agency should work to ensure that the formulation of the proposed change will meet its requirements:

o suggest the appointment of a drafting committee, with agency representation, for the proposed change;
o offer the agency's services to work with the officer who is responsible for drafting the government order/instruction; and
o if such offers are not welcome, remain in touch informally with the officers concerned.

Follow-up

Government decisionmaking on policy matters involves several levels in a department. In more important matters, several departments are involved, particularly legal, finance and personnel. The agency should follow up the progress of the proposal from table to table, department to department, until the desired order is issued.

Credit

Give credit and compliments to all who have helped, with and without enthusiasm, in the progress of the proposal.

An environment conducive to participatory development

○ Appointment of a working group for each programme consisting of senior officers, NGO representatives, academics studying the programme, and representatives of village-level organizations.
○ Policy resolution affirming government's commitment to participatory approach in a programme.
○ Pilot projects as 'learning laboratories'.
○ Action plan indicating tentative targets, responsibilities, and delegated authority.
○ Specific responsibility entrusted to a senior officer to develop the new programme.
○ Process Documentation Research to provide continuous feedback about development and emerging issues in the field.
○ Dissemination through media.
○ Fostering in the public system a culture of consultation and participation of various levels within the organization and with stakeholders outside.
○ Organizing a national support group (NSG) outside government but with active involvement of key officers of concerned government department(s), donor agencies, NGOs and academics active in the programme.[1]

22

Towards Community-sensitive Policy: influencing the Uganda National Health Plan

BEN OSUGA

The process of developing the current five-year Government of Uganda (GoU)/UNICEF health plan (1995–2000) presented an opportunity for the Uganda Community-based Health Care Association (UCBHCA) to play a strategic role in influencing health policy in Uganda. UCBHCA is an umbrella organization of health and health-related NGOs. It was represented in the various stages of the plan development process. Its involvement included participation in the review of the previous country programme, brainstorming on the key strengths and weaknesses of the previous plan, and in the development of this new five-year plan. The fora used to come up with this plan included: consultative meetings, logical-framework workshops, exchange of materials and correspondence. The process took over 15 months.

Approaches and methods used

It is extremely difficult to pinpoint any single most powerful approach or method adopted by UCBHCA for influencing this policy process. In most cases, more than one approach was used simultaneously. They included:

○ *Exploiting a previous close working relationship with the Ministry of Health and UNICEF* (UNICEF being the key funding partner). The GoU/ UNICEF partnership sought to change the relationship between UNICEF and its previous partners (including UCBHCA) from that of vertical funding to one of contractual agreements based on fee-for-service, with emphasis on district-level capacity building. The capacity that had been built for ten years within the UCBHCA membership was important in securing a central role for the association within this new set-up.
○ *Personal direct and indirect contacts.* Several meetings, both formal and informal, were arranged with key officials in strategic positions in the ministries of finance, health and local government. The meetings were on occasion engineered by inviting them to the UCBHCA's Annual General Meetings as 'distinguished guests'.[1]
○ *Exerting a strategic influence through technical assistance.* On occasion, for example, the UCBHCA has been requested to write speeches for key government officials. This has provided the opportunity to slot in strategic policy messages.
○ *Attending and facilitating aspects of planning task forces, meetings and workshops.* This involved the formation of an informal team of like-minded allies, within and outside the mainstream decisionmaking group.

Through and with these allies, strategies were developed and systematically introduced at these fora. They included:
  (i) introducing learning materials (participatory propaganda);
  (ii) introducing aspects of participatory learning and action PLA approaches as relevant;
  (iii) listening, observing and learning about group dynamics and interests in order to inform our strategy work; and
  (iv) lobbying and advocating for inclusion in the plan of community-based and community-sensitive language, paragraphs and components.

Main results

There were three main achievements of this advocacy process:

(1) *An entire component of community capacity building (CCB) was included on the five-year plan and allocated resources towards its implementation countrywide.* This meant that GoU/UNICEF embraced the concept of communities' responsibility for their own health care/ community-based health care.
(2) *PLA approaches, including relevant PRA tools, were included in the plan as key approaches to its implementation countrywide at various levels.* Notably, this will involve PRA training/follow-up and applications at parish levels.[2]
(3) *A Memorandum of Understanding has been signed by the three key actors in the CCB component.* These actors are the Ministry of Health, UNICEF and UCBHCA. The memo spells out the roles and responsibilities of each actor in the CCB process. The association's role is to facilitate the training and follow-up of government extension workers at national and district levels (as facilitators and trainers) on contractual terms. UNICEF provides the resources through the Ministry of Health.

Key challenges

The main challenges to the smooth implementation of this programme revolve around issues of organizational culture, capacity and pace of implementation. There are more questions than answers. As the UCBHCA continues to try out implementation of this tripartite agreement, it faces several fundamental challenges:

○ *The key partners in this CCB process, UNICEF and Ministry of Health, would like to see quick results.* The UCBHCA would prefer to move at the pace of the communities. Since the funds and other resources are channelled through the ministry from UNICEF – the word of the partners goes: 'He who pays the piper calls the tune', the association is powerless in these negotiations. This will have negative repercussions for communities
○ *The UCBHCA has a small secretariat and many members who have limited funds.* The secretariat therefore lacks capacity to cope with a rapid shift from grants to contractual relationships. Some seed money is

needed to keep the secretariat going as well as to recruit additional programme staff

o The UCBHCA has a wide range of resource staff trained in a number of PLA skills spread all over the country. *There is no systematic network that would ensure these resources are tapped to the benefit of the association and to influence adequately the way the CCB takes off on the ground*

o *Funds for contractual work done by the association take too long to be released*, due mainly to bureaucratic red-tape in UNICEF and the Ministry of Health. This has further disempowered the association.

These challenges need to be addressed if the UCBHCA and like-minded institutions are to play a continuing strategic role in creating a meaningful space for community-based initiatives.

23

The Research Process: sustaining quality and maximizing policy impact

IDS WORKSHOP

Participatory research is distinguished by the post-positivist paradigm within which it operates. Chapter 23 examines the implications of this distinctiveness for ensuring high quality and high impact research. Robustness of findings can be established through adhering to principles tailored to that paradigm, and findings can be strengthened through shrewd pluralism; by engaging, on its own terms, with other research approaches and data sources. Training is critical to quality and impact, and procedures for introducing and sustaining training quality, including a renewed emphasis on behaviour and attitudes, are discussed.

Approaches and methods

In addressing participatory research in general and PRA in particular, it is vital to distinguish between, on the one hand, a participatory approach or methodology and, on the other, the techniques, tools or methods with which they are associated.[1] This distinction was made very clearly by participants at a recent South–South Behaviour and Attitudes Workshop. They described the PRA approach as 'facilitating': 'seeking to empower by enabling people to express and enhance their knowledge of their conditions and lives, and to take more control by analysing, planning, acting, monitoring and evaluating'. They defined the PRA methods associated with this approach as 'open-ended, participatory and often visual as well as verbal'.[2]

Comparing approaches: positivism and post-positivism

The contemporary research community operates largely within a prevailing positivist paradigm, in which the scientific status of statements is determined through the formal construction of theories or hypotheses capable of empirical verification (Johnston *et al.*, 1986). Within this paradigm a conventional research methodology would typically use the sample survey as its main method for inquiry. The philosophical basis for its use is that behaviour can be measured, aggregated, modelled and predicted, according to statistical measures of reliability or 'robustness'. The criteria that have evolved to confirm the 'robustness' of conventional research results are termed 'internal validity', 'external validity', 'reliability' and 'objectivity' (Lincoln and Guba, 1985: 290–94; Cook and Campbell, 1979: 37; Pretty, 1993a):

○ *internal validity* means the extent to which we can infer a causal relationship between two variables;
○ *external validity* can be defined as the validity with which we can infer that the presumed causal relationship can be generalized across different types of persons, settings and times;

o *reliability* is an important precondition for validity, and can be defined as the extent to which each repetition of the same instruments will yield similar measurements; finally

o *objectivity* can be defined as the extent to which multiple observers can agree on a phenomenon, and is usually contrasted with 'subjectivity'.

The 'post-positivist', or 'constructivist',[3] paradigm encompasses a fundamentally different school of approaches to research than that of the positivist tradition. Whereas conventional inquiry is 'linear and closed', the constructivist methodology is 'iterative, interactive, hermeneutic, at times intuitive, and most certainly open' (Guba and Lincoln, 1989: 183). Within the post-positivist paradigm, participatory approaches to research such as PRA, with their attendant set of research methods, have been held up as legitimate alternatives to the conventional research approach.[4]

Participatory approaches are promoted most notably for their qualitative explanatory power in providing 'depth, richness and realism of information and analysis' (Chambers, 1994a: 14). The debates surrounding this statement are well known. Unlike the pre-established and universally applied questionnaire format, qualitative methods provide space for local people to establish their own analytical framework and thus challenge 'development from above' (Mukherjee, 1995: 27). Variables reflect local realities and priorities (Chambers, 1989).[5] Communities are heterogeneous, characterized by differences of interest and inequalities of power; participatory research disaggregates and analyses difference (Welbourn, 1991). Methods used flexibly and sequentially allow, moreover, for different groups within a community to articulate complex and non-quantifiable cause-and-effect processes. A key principle of PRA is that it seeks diversity – 'diverse events, different processes and forces explaining various relationships in local communities' (Mukherjee, 1995: 37–8) – rather than looking only for statistically significant relationships.

Trustworthiness and participatory research

These peculiar strengths of participatory research often lay it open to suspicion from within the conventional tradition as to its trustworthiness (Gill, 1991). It is argued the participatory modes of inquiry cannot stand up to the conventional tests for robustness (internal validity, external validity, reliability and objectivity), then they simply cannot be trusted. In its defence, participatory-research advocates argue that their mode of inquiry should be judged according to its own criteria, not those of another research tradition:

> To be asked about the validity or reliability of certain findings is to be asked a meaningless question. Investigators using participatory inquiry must establish trustworthiness by using equivalent, but alternative, criteria. (Pretty, 1993a: 2)

Lincoln and Guba (1985) propose a set of 'alternative trustworthiness criteria' by which research results within a post-positivist paradigm can be judged. These are: credibility (for internal validity); transferability (for external validity); dependability (for reliability); and confirmability (for objectivity).

(1) *Credibility* can be enhanced by:
   o prolonged engagement: investing sufficient time to provide scope to the study by learning about context and culture, testing for misinformation and building trust;
   o persistent observation: providing depth to the study by identifying those elements in the situation that are most relevant;
   o triangulation:[6] cross-checking information by use of multiple and different sources, methods, investigators and theories;[7]
   o peer debriefing: exposing researchers to disinterested peers in order to probe biases and explore meanings;
   o negative case analysis: continuously revising a hypothesis until it accounts for all known cases;[8]
   o referential adequacy: archiving data for future reference;[9] and
   o member checks: testing interpretations and conclusions with members of those stakeholder groups from whom data were originally collected.

(2) *Transferability* is not strictly possible within a post-positivist paradigm, certainly not in the sense of external validity in the conventional approach. According to Lincoln and Guba (1985: 316), the objective of 'constructivist' research is 'not . . . to provide an *index* of transferability . . . (but) to provide the *data* base [with working hypotheses] that make transferability judgements possible on the part of potential appliers'.

(3) *Dependability* can be enhanced through 'overlap methods' (equivalent to triangulation) and 'stepwise replication' (parallel investigations by research teams).

(4) *Confirmability* can be enhanced through the keeping of diaries (by researchers), triangulation and a 'confirmability audit' (which records the process of inquiry and the end product).[10]

Elements of these criteria are evident throughout the different chapters in this book, as illustrated by Schoonmaker Freudenberger's comments on achieving credibility with participatory methodology (Box 3.3)

Can PRA engage with the conventional research approach?

Within the prevailing positivist research paradigm, it is usually the participatory approach that must prove its utility to policymakers, not the conventional approach (Pretty, 1993a). On this basis, individual PRA methods are often promoted by their advocates as a quantitative alternative to the conventional sample-survey questionnaire, and are now commonplace, with emphasis placed on their robustness according to the conventional criterion of internal validity. Mapping exercises, for example, represent 100 per cent samples of a given population. Other PRA methods, such as ranking and scoring, are used within a 'purposive random-sampling' process (whereby populations or interest groups are selected for a purpose before being randomly sampled) which can be more statistically robust than normal random-sampling methods.

Monitoring and evaluation methods have been combined as alternatives to questionnaires (Shah, P. *et al.*, 1991; Action Aid, 1992; Vigoda, 1993;

Box 3.3   The Credibility of Qualitative Methods: lessons from Madagascar and Guinea

The purpose of conducting these participatory research studies was to inform a policy debate and to turn policymakers' attentions to the implications of their decisions on rural populations. But research can only have this impact if the results are viewed as credible and worthy of consideration.

Unfortunately, as soon as the RRA results contradict the orthodox perspective or challenge entrenched interests (and because RRAs tend to question assumptions and prevailing paradigms this is often the case) the reaction of the challenged party is invariably to question the methodology and impugn the reputation of the researchers. In most cases this involves questioning the small number of sites and the credibility of information that is obtained by 'informal' tools such as participatory mapping (as opposed to precise cartographic representations). I do not in the least resent people challenging the way RRAs are done (though I do not particularly like the fact that all qualitative methods are often assumed to be defective while all quantitative methods are assumed to be trustworthy). In fact, I think that given the many poor RRAs that try to pass themselves off as quality research, people are fully justified in questioning how the methods have been used. This means, however, that the teams have to take extraordinary precautions in their use of the methods so that they will be in a position to persuasively defend their use of the methodology.

Being able to defend the methodology requires that deliberate and systematic steps are taken to ensure that (i) methodological principles are followed with the greatest attention and (ii) that the process is well documented. In my experience, when I have taken the trouble to explain the careful process by which the sites were selected and the teams' scrupulous attention to reducing bias through triangulation of team members, village respondents, and the use of diverse tools, most discussion of the methods is dispatched, allowing people to focus again on the substantive results of the work. To the extent that information from other methods (surveys or remote sensing techniques) can be brought in to corroborate the qualitative findings, this helps to further assuage the doubters.

Finally, in more than one instance, villagers themselves have leaped to the defence of the research team. We have tried to make it a practice to invite representatives from the sites studied to at least the regional workshops held to discuss the results. In one case, when one of the functionaries in attendance began to rail against the team and suggest that the findings from the study could not possibly be accurate, an elder of the village rose with great dignity and proceeded to indignantly refute the challenge. He noted that the team had conducted a highly serious study and captured exactly the reality of their village. He added that he would be happy to take the bureaucrat or any others who doubted the results back home with him to show them that not only was this the reality in their village but that it was common practice throughout the zone. I don't think the bureaucrat took him up on his offer, but neither did he cause us any further problems during the workshop.

Source: Karen Schoonmaker Freudenberger, pers. comm.

Adams *et al.*, 1993; Rajaratnam *et al.*, 1993), proving both more cost-effective and more popular than the latter. When employed for impact assessment, their use has not been limited to a qualitative explanation of observed trends and outcomes, but has been extended to incorporate quantitatively measured variables, elicited using recall methods,[11] to establish 'over-time' comparisons of the project population before and after. Generally, participatory methods have been used as alternatives to questionnaires for data gathering in many contexts, often proving cheaper, quicker and less prone to error (Chambers, 1994a: 17).

Despite increasing acceptance of the internal validity of PRA methods, problems emerge when the research process needs to be scaled up. Effective synthesis research requires a minimum degree of standardization of information, raising questions as to the external validity – or statistical defensibility across population groups – of PRA methods.

In a conventional research mode, standardization requires that a series of internally valid exercises over various locations and population groups utilizes similar exercises and directly comparable indicators. Within the PRA tradition, there seems to be an inherent contradiction between its emphasis on diversity and the need in central analysis for commensurate data (Chambers, 1994a). While there is no problem with aggregating certain forms of data where discrete units can be counted, such as numbers of children immunized or animals owned, there is a greater tendency for PRA methods to emphasize relative values, necessitating a shift from measuring to comparing (Chambers 1994b: 1264) and seemingly preventing comparability across populations.

Efforts have been made, however, to adapt post-positivist approaches in an attempt to reconcile a prevailing external demand for quantifiable indicators with the self-evident qualitative strengths of PRA methods. For example, the Kenyan and Tanzanian PPAs adopted a notably more standardized and statistical approach to the participatory research process when compared with the PPAs discussed in Part 2. The Kenya PPA was designed specifically to complement the statistical findings on poverty arising out of the government's December 1992 Welfare Monitoring Survey (WMS).[12] Through mapping and wealth-ranking exercises, local participants were encouraged to identify and discuss the characteristics of people in their village according to four categories: very poor, poor, average and rich. The results of this participatory categorization process were then compared across districts and cross-tabulated by headship in each district.[13] By adopting this standardized approach, the study was also able to compare the participatory poverty-line data of each district with the poverty lines established through the conventional absolute poverty approach.

In both Kenya and Tanzania, SARAR[14] techniques were used in community-based ranking exercises, with pre-established categories introduced to analysts through picture cards. This method was adopted in order 'to avoid introducing sectoral bias' (Narayan and Nyamwaya, 1996: 9), but also enabled ease of comparison and data aggregation across communities, adding weight to conclusions and policy recommendations. For a problem-identification exercise conducted during the Kenya PPA, for instance, a set of some two dozen drawings was developed, depicting a variety of problems and issues. These were used, along with blank paper for additional local problems not covered by the drawings, by local analysts for ranking their five most important problems.

The approach towards standardization and aggregation adopted by the Kenya and Tanzania PPAs represents a significant shift in the way that participatory research data are being analysed, a move that is not without attendant uncertainty. At the centre of this doubt is the validity of the assumptions that underlie such analysis. Quantitative data collected within a participatory methodology tend to consist of ordinal rather than cardinal measures of well-being, 'adequate for *relative* wealth ranking of different groups' (Shaffer, 1996: 25, emphasis added). There is no reason to suppose, for example, that people in different communities will have the same cut-off points when they categorize 'wealth'. Within the context of post-positivist trustworthiness, the efforts made in the Kenya and Tanzania PPAs to establish external validity might be replaced by an emphasis on providing contextualized but transferable data.

The inherent difficulties of aggregating and standardizing data collected with participatory tools are compounded further by the intensive nature of participatory research, which does not easily lend itself to the large-scale reproduction required for conventional external validity. Schoonmaker Freudenberger argues that good participatory research requires 'time, money and, especially, energetic, inquisitive researchers' (Chapter 8). It is not possible, she argues, for energy, enthusiasm and creativity to be sustained through a string of exercises, and the alternative of bringing a large number of people into the process raises the issue of a trade-off between quality of research and its representativeness. Understanding issues and behaviour, rather than providing the basis for extrapolation, lies at the heart of good participatory policy-influencing research. Its sustained effectiveness lies, not in trying to transform itself, but in combining its eye for detail with the broader brush stokes of other traditions.

Methodologies, methods and policy change

So where do we go with participatory research? Do methodologies that attempt to engage with the positivist research paradigm serve only to imbue the participatory approach with greater conventional robustness than it merits? Furthermore, do attempts to engage with the conventional research mode of enquiry undermine the *raison d'être* for the participatory approach?

Schoonmaker Freudenberger (Chapter 8) argues that participatory researchers should resist such engagement on the basis that 'it is impossible to satisfy those who doubt anything that is not based on statistical significance'. Certainly, given the peculiar strengths of the PRA tradition and attendant concerns about the quality-representativeness trade-off, it would seem unwise to try to fashion participatory research methodologies too closely in the image of more empiricist traditions when looking to influence policy.

Ultimately, we should not forget that the context is one of projecting local voices into the policy process. There is an alternative, and perhaps given this context a more useful, approach which eschews epistemological exclusiveness and views approaches and methods as independent yet interchangeable:

It is getting harder to find any methodologists solidly encamped in one epistemology or the other. More and more 'quantitative' methodologists, operating from a logical positivist stance, are using naturalistic and phenomenological approaches to complement tests, surveys and structured interviews. On the other side, an increasing number of ethnographers and qualitative researchers are using pre-designed conceptual frameworks and pre-structured instrumentation, especially when dealing with more than one institution or community . . . we contend that researchers should pursue their work, be open to an ecumenical blend of epistemologies and procedures, and leave the grand debate to those who care most about it (Miles and Huberman, 1984: 20, cited in Guba and Lincoln, 1989: 158).

A pluralistic-use research method emerges as a key criterion of trustworthiness when presenting policy-relevant information. Workshop participants stressed the importance of extending the triangulation process beyond the immediate range of PRA methods. Just as it is recognized that there are multiple strategies to influence policymakers so too, it is argued, participatory methodologies and methods for policy-focused research should not be adopted in isolation but should be seen as powerful research instruments when combined with other methodologies and traditions. This is demonstrated by the importance of Milimo's anthropological insights in Booth's case study (Chapter 4), as well as the usefulness of accommodating and complementing the broader spatial and numerical dimensions provided by quantitative surveys. The sequencing of questionnaire surveys and participatory research, with questionnaires both preceding and following the participatory exercises, was integral to several PPA exercises discussed by Robb (Chapter 16). The uses and advantages of sequencing these methodologies, along with presentations of further case studies, are discussed in some detail by Mukherjee (1995: 93–102). Recall data are open to considerable bias, while baseline survey data may be inaccurate or incomplete. Triangulation means making the most of the approaches and methods to cross-check results, and of secondary sources as baselines or comparisons. There is little room, it appears, for epistemological exclusiveness.

There are strong objections to this ecumenical position. Guba and Lincoln (1989: 183) warn of the dangers of confusing methods with methodologies. A methodology is more than just a matter of selecting among methods: it 'involves the researcher utterly – from unconscious world-view to enactment of that world-view via the inquiry process'.

Parmesh Shah (1993: 3), on the other hand, believes a change of methods can engender a change of methodology; participatory research methods can be used not only as a challenge to the validity and reliability of conventional methods, but their use can encourage a change in the mind-set of a researcher schooled in the positivist research paradigm. This change involves a shift from an extractive to a participatory mode, whereby research becomes 'an open-ended process in which people are given an opportunity to participate in designing a questionnaire, developing criteria and indicators, discussing the issues which need to be explored and collecting and analysing data through use of a range of verbal and visual methods including questionnaires'.

Ultimately, shrewd pluralism and inventiveness in the use of approaches and methods can provide the most powerful means to influence policy. The question for researchers then becomes: 'which techniques and tools are appropriate and in which contexts?' In order to influence policy most effectively, this also means proactively building perceived policy needs into the research design and implementation. Variables informing the choice of field site can include the potential demands of the policymakers themselves, while selected populations can be representative of a clientele that interests policymakers. Similarly, individual PRA methods can be 'sharpened' in order to influence policymakers more effectively. Milimo *et al.* (Chapter 13), for instance, reflect that the application of trend analysis to specific trends during the Zambia PPA would have made this particular technique a powerful instrument for strengthening policy messages. Finally, greater self-confidence and knowledge of the statistical rigour of many PRA methods would strengthen their legitimacy and lend policy recommendations greater conviction.

Training for participatory policy-focused research

The distinction between approach and methods is particularly important for training in participatory research. Booth (Chapter 4) raises the issue of relative emphasis in PRA training, arguing that PRA will be effective in influencing sectoral policy 'only if emphasis is placed on its generic principles – learning reversal, optimal ignorance, offsetting biases, triangulation, etc. – and not if it is treated in practice mainly as a technical repertoire'. Warning of the possible deleterious effect of a 'toolkit approach', he comments: 'more techniques could easily have produced less understanding'.

During the IDS workshop, various aspects of PRA were specified as needing a training component in order to build capacity and sustain quality:

o training in the philosophical differences between research traditions, and in defending PRA against criticisms rooted in other traditions;
o training in analysis is seen as critical by several contributors, with debates surrounding the analytical process elaborated on by Norton (Chapter 24);
o training in report writing; to 'translate' discourse to the official level and present information in a policy-friendly format but without losing the voice of the local participants. The management committee of the South African PPA held a training workshop on policy and report writing, to which each participating research organization was required to send at least one person (*SA PPA Newsletter*, 1995);
o training for dissemination, for the effective linking of research analysis to policy outcomes through strategic efforts, as discussed above.

Time is often a fundamental constraint when considering quality in training. Additional time demands are placed on trainers as the distinction is increasingly made between the tools and techniques of PRA and associated attitudes and behaviour; between 'doing' and 'being' (*Face to Face*, 1996a). Hence, in addition to the time needed to explain the wide range of PRA methods and their applications, relative emphasis in training has shifted from methods to approach:

PRA practitioners have come to stress personal behaviour and attitudes, role reversals, facilitating participation through group processes and visualization, critical self-awareness, embracing error and sharing without boundaries. We believe that these principles and concepts must be placed at the centre of all participatory development activities (Absalom *et al.*, 1995).

To cope with these increasing demands placed upon them, PRA trainers have developed quick but effective exercises, using role play and/or discussion for instilling[15] in trainees the self-critical awareness necessary to 'discover' a range of principles common to participatory research approaches,[16] including: respecting and instilling confidence in others; being a good listener; passing over initiative and responsibility; being flexible; and embracing error. In one exercise, for instance, trainees are each handed a card, noting a different principle, and asked to think about why this could be important when using PRA, or if they could recount an occasion on which it affected their work in the past (*Hlabisa PRA Training Report*, 1995). 'Dominator' is a game designed to enhance awareness of dominant and submissive behaviour, both verbal and non-verbal, through role-play and discussion (Chambers, 1995, mimeo). Another game, 'Saboteur', aims to demonstrate how communication and group work can be easily disrupted and creates a group strategy for recognizing and dealing with sabotage (Pretty *et al.*, 1995). 'Listening Pairs' aims to help participants realize the importance of listening skills to good communication (Welbourn, 1995). The objective of 'Cooperative Squares' is to experience and analyse some of the elements of cooperation and for individuals to look at their own behaviour when working in a group (Pretty *et al.*, 1995). 'Shoulder Tapping' is a means of alerting colleagues to their dominant behaviour (Shah, A.C., 1991). These, and many other exercises have proved to be simple but effective ways of fundamentally challenging behaviour and attitudes.

Looking beyond introducing good practice in training, the sustainability of standards in training becomes a critical issue. Is it possible to ensure that as training is spread it is self-improving? Kane *et al.* (Chapter 5) argue that a tension surfaces between the imperative to 'make ourselves redundant' in the training process and the need to ensure sustained quality in different areas of the PRA process. They argue that training and the reproduction of training, like a video tape played and replayed, are susceptible to an ongoing process of erosion of quality. With each successive training process something is lost, particularly with respect to the quality of analysis.

An alternative perspective posits that rather than quality being lost, something could be gained – a method refined or an approach enriched – through the replication process.[17] The 'cascade' effect of the dissemination of PRA training ensures that new people with new ideas, but with a shared underlying philosophy, are brought into the process. In this way, PRA avoids becoming a clone of itself but evolves and improves according to each new context. Emphasis shifts from the refining of a blueprint training process to creating ways in which people can come together in their own contexts to develop their own theory.

24

Analysing Participatory Research for Policy Change

ANDREW NORTON[1]

The main objective of this chapter is to share some of the experience gained in the process of working on Participatory Poverty Assessments in Ghana, Zambia and South Africa (see Norton et al., 1994; May with Attwood et al., 1996; Norton et al., 1995). The brief introduction deals with some of the conceptual and ethical issues raised. The process of analysis of research generated through using participatory methods is then examined. Later sections are designed to give practical guidance for development practitioners seeking to develop their capacity to carry out participatory policy research.

From extractive research to participatory development practice

In describing the transition from an 'extractive' research approach to that of a participatory development practitioner a key dimension in the opposition presented is generally that between 'ownership' of the information generated by the 'outsider/researcher' and ownership by the 'insider/participant'. This transition is also frequently presented as part of a broader transformation in which the role of analyst passes from the researcher to the (local) participant. The transition from informant to analyst on the part of the local participant is matched by one from analyst to facilitator by the outsider/researcher (see Chambers, 1992). The various dualisms presented above are all clearly limited and potentially problematic. In particular in mixed research teams containing both community members and outsiders the boundaries between outsider and local are both theoretically and practically invalid.

In reality, however, most interactions in the practice of development still carry with them the kinds of imbalances of power, authority and control over resources that make the binary frameworks referred to above instantly applicable and recognizable. In this context the general concept of 'reversal' has been an important element promoting new participatory forms of development practice. The practical benefits have been in developing new forms of action and learning which open the possibility for the intended beneficiaries of development processes to define more of the content, priorities and outcomes of those processes.

Within this framework of understanding, the position of participatory research for policy formulation is evidently problematic. Techniques and methods can be used which help members of poor urban and rural communities generate analyses of their situation, the constraints which impede improved well-being (whether social, economic, environmental etc.), and appropriate action which can be taken to overcome those constraints. In the context of the local field-research 'event', the transformation referred to above (community members becoming analysts, outside practitioners becoming facilitators) can be seen as taking place. In aggregating the results of such exercises to produce material which is relevant to national policy frameworks, however, an analytical process takes place which is outside the control of the local participants. Even if the material is presented in strongly testimonial forms (case histories, direct quotation, video clips of villagers talking) decisions have been made about which voices are selected, what elements of what they had to say were relevant, and so on. Practitioners of participatory development approaches who work exclusively with the goal of empowering people to take action at the community level are therefore often uncomfortable with the use of such methodologies to produce inputs to policy formulation. On the other hand, without the use of methods which can present key elements of the realities and priorities of poor people, it is likely that social policy will remain driven by technocratic models in which the dominant factors taken into account will be those which fit with the theoretical paradigm of the group designing the research. The policy directions that emerge risk being constrained by a narrow, technocratic vision, grounded in the assumptions and experiences of outsiders. The chapters in this book provide many examples of instances where the use of participatory research methods has enriched the process of policy formulation.[2]

The following basic principles for policy research that uses participatory methods can be noted:

○ *In participatory policy research analysis takes place at different levels and with different actors.* Typically this involves at least two groups: community members and members of research teams. In the larger exercises a distinction can also often be seen between the analysis of members of research teams, and the contribution of the report authors. The process of analysis should be as transparent as possible, and every effort should be made to distinguish each group's contribution.

○ *Participatory policy research does not have as its sole, or even primary goal, direct community-level empowerment.* The primary rationale for such exercises is generally the need to make policy more responsive to the needs and realities of affected people, though the methods which are used (PLA, PRA) typically derive from a tradition where direct empowerment is seen as the primary objective of legitimate social action.[3]

In relation to both of these points it is helpful to be clear about the shift in the context in which participatory methods are applied (from community-level action to policy formulation); likewise, it is unhelpful to make exaggerated claims about the outcomes in terms of participation or empowerment.

Bearing in mind these principles, the following is intended to provide practical guidance, outlining some useful principles for engaging in policy research using participatory research methods. On the premise that the institutions involved in such research do not always have prior experience of applied research the guidance attempts to be comprehensive.

Preparing for the research

This section indicates some useful tools and issues to consider when pre-paring for an exercise of this kind. Perhaps the most useful starting-point is to 'think the process backwards' from the anticipated desired result: to whom are the results to be presented and how? whom is it hoped to influence and with what kinds of outcomes? As with much of the other guidance presented below the need to engage in a reasonable amount of forward planning should be balanced against the importance of maintain-ing flexibility in the research without which the participatory character of the exercise will be lost.

Policy-based research often involves a number of key stakeholders be-fore the nature and objectives of the exercise have been finalized. In the case of the South Africa PPA, for example, several levels of stakeholder existed from the beginning of the process: the South African government (represented by the office of the Reconstruction and Development Pro-gramme); donor agencies (the World Bank, ODA and the Dutch gov-ernment); the coordinating institution (Data Research Africa); and the participating researchers and research institutions (academics, NGOs, CBOs). These organizations can be expected to have different interests and motivations for engaging in the research. This makes it particularly important that the group which is to carry out the project negotiates a clear and satisfactory understanding of its nature. This typically involves bureau-cratic processes and instruments (contracts, terms of reference), but the sharing of documentation which outlines objectives, principles and pro-cesses also contributes to building a shared understanding of the nature of the project. It is impossible to guarantee that results will influence policy, but the presence of committed individuals in policy positions in agencies which it is hoped to influence give the project a reasonable chance of promoting change. Although the final results in terms of policy influence are never fully predictable, identifying particular policy areas and tailoring the selection of methods and research participants to deal with these are clearly important. There will, however, be a greater tendency than in con-ventional approaches towards having to deal with multiple stakeholders, expressing diverse interests through varying objectives. In this kind of context an NGO engaging in research with a variety of partners (donors, government, communities) needs to be very clear about its own goals, whether in terms of policy influence, advocacy or capacity building.

It is also important to spend time on developing the research design. For smaller-scale thematic studies this might be relatively simple, and possibly emerge fairly naturally from the ongoing work of an NGO; for a larger exercise such as a national poverty study, more forward thinking will be necessary, including: the research questions to be investigated and how these fit in with the objectives; an indicative guide to the research methods to be used (both in general and in relation to specific research questions where appropriate); methods for selection of field sites and participants; composition of research teams (by gender, specialization, institutional background, language skills etc.); and a schedule for carrying out the re-search, including provision for analysing the results. While this might seem an obvious point, experience shows that time invested in this is generally of great benefit. For larger exercises a basic field guide for the research teams is essential. Unlike field enumerators for a quantitative survey, teams using participatory methods must share a common understanding of the nature of the project in order to generate comparable results from which coherent policy conclusions can be developed. The training which the teams receive is critical to this cohesion, but a field guide is a useful supplementary tool. Its use must not, however, restrict flexibility and the iterative quality that is essential to good participatory research.

In developing the research design and proposal there may be a tension between strengthening the participation of local communities in the process of analysis and generation of policy results, and allowing for an implementation schedule that produces policy results quickly and cost effectively. In particular, if research participants are to have any opportunity to assess the final policy conclusions of their work, a second round of field visits has to be programmed for these consultations. While this may slow things down and increase costs, it is clearly good practice.

In developing the overall plan for the training of field teams it is useful to include the kinds of analytical points which are dealt with in this chapter. If the researchers have no experience whatsoever of report-writing then a certain amount of very basic training in this area (structure, style etc.) is also desirable. Bringing new actors with special views, experiences and commitments into the field of policy research is an exciting process which promises real long-term benefits for the societies involved.

Analysis and reporting in the field

In both Zambia and Ghana the PPA teams prepared field-site reports in between visiting different communities. This proved to be extremely important for a number of reasons: the teams started to develop an improved understanding of methods through carrying out preliminary synthesis and analysis; comparative issues which could be investigated in subsequent field sites emerged clearly; striking findings from particular environments were written up while the experience was vivid in the researchers' minds; the process of compiling field reports meant that a huge amount of preparatory work carried out enabled the final report to focus on generating key policy messages. If the schedule allows for this, presenting the results back to the local-level research participants is an invaluable aid to improving the rigour of the findings, testing conclusions and ensuring the greatest possible involvement of some or all of the participants in generating policy conclusions.

It is important for institutions used to participatory methods for community animation and empowerment ends to realize that for policy research the quality of recording and reporting of field exercises is critical. To illustrate, Box 3.4 is derived from material generated at research workshops in Zambia and South Africa. It comprises a checklist of the key elements to be recorded in conducting PRA.

For large research exercises involving a number of field sites, therefore, attention has to be paid to recording and reporting at various different

---

Box 3.4   Key elements to record during PRA

Basic recording of PRA exercises

○ place, location (any particular characteristics of the location that are significant – e.g. public space or private)
○ date, time of day, duration of the exercise
○ participants (numbers, gender, ethnicity, generation, names where appropriate, specific key individuals present)
○ facilitators/researchers present
○ language issues (translation etc.)
○ materials used for the exercise

Recording the process

○ who participates? how does the quality of participation change during the exercise?
○ how was the exercise initiated and by whom?
○ relevant aspects of the context for the exercise (e.g. aspects of social context known to be relevant, previous information gained on the subject)
○ full reporting on the content of the discussion generated while the exercise is being carried out
○ key quotations from participants
○ points of interpretation essential to understanding the visual (e.g. on a seasonality matrix recording sources of income: are the scorings consistent between the different lines or is the matrix in fact a series of independent graphs which would have to be triangulated with another exercise to assess the relative importance of the different income sources? From the output alone this is not transparent; frequently the correct interpretation of an output is not possible without notes from the researchers who were present
○ decisions taken during the exercise by the team (e.g. not to follow up with a planned exercise for a specific reason)

After the PRA exercise

○ follow-up interviews
○ verification/cross-checking: in writing up the exercise researchers can note relevant information picked up from other exercises

---

stages. Good daily recording in the field enables messages to be captured in field-site reports which then feed into the final analysis and presentation of results. Regular discussion of findings and methods among the research teams helps this along. The quality of teamwork among the researchers often seems to be the most important factor in determining the quality and impact of the final results.

Policy analysis with participatory research findings

The analysis of participatory research results is time-consuming and there are few general rules about how to go about it. The key is for those who compile reports to familiarize themselves as thoroughly as possible with the material that has been collected. Visual PRA 'outputs' can rarely be simplistically aggregated or analysed quantitatively, reflecting as they do categories of analysis generated by different groups of participants which are rarely consistent.[4] Separation of the description of the research results from analysis is in practice not possible. Nonetheless, comparative processes are always a possibility, and the existence of well-documented results from a wide range of different methods which have been used across a spectrum of social groups provides rich testimony which is not difficult to apply to specific policy issues.

It is first useful, however, to think through what is meant in different contexts by the word 'policy'. Policy is clearly more than a set of goals and procedures. It can refer to: processes of resource allocation; institutional mechanisms and procedures for public and non-governmental institutions; legal and regulatory frameworks applied by the state; and issues of access, quality, efficiency and relevance in the delivery of public services. Whatever its nature, policy is generally negotiated among a set of different stakeholders who vary in terms of: influence, power, access to information, perspectives and interests. Key policy messages are often in the nature of advocacy, and are likely to be influential only by virtue of how powerfully they emerge from the information presented. It is not just the message that is important, but how convincing is the case made for it. The testimonial quality of PRA visual exercises can be extremely powerful.

In order to make the most of this it is important that material which is presented is put clearly in context. Presented with an institutional diagram, a seasonality chart or a flow diagram, readers not familiar with PRA processes will tend to assume that the research team have constructed these themselves unless it is clear that they are the results of analysis carried out by local people in their own communities. The extensive use of verbatim reporting (testimony) from participants, where this is strong and best illustrates a point, will also strengthen the force with which conclusions are presented. For an audience not familiar with participatory or qualitative research methods (i.e. most policymakers in government or international agencies), the direct presentation of field results is particularly important, if necessary in the form of annexes. This helps to convey the methodological rigour and professional process which lie behind the conclusions of a study.

The process of generating policy conclusions and recommendations generally needs to consider the capacities and potential for action of institutions at different levels, for example:

○ community-based organizations (CBOs)
○ NGOs
○ local-level service providers
○ district-level line ministry managers
○ local government
○ donor agencies

o national government (including Finance Ministry and various line ministries)

In most cases the specific purpose of policy research using participatory methods is to make available to secondary stakeholders certain kinds of information about how primary stakeholders view and analyse key issues in their lives. The eventual results of this in terms of policy change will usually be influenced by a variety of other processes. The more complex the institutional field involved the more this will be the case. Under most conditions the end results are unpredictable. For example, the recent Africa Region Poverty Task Force Report from the World Bank (1996a) identified that rural infrastructure (particularly water and rural roads) has been a neglected area for investment by the Bank. The identification of this as a priority area was due largely to the influence of various participatory poverty assessments carried out over the previous two years, which had identified physical isolation and lack of access to water consistently as significant issues for poor rural communities. Placing primary stakeholders' priorities on the agenda for policymakers can have long-term influence in ways which are hard to predict and go beyond the specific messages of a single report.

Social analysis using PRA material

The specific research exercises that I have been involved in have mostly used the PRA/PLA family of methods and approaches to some degree. There is a commonality to the character of the material generated through these methods, whose use in social analysis presents specific challenges which have not yet been widely explored. While there is often a tendency to assume that participatory research has a specifically social research character, the roots of PRA are diverse, and include substantial inputs from farming systems and agro-ecosystems research (see Chambers, 1992). Bringing the methods and approach of PRA together with a social-analysis perspective means predominantly two things: to inform analysis with an understanding of social and cultural processes and systems; and to bring to the analysis and research an awareness of the social heterogeneity of groups and communities (gender, class, ethnicity, generation etc.). The following notes relate in particular to poverty analysis using PRA/PLA material.

Analysis of difference[5]

This process consists essentially of generating meaning from material through comparing data, perceptions, priorities or analyses generated by different social groups. These groups may be defined by a range of different characteristics, including gender, age/generation, region, community, wealth, social status, ethnicity or a range of distinctions specific to particular environments (e.g. migrants vs non-migrants, farm workers vs smallholders, the unemployed vs the employed). At the most basic level this process involves looking for contrast or consistency in the findings generated both within and across field sites. Distinctions in the priorities expressed by different genders or age groups can then be related to other

185

information about livelihood and social systems. This kind of analysis is important to ensure that policy conclusions take account of social and economic heterogeneity, and illustrate the different impacts that policy change can have on different social groups. In the Zambia PPA, for example, water supply emerged as one of the most consistent elements of priority ranking and other analyses carried out with rural women. Exercises carried out with men were more varied; water featured as a priority need essentially where it was related to livelihood activities controlled by men (especially livestock).

Triangulation between different exercises

Triangulation using multiple sources, methods and investigators is a key tool in establishing the 'trustworthiness' of participatory research results. This process of cross-checking to test results and seek a more complete understanding should occur at all stages of the research – in the field, in preliminary analysis and in the preparation of the final results.

To take one example. We can look at the process of generating conclusions on what people in poor communities see as the key constraints which prevent them from improving their situation, and the key actions which can be taken by institutions at various levels to overcome these. This tends to be seen by policymakers as one of the more valuable results of participatory research in terms of 'upstream' policy work as it provides a perspective on cross-sectoral priorities in resource allocation, an area where more conventional economic analyses generally do not produce firm conclusions. The results of needs-ranking, priority-ranking and problem-ranking exercises can have significant influence. The interpretation of these activities, however, generally needs great care. For example, in community-level discussions about 'needs' priorities are often expressed through a perceived need for a particular piece of infrastructure ('we need a clinic'). To what extent is it valid to see this a proxy for dissatisfaction with the level of access or quality of health services in general? People may fail to rank a new school as a priority for a variety of reasons:

○ they place a low value on basic education;
○ they place a high value on education, but are satisfied with access;
○ they value education for their children, but are disillusioned with the quality of the service;
○ they do not think a new school would do any good; or
○ they do not believe they would be able to afford to send their children to school.

Information from discussions, interviews and other exercises will help to confirm or deny these possible interpretations. For example, if the school/ PTA appears prominently and regularly in institutional diagrams it would indicate that the school is valued by the community. Therefore the second interpretation would be the most likely reason for the non-appearance of education in the list of priority needs.

To take another example, information on the key components of livelihood strategies can be derived from the majority of exercises carried out with a given social group (wealth ranking, seasonality analyses, institutional diagrams, ranking or scoring of problems/constraints, discussions etc.). As with other forms of investigation involving large amounts of 'thick description' (social anthropology, ethnography) a thorough familiarity with the context and material will produce greater understanding of causal links and systemic patterns underlying the issues being investigated.

'Breaking down' issues

It is often helpful to seek to 'break down' issues that have been investigated to help/order the material for analysis. In Ghana, for example, a wealth of data on education services and the poor started to appear a great deal more coherent when the researchers began to break it down into issues of access, quality and relevance (see Korobe, 1995). Each of these can, of course, be broken down further in turn. For example, access into cost and non-cost barriers (flooded roads, distance, overcrowding of schools). The cost barriers can be broken down into cash costs and opportunity costs (the loss of the child's productive and domestic labour). Cash costs can be broken down into formal charges (school fees, examination fees) and informal costs (PTA fees, uniform/equipment costs; transport charges; bribes to place children in schools). All these are helpful in challenging policymaker assumptions about the conditions of access to schooling and the real constraints to getting more children into school.

Notes on poverty analysis using PLA/PRA methods

Much of the literature on the assessment and analysis of poverty is derived from a positivist tradition where the key information source is household questionnaire surveys, and the conception of poverty is dominated by a single measure (an assessment of household consumption levels constructed from both cash expenditure and cash values imputed to consumption of self-produced goods, especially food, which is then used as a base for a 'poverty line'). The key examples of this would be the major World Bank texts, the 1990 *World Development Report* on poverty and the *Poverty Reduction Handbook* (1992).

As has been repeatedly stressed the kinds of research described here illuminate a very different view of poverty, which encompasses a variety of dimensions of the experience, but does not necessarily see household income and expenditure levels as the key issue.[6] Local views of poverty and vulnerability do not generate one-dimensional indicators such as the poverty line. They relate instead to fundamental values about basic entitlements and need. These vary substantially between and within different social groups as well as between different spatial areas. How, then, can we apply concepts which will allow for policy conclusions to be reached?

There is a helpful theoretical literature which provides an alternative framework for describing and analysing issues related to poverty. Key texts include Chambers (1983; 1995b), Moser (1996) and IDS Bulletin (1989) as well as the PPAs described in this chapter and elsewhere in this book. The following is a brief synthesis of the main points from this literature.

187

The unit of analysis

Different aspects of poverty and deprivation apply at different levels of social organization. For example, lack of street-lighting, electricity, water, access to schooling, access to markets may apply predominantly at the level of the settlement or community, while food security and income may be seen as issues which apply at the household level. Different participatory research exercises will tend to produce conclusions stressing dimensions of poverty which apply at different levels. For example, needs-ranking exercises usually produce information on aspects of deprivation which apply predominantly at the community level (however defined), while wealth ranking focuses on dimensions of poverty which differentiate between households.

If a PPA is being carried out to complement a conventional poverty analysis using household-consumption data, it is vital to explore dimensions of deprivation within household units (gender, age) which are completely hidden by methods which treat the household as a 'black box' and assume: (i) that all resources and income are pooled; and (ii) that the distribution of goods within is equitable. Although, as Kabeer (1996) observes, participatory research is only as gender-aware as its practitioners, there is a specific obligation in this kind of research to reveal aspects of experience that are normally invisible, due to dominant structures of power and the conceptual understandings which go with them.

Vulnerability vs poverty

Concepts of vulnerability have a more dynamic character than those of poverty. They deal essentially with the process dimensions of poverty, i.e. the conditions under which specific groups of people with specific social characteristics are vulnerable to a rapid deterioration in their well-being. There are essentially two aspects to the analysis of vulnerability: (i) the nature of the 'threat', which may be derived from the social, political, economic or physical environment; and (ii) the capacity of the group in question to respond to threats, either in terms of resisting the negative impact or in recovering their position afterwards – which depends primarily on the assets upon which they can call.

Typically the type of external threat is described either in terms of 'shocks', 'cycles' or 'trends'. These are descriptive metaphors which are fairly clear in their application, although there can be grey areas (persistent declining rainfall is a 'trend' but drought is a 'shock', yet both terms may be used to describe a similar set of events). The commonest form of cyclical impact is the influence of seasonality in different environments on a whole range of key aspects of well-being (e.g. food security, health, income). Seasonal poverty is of particular relevance to policy analysis due both to its wide significance and because its relative predictability allows for the possibility of a wide range of interventions to counter its impact (provision of sources of food or income which will help in the lean periods, staggering of expenses in areas such as school fees so they do not all fall at the worst time of year).

Assets

The analysis of assets is a useful link between the discussion of the unit of analysis and that of vulnerability above. Frameworks of analysis which examine assets held by different social groups or individuals at different social levels are valuable in determining which kinds of people are vulnerable to what sort of negative impact, and what kinds of assets will be of particular help.[7] Assets are commonly categorized into a variety of different groupings:

(1) *Examines the nature of the asset through a threefold division into 'stores', 'claims' and 'investments'.* 'Stores' of wealth refer essentially to assets which can be converted into basic consumption goods through sale or direct consumption (e.g. cattle, money, grain, jewellery); 'claims' refers to assets in the sense of social relationships or obligations which can be called upon from, for example, kin, community members, friends, charitable organizations, government bodies for assistance in times of need; and 'investments' refer to actions where groups or individuals invest in assets which will assist their long-term capacity to be productive and sustain their livelihoods (including human investments, such as health and education, as well as investments in material items to assist production).

(2) *Distinguishes according to different understandings of the form of capital involved.* While material capital refers to man-made and natural items over which rights and ownership can be asserted, human capital refers to the individual (or household, community) capabilities in terms of strength, skills, education, labour power, physical health. The term 'social capital' has recently gained currency to describe assets which households or individuals can draw on not only to mobilize claims but also to take collective action to deal with problems. It is generally understood to refer to the norms, trust and reciprocity networks that facilitate mutually beneficial cooperation among a given social group or community.[8]

These two typologies can be seen as linked, insofar as the first (stores, claims, investments) refers to the relationship between the person or social groups and the assets available, while the second categorises the assets themselves.

Dangerous assumptions!

Because a research team begins work with a community professing a commitment to understanding their realities and conditions does not mean that wrong and misleading assumptions are necessarily left behind. Even the methods applied may tend towards reinforcing biases unless researchers are constantly prepared to challenge their own assumptions. To take one example. PRA is derived predominantly from rural research traditions. In common with much other investigation it tends towards the unthinking adoption of some ideas which are unhelpful in either policy research or community-level participatory planning. These assumptions are particularly characteristic of much rural research, and raise particular practical problems when PRA methods are used in urban areas. They may also be problematic and unhelpful in rural research too. We can highlight the following:

(1) *The assumption of community*: a series of assumptions about the nature of communities characterizes much rural research. Specifically communities are considered: homogeneous; to have clearly defined boundaries; to take collective decisions (with everyone allowed to participate in that process); to be 'natural'/'traditional' units which have emerged through long-standing autonomous processes. Good practice in PRA seeks to break down the first of these assumptions through seeking out the powerless, poorer, less-visible members of communities and assuring to the greatest possible degree their opportunity to participate in the process of analysis and research. This, however, does not guarantee that PRA practitioners do not fall into any of these traps. In order to avoid assumptions of this kind, the following principles are useful: examining the issue of community with the research participants in order to explore their concepts; being aware of our own assumptions and constantly testing these against the results of the research; being aware that 'community' can be a flexible concept which refers to different boundaries under different circumstances.

(2) *The assumption of homogeneity of livelihoods:* some exercises carried out in group contexts involve an assumption that the livelihoods of the group are similar and follow comparable patterns. For example, seasonality of income or food security in a rural community follows set patterns for all farmers to the extent that they are depending on a similar mix of crops and supplementary income-earning strategies. This may or may not be the case, and investigation with diverse groups would be needed to be sure that stress points identified in seasonality analysis were relevant to all community members. This kind of assumption tends to be particularly flawed for livelihood issues in urban contexts (unless a particular group has been selected by occupation).

(3) *The assumption of mutual knowledge:* some PRA exercises (notably wealth ranking) involve an assumption that within a particular social group or community people have intimate knowledge of their neighbours. In some contexts (particularly some urban areas) this assumption may not be valid. In Ghana some members of poor urban communities refused to attempt wealth ranking, saying: 'it is only when someone faces a crisis, like having to send a child to hospital, that you can really see the resources they have, when a rich relative will come forward to pay'. By contrast, in rural areas the kinds of resources in terms of claims on others for assistance that individuals or households can draw on tend to be coded publicly in networks of kinship and community.

Opening doors – new actors in policy research

In conclusion, it is worth offering a few observations on the kinds of actors that have been involved in the PPA exercises which form the basis for the experience described in this chapter. One of the strengths of the processes described has been the inclusion in the research teams of people who were not formal researchers, whether from NGOs or from government service, alongside experienced social scientists. This has had a number of benefits, both in terms of developing the capacities of organizations like CEDEP in Ghana, the PAG in Zambia or the various NGOs involved in the South African PPA to contribute to policy research and strategic advocacy exercises, and in terms of bringing to the research itself practitioner perspectives which have enriched the enquiry. This would have been extremely difficult without the development of a group of participatory research methodologies which do not assume as a starting-point specific research expertise in an academic sense, and which stress processes of team building out of diverse participant groups. There is a need, in keeping with this approach, to develop an inclusive language and approach for the kinds of social analysis described in this chapter. There is considerable scope for development in the analytical approaches to working with participatory research material for policy research, and the chapters in this book represent no more than a useful starting-point. In developing these ideas there will be a need to keep the language and methods of analysis, as well as those for field research and action, accessible to the widest possible range of participants.

25

Participation, Policy Change and Empowerment

IDS WORKSHOP

Participatory jargon pervades the development community. PRA, argues Johansson (1994: 2), 'is about to become just another cookbook recipe from a whimsical development industry'. The challenge for us – development professionals – is to ensure that the principles of participation are not lost as the language of participation becomes institutionalized. The institutionalization of participation is the subject of an accompanying volume to this book (see Blackburn with Holland, 1997). It is important to consider here, however: (i) who can be empowered by participatory policy-focused research; and (ii) in what circumstances certain groups are empowered. In answering these questions, we development professionals must disempower ourselves at every opportunity. The success or otherwise of doing so depends very much on where the motivation for a participatory approach to policy change lies.[1]

Whose empowerment does what?

PRA is a broadly empowering experience, with different groups of people gaining different types of power. First, there is 'the community', 'local people', 'the poor', 'beneficiaries', 'primary stakeholders', a group perhaps characterized by as many conflicts of interest and inequities of power as by commonalities that bind them to these group labels. Then there is the range of institutions within the policy process that make up 'secondary' (or institutional) stakeholders. They include CBOs, NGOs, local-level service providers, district-level line ministry managers, local government, donor agencies and national government (see Chapter 24).

It is important to realize that different stakeholders are and should be empowered by the participatory policy process in different ways. In development, power is usually seen as 'an asset, a means to getting things done' (Chambers, 1997: 76). Chambers argues the counterpoint, of power as disability, as preventing those who have it from learning. It is perhaps more useful to talk therefore about disempowerment through the development process; and yet it is more difficult for 'us' to disempower 'ourselves' than to empower 'them', local people: 'to put the last first is the easier half. Putting the first last is harder' (ibid.: 2). Through the participatory policy process, there is a tendency for power to get stuck at every level, often with corrupting outcomes. University researchers, for instance, may become élites and advocates, retaining control over what they believe are community perceptions. A community 'gatekeeper' may be corrupted by the power bestowed through negotiating entry with outsiders. Through the disabling effect of power, limits are placed on the full participation in the policy process of those whose lives are truly being affected by it.

Empowerment and local-level conflict

Empowerment often threatens vested interests, and such threats create conflict. By challenging the concept of top-down policy intervention, a participatory approach also challenges the myth of the homogeneous 'community' and brings to light latent conflicts of interest at the local level. Yet while PRA reveals conflicts it can also help to resolve them. The role of conflict resolution becomes an important component of PRA in bridging political divisions at the local level and between the local level and outsiders.

Ultimately, consensus-building will often depend on the willingness of vested interests to cede control over resources. As Gujja *et al.* (Chapter 7) emphasize, the success of policies for joint protected-area management of the Ucchali and Keoladeo wetland complexes will depend on addressing 'larger questions' of land alienation, land scarcity and grazing rights. If left out of the policy-reform process, existing inequities will serve only to perpetuate the conflicts which such schemes attempt to mediate.

Despite these fundamental obstacles to consensus, Welbourn (1993) believes that PRA holds great potential for helping people address and resolve conflict, because of its emphasis on communication skills. It is necessary for development workers to recognize that conflict as a political process is present in any community, and to become skilled in the facilitation and arbitration of conflicts as they arise through the PRA process.

Mukherjee (1996) argues for the building of better relationships between stakeholders, on the grounds that misconceptions create conflict. For example, local people from villages bordering a wildlife sanctuary in Uttar Pradesh were excluded from accessing the area by new laws designed to conserve biodiversity and wildlife. Villagers suffered as a result of the constraints this imposed on their livelihoods, and conflicts frequently arose with the local revenue, forest and wildlife administration over encroachment on sanctuary land. Participatory sessions with villagers revealed their wealth of knowledge about sanctuary resources and allowed them to explain in detail the precise problems that their exclusion from the sanctuary had created. The policy outcome of this process remains to be seen. Acceptance and participation of local people in the policy process is, however, she argues, fundamental to the future sustainability of both village livelihoods and of the sanctuary itself. Policy change for a sustainable solution requires the disempowerment of sanctuary managers and their teams through their sensitization to the needs of local communities. This could be initiated through joint sessions of the two groups of stakeholders in the presence of local or outside mediators.

Participatory process or policy product?

Any discussion of participation in the context of policy-focused research raises the more specific tensions that exist between the requirements of policymakers and those of a participatory process, tensions that do not seem immediately reconcilable. Policymakers require a policy product. In the worst-case scenario, participatory methods are used merely to legitimize pre-set programmes by encouraging local people to express as priorities what they know they are going to get. Planners designing a new village layout in the wake of the Maharashtra earthquake of 1993 defended their preference for a grid layout on the grounds that it had been a participatory process. Subsequent PRA by Meera Shah revealed that the earlier 'participatory' process had been loaded from the outset. Furthermore, villagers knew that the outsiders preferred the grid layout and believed that they would get the housing quicker if they agreed. Through PRA, the older people of the village decided on a pattern that more accurately reflected their social realities (Shah, M. K., 1996 and pers. comm., cited in Chambers, 1997: 90).

On the other hand, it has been demonstrated that what Booth (Chapter 4) terms '"rapid" interactive fieldwork of the PRA type' can be a very effective mechanism for sensitizing policymakers to the needs, capacities and perspectives of the poor. If a document with recommendations is the product of participatory research, this product alone may have the effect of giving the people concerned more power.

In contrast to the emphasis of policymakers on a policy outcome or 'product', the central plank of PRA is the participatory process itself. The gulf between the open-agenda ethos of PRA and focused (pre-defined) agenda often set by policy-focused research underlines this distinction still further. Can PRA combine an emphasis on community empowerment with a concern for policy outcomes?

During one small-group discussion at the IDS workshop, a threefold outcome of PRA was identified:

○ PRA can help influence local action;
○ it can influence local action and policy; or
○ influence policy only, without consideration for community interests.

This group considered it unethical if the 'PRA' fits into the third category, with PRA methods used in an extractive mode simply to influence policy without any link back to the local community.

While it is unhelpful to make exaggerated claims about the outcomes of policy-focused research in terms of empowerment (see Norton, Chapter 24), it should be acknowledged that local action can still be an indirect outcome of an essentially extractive research process. Schoonmaker Freudenberger (Chapter 8) points out that RRA analysis facilitates villagers' ability to analyse their realities in a systematic fashion that policymakers can understand. It facilitates local reflections on impacts of policy or proposed policy changes, and enables local people to express and stand up for their interests, with in one instance villagers successfully confronting local authorities after an RRA study.

Furthermore, emphasis of participatory policy-focused research need not be exclusively on delivering a specific policy recommendation but can emphasize the provision of a learning experience for policymakers, challenging their attitudes and behaviour through their face-to-face interaction with local people, as discussed in Chapter 19. Care can also be taken in design to link policy-focused research to institutions involved with continuing community-based initiatives, as was demonstrated by the designers of the South African PPA (see Attwood and May, Chapter 15). The agenda of much policy-focused PRA need not be rigidly pre-defined, with flexibility increased if researchers feel it appropriate to change their agendas in the field in response to the priority issues emerging through analysis by local participants.

Finally, the ethical questioning of 'product'-based participatory research is further clouded when the possible local empowering impacts of policy change itself are considered. Gill (Chapter 3), discussing the use of PRA methods by the Tarai Research Network, recognizes that the nature of the process is inherently less participatory and yet the underlying motive is not exploitative, being intended ultimately to benefit local people.

Promoting PRA best practice in policy-focused research

This debate can be resolved to some extent by adopting the attitude that if certain outcomes are more likely to happen by design rather than by accident, then product-based participatory research can be justified with greater confidence. On this basis, there are certain principles which can be built into policy-based research to ensure capacity building and the filtering down of power through stakeholders and through levels:

○ *Collaborate with and build the capacity of local institutions such as universities, NGOs and community groups.* Local capacity building emerged as one of the most important aspects of the PPA experiences discussed in Part 2, not simply in terms of the effectiveness of the research process but more significantly as an outcome in itself of the process. In both Guinea and Madagascar, the research teams also included NGO representatives, some of whom were selected from the national headquarters but at least one of whom came from the zone where the case study was carried out. This was important to diversify the perspectives on the team, but it also helped ensure that information collected in the studies could be put to immediate use by local development practitioners working in the area. Since the benefits to the local population of the policy assessment were distant at best (and nonexistent at worst), participation by NGOs working on local-resource management questions increased the chance that participating villages would gain some direct benefits as a result of the studies. In fact, there were numerous examples of this. In some cases the NGOs stepped in to respond to specific needs identified in the studies, in others they refined and improved their projects in light of information that was gathered.

○ *Ensure that analysis is always taken back to the community, e.g. through a primary stakeholder workshop.* Booth (Chapter 4) argues that at the very least policy-focused PRA should be a learning and not a disempowering experience. In the case of the Zambia cost-recovery study, report-back was achieved to some extent through the formation and follow-up activity of the Participatory Assessment Group (PAG). Johansson's experience of taking videod PRA back to local analysts in Tanzanian fishing villages had the dramatic effect of inspiring community mobilization and action in villages up and down the coast (see Box 3.1).

○ *Build in a follow-up component when engaging in 'experimental' research.* There is a danger of PRA being a 'one-off' exercise, whether for policy or local action. How often do researchers and policymakers return and look at what happens as a result of this research intervention? PRA practitioners are increasingly aware of the twin dangers of raising local expectations for external assistance and of 'PRA fatigue' engendered by repeated return visits to local communities. The design of the research 'intervention' becomes critical to avoiding these pitfalls. For example, in the case study on girls' education in the Gambia presented in Chapter 5 the research process started with priority actions that the community could instigate by itself, only then evolving to doing things for which it could get external funding.

○ *Build on existing community management and decision-making practices. Provide supportive space for local groups to function and recognize the legitimacy of (new) local groups.* Applying the principle of inclusion to local management and decision-making practices through PRA can facilitate local empowerment. The South African PPA, for example, was conducted by a range of CBO and NGO researchers who had proposed studies that were part of their existing and continuing working relations with local communities and community-based initiatives (Chapter 15). The final design of the Jamaican Social Investment Fund took into account the need to include and support local groups and decisionmakers, both formal and informal, in the subproject cycle, rather than impose 'project committees' as had happened with other social funds.

○ *Learn to let go, having adequately equipped people.* The disempowering process means making ourselves redundant. Power must not get stuck. In the context of policy-focused research, this means enabling local people to develop their participation in the policy process in their own way.

Applying principles is not straightforward. The drive towards a self-sustaining process of participation in the policy process is continually challenged by contesting claims to ownership of that process. This reality presents itself, for example, through constraints imposed by a lack of control over financing and timing of projects at the local level. Schoonmaker Freudenberger highlights in Chapter 8 the inherent financial vulnerability of a research process reliant on donor funds, which in the case of Guinea were withdrawn part-way through the process. Owen (Chapter 14) underlines the barriers to local ownership of a research process when multiple claims of ownership of that process result in insensitively timetabled demands for outputs. Yet the importance of principles is that they should be striven for despite the challenges that may be thrown up. Participatory principles are emerging throughout the policy world. There is, increasingly, a recognition that 'demand-driven' policymaking requires a fundamental change in attitudes and behaviour, a 'disempowerment' on the part of the policymakers themselves.

Afterword

ROBERT CHAMBERS

Making a difference

Empowering poor people to conduct their own appraisal and analysis, and to present their realities, is one thing. Whether their voices are heard, understood and acted on is another. There are two weak links: from voice to policy change (policy-in-principle); and from policy change to practice (policy-in-practice).

For two reasons, there is less evidence in this book about these two links than about the participatory research itself:

(1) The work is recent. Often there has not yet been time for findings and presentations to work their way through into policy-in-principle, and still less to policy-in-practice.
(2) Causes and effects with policy change are often complex and hidden. Linear cause–effect relations cannot be established.

Partial exceptions are some of the cases reported: priority to rural infrastructure in Ghana; balance between sectors, and influence on health policies in Zambia; the timing of school-fee payments and rules for girls' school uniforms in The Gambia. More common are changes with multiple and obscure causality, with participatory research as one factor. Scottish forest policy is an enlightening case, where the researchers (Inglis and Guy, Chapter 9) could not find direct evidence connecting the PRA events and the subsequent policy change, although in their judgement some causal links were probably there.

From voice to policy

There are, all the same, practical lessons to be drawn about the link between voice and policy change. These concern ownership, credibility and process.

(1) *Ownership* affects likelihood of change. There is no one best approach. Sometimes ownership at first by groups in civil society may be unavoidable: policy-related research may have to be initiated without explicit government support. This can then lead to confronting policymakers with evidence about desirable change. Early changes in policy may, however, be more likely if the research process is owned by policymakers from the start, and especially if they themselves or their colleagues take part in the field. In practice. much participatory policy research to date has been undertaken with donor support, which can have both negative and positive effects. Negative effects can include lack of continuity: the fickle behaviour of USAID in Guinea (see

Chapter 8) in abandoning support is a warning to governments to choose stable and reliable donors. More positive in the longer term is for donors to negotiate government partnership and ownership. In South Africa the PPA process was taken over and managed by South Africans, leading to its findings being taken seriously at the cabinet level (see Chapter 15).

(2) *Credibility* is needed to convince policymakers. In practice, credibility has come in three ways: researchers have carried conviction by being transparent and self-critical about their methods and findings; reports and outputs have included 'voices' in the form of what people have said, and visuals in the form of diagrams which they have made; and those presenting to policymakers have variously spoken on behalf of the poor, and/or been officials, and/or local people themselves.

(3) *Process* is critical. Anil Shah (Chapter 20) illustrates the range of levels of policy, each with its own time-scale. He and Ben Osuga (Chapter 22) describe sequences and tactics that may be appropriate. Process is far more than just presenting a report. Perhaps most important is sensitive tenacity, sometimes waiting, sometimes acting decisively to seize an opportunity. As with conservation policy (Chapter 7), a long process may be entailed in local, national and international fora.

From policy to practice

The link between policy-in-principle and policy-in-practice has been less explored. Implementability will vary. Some changes can have potentially big effects for poor people at low cost, for example changing the dates for payment of school expenses, or training health staff to be polite and considerate. Others, for example rural infrastructure, may appeal to some donors; others, which confront vested interests or entrenched custom, may require long campaigns.

Thematic research can play a part through feedback on field realities. In Zambia, contrary to policy, many of the poorest were found being excluded from health and education services (see Chapter 4). Revisits to communities can indicate changes which are occurring. Perhaps most of all, in the longer run, participatory monitoring and evaluation by communities and groups themselves, with their own baselines, will serve to close the circle, with feedback to policymakers on grassroots developments.

The future

The practical scope for policy-related participatory research is expanding. In most of the experiences reported in this book, teams had initially to be trained in PRA. Now local capabilities are multiplying. CEDEP in Ghana (Chapter 12) and PAG in Zambia (Chapter 13) both received their initial training for a PPA and then continued with their teams to provide a national capability for PRA-type policy-related studies. In many countries, initial training and orientation will soon be less lengthy because in-country capabilities will already be there. Participatory research into the realities of the poor will be a widespread, if not universal, option.

The opportunities opened up by this book are, then, immense. They are for new ways in which the powerful can learn from the weak, and in which the weak can express their realities with authority and credibility, and so influence policy and practice. The approaches and methods are continuously being invented and developed. There will never be, and should never be any blueprint for what to do and how to do it. In a spirit of pluralism, lessons can continuously be learnt from experiences like those reported and analysed here. Each is, and should be planned, invented and improvised as a new and unique process. Already, through the diversity this book shows, practical experience is impressive. Readers may agree that these approaches and methods should continue to be developed, adopted and adapted worldwide, by governments, by civil society, and more and more by the poor and powerless themselves through their organizations.

Governments, NGOs and other bodies now have a menu of options to choose between or combine. This includes:

(1) *Sectoral research networks.* The Tarai Research Network (see Chapter 3) is a model amenable to widespread adoption and adaptation by governments which need quick insight into and feedback on local realities, including policy issues and policy-in-practice.
(2) *Thematic studies.* These can be on almost any sector or issue, not limited to the examples presented in Part 1.
(3) *Participatory poverty assessments.* These can be in a variety of modes, and at a national or local level.
(4) *Direct interaction and learning* between decisionmakers and poor people. Decisionmakers can be involved in the participatory research, as in Guinea (see Chapter 8), or through poor people going to decisionmakers and presenting evidence in visual as well as verbal form. The decision of James Wolfensohn, President of the World Bank, that all senior World Bank staff members should spend a week of total immersion in a village or slum sets an example which other donors, and national governments, could follow. The potential here is to transform insight and commitment among policymakers through direct experience of a type they are normally denied.

In making any list, or outlining categories, there is a danger of closure. Participatory research for policy is evolving rapidly. This book cannot and should not set firm patterns. At the same time, good advice is available, drawing on experience to date (see Chapter 24). The essence of good participatory research is methodological pluralism and improvisation. After initial inventiveness, innovations tend to settle into stable patterns and ritual sequences. The antidote is to invent each process anew, drawing eclectically on past experience, and always experimenting and exploring better ways of doing things.

The experiences reported and analysed here are, then, only a beginning. They point towards a potential the magnitude of which is difficult to grasp: that throughout the world participatory research in a PRA mode could give voice to the unheard, and persuade and change the powerful; that the realities of those who are last could be presented personally and credibly to those who are first; and that the needs and priorities of the last could come more and more to be understood by others and to count.

After *Whose Voice?* one is tempted to say that the world should never be the same again. It will, however, repeat itself in denying the realities of the poor, weak and vulnerable. What cannot now be repeated is any assertion that the poor are incapable of their own analysis, or any assertion that the powerful lack the approaches and methods to enable them to undertake that analysis. Verbally, there have always been ways. Visually, now, there is a new additional repertoire. Behaviourally, too, we now know better how critical are the ways we interact, and how what sort of people we are affects our interactions. There are now fewer excuses than ever before for ignoring the needs and priorities of the poor.

Caroline Robb

Country	Timing	Context (Bank)	Context (in-country)	Institutions involved	Methodology	Level of participation of the poor	Level of participation of other stakeholders
Africa region							
Benin	Partial PPA completed; 3 weeks field-work in 1993	The manager of the PPA was also responsible for the overall PA. An outside consultant assisted in the PPA. Various departments in the Bank were consulted at all stages.	Limited permission from central government was sought. Local government was extensively involved. Central government was supportive however, of the approach. Stable political environment.	A unit in the Ministry of Planning assisted in the coordination	5 out of the 6 regions were covered. (The sixth had already been extensively covered.) 23 villages and some urban communities. RRAs.	Information sharing	The government was cooperative and receptive
Cameroon	March–September 1994	Country economist was not involved. During the preparation of the PA, the country department was restructured and the management team changed. CFA devaluation meant the COD spent more time on new lending and adjustment.	Debt-distressed country. No longer IBRD country. CFA devaluation. Some key policymakers reticent to support the PPA process.	CARE-Cameroon with support from CARE-Canada provided a technical advisor for the PPA and carried out 2 of the 5 regional assessments. University of Yaounde, ASAFE, PAID also involved in the PPA.	In-country 1-day technical workshop followed by national-level conference for 4 days. Beneficiary assessments (BA) used in 6 regions. 1559 households in selected study zones, and over 150 interviews with key informants – local-government officials, community leaders, service providers and church and women's groups. 50% of those interviewed were women.	Information sharing	Information sharing with selected institutions and with the government at different levels

Annexe 1: *(Continued)*

Country	Timing	Context (Bank)	Context (in-country)	Institutions involved	Methodology	Level of participation of the poor	Level of participation of other stakeholders
Equatorial Guinea	2 week fieldwork 1995; near completion	The PA was renamed a Poverty Note. The COD required that a PPA should be conducted.	Government involvement not extensive	FAO. Government officials at lower levels	RRAs; 15 villages and 2 urban communities in the capital and 3 in another city.	Information sharing	Limited dialogue with key stakeholders
Ghana	May/June 1993, April/ May 1994, Nov 1994. Conducted after quantitative survey (Oct 1991/ Sept 1992)	Clear lines of communication established between the manager of the PA and technical department.	Stable political environment. Government involvement initially limited but now supportive.	Teams from academic institutions, Ministry of Local Government and Rural Development, NGOs and international aid agencies (especially UNICEF)	Three phases, 15 communities, rural and urban; focus groups and PRAs.	Information sharing	Key policymakers not involved extensively at the beginning until a greater understanding of the PPA was gained
Kenya	Preparation: Feb 1994; fieldwork: March 1994; write up: April and May 1994; final document published in 1995	Manager of the PA was initially cautious. Both the manager of the PA and the PPA were involved in drafting the terms of reference and in the preparation of the PPA. The manager of the PPA coordinated most of work in-country.	Relatively economically stable for Africa; Government centralized.	Central Bureau of Statistics (CBS), Ministry of Planning, AMREF (Regional NGO) and the ODA.UK. Final document published by UNICEF/ODA and AMREF.	SARAR, PRAs and household questionnaires. Community groups and school children. Six districts were selected using information from the censor cluster samples. The poorest communities were then selected.	Information sharing	Local government was more involved than central government

Lesotho	Two qualitative surveys conducted in 1991 and 1993		New government is open to the inclusion of stakeholders in the analysis of poverty. There is a representative body of NGOs which is supported by the government but its capacity is limited.	UNICEF, Red Cross, NGO from Zambia, council of NGOs, and local government. A private consulting firm, Sechaba, undertook the PRA.	PRAs. The original PA had no action plan. At a three-day workshop the government, NGOs and World Bank agreed to draft the action plan. Participant observation, case studies, individual and group interviews in rural and urban areas.	Information sharing	The action plan received extensive support from a cross-section of the stakeholders
Madagascar	One year, commencing November 1993	The manager of the PA was committed to the approach and worked closely with the manager of the PPA. However, change in management of the division meant follow-up has not been extensive.	1991 civil service went on strike to change the presidency. The PPA was supported by the ministry of the Economy, Planning and Communications, and Culture but this support is fragmented.	Steering committee comprised of key line ministries, parliamentarians, NGOs, national consultancy firm and the university. The PPA was carried out by the Malagasy. A local consulting firm for 2 regions and 2 groups of academics for the other 2 regions. Several Malagasy consultants and 1 Canadian consultant coordinated the activities.	BA. 2600 qualitative interviews conducted. Periodic progress reviews with UNDP and government committees.	Information sharing	Key policymakers have been fully involved in a process of consultation from the beginning

Annexe 1: *(Continued)*

Country	Timing	Context (Bank)	Context (in-country)	Institutions involved	Methodology	Level of participation of the poor	Level of participation of other stakeholders
Mali	Three weeks fieldwork in 1993	The managers of the PA and PPA were able to communicate clearly.	Government was not supportive of the methodology. The PPA was renamed a Living Conditions Survey. A household survey was conducted but the results have not been published.	Save the Children	BA conducted in Bamako	Information sharing	Initially limited participation of key stakeholders
Mozambique	Ongoing. First phase July 1995	Freestanding document – not linked to a PA. Manager of the PPA located in Moputo had much experience having been involved in the Zambia PPA. Continued Bank support now unclear.	Government very supportive of the process of collecting qualitative information. Government has undertaken its own PA which the PPA will feed into.	Poverty Alleviation Unit, established by the World Bank, and the university undertook the PRA surveys. NGOs were extensively involved especially with problem ranking and prioritization.	PRAs		One of the main objectives of the PPA has been to involve a wide range of stakeholders from the beginning

					Information sharing
	1994, 3 months in the field	proached the ODA for technical assistance in the form of an economist but instead a social scientist was selected by the ODA. After seeing the value added to the analysis of poverty through the qualitative information, the country team became more supportive of the PPA.	supportive. As the process developed, however, support increased. It now runs its own programme.	groups. 2000 people in 98 locations in rural and urban areas.	and UNICEF. No local NGOs were involved in the PPA work but since the government has taken over, local NGOs are now involved.	Government included from the beginning and became more involved as the value of the qualitative information became apparent.
South Africa	On-going. PPA workshop convened in Feb. 1995. Final document due out in draft in Jan 1996.	The PPA was initiated to complement the household survey which had been completed in Aug. 1994. Managers of the PPA and the PA worked closely throughout the process.	Government involvement sought from the beginning. Initially distant but later very involved and committed through the RDP office. Approval for the collaboration between UNDP and the World Bank was sought at the cabinet level. It was decided that the PA would be named the Poverty and Inequality Report of South Africa. Currently, South Africa is not borrowing from the Bank.	Worked with a private-sector market-research consultancy and NGOs. The consultancy established an MC which comprised a cross-section of stakeholders, selected during the initial workshop. The government was represented through the RD. UNDP was also involved. Co-funded by the ODA.	PRA. Not roving teams. Regionally targeted. The three poorest provinces were selected representing 62% of the poor. The household survey was used to identify the poor used. 30–30 communities were involved. The approach was to build upon the existing network of NGOs rather than create a parallel system. PRA training was provided. The existing network had already established trust in many of the communities.	Broad initial consultative workshop. The PPA process has so far stressed the importance of including a continous cross-section of stakeholders. Very strong government ownership.

Annexe 1: *(Continued)*

Country	Timing	Context (Bank)	Context (in-country)	Institutions involved	Methodology	Level of participation of the poor	Level of participation of other stakeholders
Swaziland	Fieldwork completed. Report forthcoming.	The Bank's focus has been on the education section. Freestanding PPA, not part of a PA.	Government initially reluctant to become involved in the PPA.	PPA was not part of a Bank PA. The UNDP used the information in its poverty strategy.	600 households, 100 focus group in 63 communities throughout Swaziland. Regional workshops. Focus discussion groups, PRAs and interviews.	Information sharing	The government and NGOs became increasingly involved
Tanzania	Preparation: Feb/March 1995; fieldwork: May; report writing: ongoing	Manager of the PA was interested in and aware of the work being carried out in Tanzania	Government was cooperative and fully involved at the district	University of Tanzania (but capacity limited)	SARAR, PRAs. A team of 36 people visited 85 villages over 40 days. 6000 people involved.	Information sharing with no immediate follow-up	Government was co-operative and attended policy workshops, which were coordinated with the Bank's social-sector review and Country Economic Memorandum preparation
Togo	2 weeks Nov 1994; 1 week Feb 1995	The PA was completed alongside the environmental assessment. The COD was supportive and committed to the approach. Lines of communications were clearly established. The resident mission was cooperative.	Government is centralized; debt problem; social unrest prevailed from 1992–3. Before the PPA, the government and the UNDP had already begun a policy debate about poverty.	UNDP, local consulting firm through UNDP; 15 unemployed graduates were trained; one team of 5 and a second team of 10 led by a UNDP Dutch consultant.	RRAs; semi-structured interviews; information sheets; children's drawings depicting poverty.	Information sharing	Donor participation more extensive than government's
Uganda	One week 1993. One of the first PPAs.	The PPA was conducted with the PA	Civil war in certain areas. Government willing to accept that poverty exists	Ministry of Planning and UNDP	RRAs, pictorial drawings. The PPA was only conducted in areas where quantitative	Information sharing	Involvement of other institutions limited due to time constants

Zambia	Research Sept–Nov 1993	The PA and PPA managers worked closely throughout the process. The PA manager had supported qualitative techniques in a previous Bank project in Zambia (Social Recovery Project) and promoted the BA/PRA approach in the Bank.	Government gradually included through the Systematic Client Consultation approach	9-person interdisciplinary team of researchers. The team later formed an NGO called the Participatory Assessment Group.	Mix of methods included BA and PRAs. Interview Guide for semi-structured interviews with individuals and groups; 10 research sites over a variety of communities (urban and rural).	Moved beyond information sharing – the poor were consulted on an ongoing basis	Extensive stakeholder consultation
Latin America and the Carribbean							
Argentina	PPA started in Oct 1995. Estimated duration 6 months. PA already completed.	Before PPA had been undertaken, time was spent building up understanding between the technical team and the COD. Engendered a positive attitude towards the PPA from the outset. Some questions were raised by the COD on whether the information will be 'sound-bites' focused.	Government requested the assistance of the Bank in conducting qualitative research. Good level of coordination between government agencies.	Ministry of Social Welfare through the direct involvement of the minister; NGOs	BA with conversational interviews and partial observation	Information sharing	Ministry and Minister of Social Welfare fully involved. In this ministry a unit has been established to monitor poverty and social programme. A seminar has been held with high-level government officials. Strong interest has been expressed already by other departments. NGOs will be involved in the execution work. The dialogue between government and the NGOs has gradually increased.

207

Annexe 1: *(Continued)*

Country	Timing	Context (Bank)	Context (in-country)	Institutions involved	Methodology	Level of participation of the poor	Level of participation of other stakeholders
Brazil	9 months	Focus on education and employment	Strong interest by government in the qualitative approach	BA	Information sharing	Information sharing	Local state and federal governments
Costa Rica	1992: 2 months fieldwork	Coordinated with the PA manager who lives in Honduras. This often meant that lines of communication between the managers of the PA and PPA were not always clear.	Government was supportive of the process. Senior officials from the Ministry of Economic Planning were involved from the beginning.	No NGOs were involved. The government wants to include them extensively at the dissemination phase.	BA in four regions. 262 interviews.	Information sharing	Government extensively involved from the beginning
Ecuador	Preparation April 1994; fieldwork: May 1994; Meetings with stakeholders: October 1995	The manager of the PA had no access to funds from the Bank and had to raise the funding. As such he was unable to recruit consultants from the Bank's technical department. From the beginning, the manager was able clearly to define the information he considered to be	Government neither supported nor objected to the PA or the PPA.	UNICEF co-financed the process. Two NGOs were involved in both the rural and urban areas. Government institutions were not extensively involved at any level.	7 villages and 1 urban community. PRAs, SSIs and workshops.	PPA was called a Rural Qualitative Survey as it was feld that the process was not participatory but more one of information sharing. NGOs went back to share the results of the studies with several communities.	Participation of government institutions was minimal. The NGOs were extensively involved. Interest of non-participating NGOs is very high.

Guatemala	4 months	The PPA was undertaken without extensive consultations with the Country Department	Government would have liked to have been more involved in the decisionmaking process of the PPA	Liaised with the university but relations between it and the Bank have not been strong. UNDP and UNICEF initially supportive.	BA	Information sharing	Government produced its own publication using the results of the BA
Mexico	Interviews conducted with the PA in February and March 1995	Clear lines of communication established between the PPA advisor and the manager of the PA. However, communications with the supervisor undertaking the PPA in the field were difficult.	Major devaluation. Strong initial support lessened a other priorities took over.	Secretarie Desarrollo Social SDS (Government Poverty Agency) participated actively in the fieldwork. All consultants hired were from NGOs.	BA. 4 teams interviewed 722 people in four areas (2 urban, 2 rural). Qualitative research and conversational interviews.	Information sharing	UNDP and UNICEF co-financed. The capacity of the SDS to conduct qualitative assessments increased.
Europe and Central Asia Armenia	Started in 1994; completion date April	Wanted to coordinate the PA with the Social Investment Fund. Good relations with COD. Senior management support.	Ministry of Economy	Armenian Assembly of Armenia (AAA). Most other NGOs were involved in emergency aid. Church also involved. University also assisted in the survey.			

Annexe 1: *(Continued)*

Country	Timing	Context (Bank)	Context (in-country)	Institutions involved	Methodology	Level of participation of the poor	Level of participation of other stakeholders
South Asia Pakistan	Feb–July 1994. Fieldwork for two months.	Manager of the PA given limited time to complete. Many felt that the PPA information was not adequately represented in the PA. The PPA was conducted after the household survey analysis was completed. The supervisor of the PPA was an outside consultant. The Human Resources Divisions and the COD managed the PPA.	Government did not support or oppose the PPA. However, some of the government officials and NGOs disagreed with the PAs conclusions. Although there was consultation, some stakeholders felt their views were not considered and that the ongoing national poverty debate was not presented in the final PA.	Federal Bureau of Statistics was involved in selecting the study communities.	Local consultants were recruited. Roving teams were used. PRAs.	Information sharing	Workshops were held with a wide cross-section of stakeholders for the PA.

Abbreviations
BA   Beneficiary Assessments
COD Country Operations Department
PA   Poverty Assessment
PPA Participatory Poverty Assessments
PRA Participatory Rural Appraisals

210

Caroline Robb

Country	Value added through the PPA information	Impact upon the World Bank	Impact upon the borrower	Impact upon other institutions	Lessons learnt
Africa Region					
Benin		This was one of the first PPAs in the Bank and its results initiated the ongoing dialogue on the use of qualitative and quantitative information.	The PPAs strengthen the capacity of the Ministry of Planning to conduct qualitative assessments.		
Burkina Faso					
Cameroon	In the PA, the information was of a generic nature. Interpretation of the data in the Bank was limited because of a lack of time.	Limited follow-through of information into the PA and into the Country Assistance Strategy (overally policy document guiding the Bank's projects and programmes in a specific country). Time constraints. Limited impact on sector work. Some viewed the qualitative information as having limited credibility.	Ownership developed within the ministries which were directly involved in the PPA but not amongst key policymakers. To some extent, the PPA put issues of governance of the agenda for discussion. However, there was limited scope to build upon the PPA and PA as the government was not extensively involved.	NGOs and other institutions involved in the PPAs understood the value of the approach. Interest has been generated among local government and NGOs to continue the approach initiated through the PPA. But as yet there has been no demand.	Working with NGOs in preparing the PA and PPA provided a highly cost-effective means of tapping into expertise and capacity. A technical workshop was organized in Kribi and a national conference in Yaounde in November 1994. At these workshops, broad-based discussions of the PA and the views of the poor and some key NGOs were used to redefine key priorities for the poverty-reduction strategy. However, there were institutional constraints in-country and in the Bank. Limited room for manoeuvre at the government level has meant that the exercise has been one of information gathering with limited room for learning and shifting of attitudes. Thus the value of conducting the PPA has been limited. The composition of the team involved within the Bank affects the way in which the information is managed, disseminated and analysed. The results of the PPA were published without extensive government support.

211

Annexe 2: *(Continued)*

Country	Value added through the PPA information	Impact upon the World Bank	Impact upon the borrower	Impact upon other institutions	Lessons learnt
Equatorial Guinea		The report has been rewritten	Government has not as yet seen the final version		The information may be accurate but if the institutional framework of the borrower and the Bank is unable to embrace the results, the impact will be limited.
Ghana	The PPA complemented the quantitative information. However, it also provided further information such as the problems of female-headed households in the north. The importance of rural infrastructure and the quality and access of education and health were highlighted.	The information from the PPA is relatively complex and extensive, thus making incorporation of its analysis into other Bank reports often time-consuming and difficult. However, the Country Economic Memorandum (CEM) – an influential Bank instrument – had a poverty focus which, in part, was influenced by the results of the PA. The government was initially unreceptive towards the results of the PA and PPA until the CEM incorporated poverty issues. The formulation of a poverty policy through joint-donor action and a Consultative Group meeting in Paris is now being developed.	The information from the PPA and PA has been analysed in a UNICEF report, which was later disseminated by at a national conference attended by key policymakers. An ongoing process of dialogue has now developed between the Bank and the government regarding poverty.	Other institutions were already involved in promoting a dialogue on poverty. As such, it is difficult to assess the impact of the PPA alone on other institutions.	Initially key stakeholders were reluctant to become involved. However, a process approach was adopted whereby the PPA and PA were viewed only as means of initiating dialogue and not as ends. For such an approach, Bank follow-up is vital. To influence policymakers, it may be appropriate to understand which documents and mechanisms have more credibility in-country.

Kenya	The information in the PPA was used to design a more effective and focused quantitative questionnaire. The PPA stressed issues such as social capital, coping strategies, female-headed households and water. It highlighted the fact that people defined female-headed households differently. Some argued, however, that the information in the PPA was not representative as it focuses only on the poor.	The PA does reflect the major findings of the PPA. Some argued that the PA and PPA could have been more extensively incorporated into country reports.	Some in government were initially sceptical and not willing to become involved directly. The benefits of adopting the approach were not clear to them. However, after the first PPA analysis, the government has initiated a second round with the NGOs. This is being funded by the ODA.	Capacity in-country to conduct qualitative assessments has increased.	Sequencing of the PPA and quantitative analysis is important. More time is required to develop dialogue with key stakeholders.
Lesotho	Three key additional themes emerged from the PPA: alcoholism; political factors such as injustice and corruption; and a hatred of witchcraft. These issues fed into the policy level through the action plan. As government ownership increased, such issues as corruption and the role of local government appeared in speeches and documents.		Initially limited ownership from government. Some in government felt that the draft PA was not a clear policy document.		Initially there was limited ownership. Local ownership was created only after the drafting of the action plan, which was formulated with a cross-section of stakeholders.

Annexe 2: *(Continued)*

Country	Value added through the PPA information	Impact upon the World Bank	Impact upon the borrower	Impact upon other institutions	Lessons learnt
Madagascar	The PA information put such issues as access to social services and security on the agenda for discussion. However, follow-up by the Bank was not extensive.	Impact upon Bank documents has been limited to date.	Government commitment and ownership of the problem vary. Those who were involved are now committed. Government officials have visited the Bank on several occasions in order to follow up the results of the PPA.	Impact on other key institutions in-country which were involved in the PPA has been high.	Because the initial approach was not just a one-off intervention of information gathering, but part of a process of building up dialogue at different levels with various stakeholders, government ownership has developed. However, because Bank follow-up has not been extensive, it has not been possible to consolidate all the advances in policy dialogue.
Mali	The information from the qualitative survey explained the perceived anomalies from the quantitative survey. For example, the disproportionate amount of money spent on clothing was explained by the fact that clothing and jewelry are also an investment.				
Mozambique		Too early to assess policy impact	The PPA process was successfully internalized in the Ministry of Planning. High degree of local ownership.	Other stakeholders have been included through widespread dissemination of the PPA material from the beginning.	There was a trade-off between local ownership and quality control. For increased impact, the PPA reports should be written in a more concise manner. In the first phase there was an overcrowding of the research agenda and the interview guide was too broad. Careful matching of the research issues to methods of investigation is required. A major problem has been catering to multiple stakeholders. The World Bank had its own internal deadlines to respond to but the Bank PPA manager, located in Moputo, had

Nigeria	Before the PPA, the Bank was focusing on health and education. The PPA highlighted that the poor viewed water and roads as their priorities. In addition, the weakness of the coping mechanisms was highlighted.	The results of the PPA have impacted upon the Bank's sector work especially in the social sectors and infrastructure.	In-country the PPA has initiated an on-going and gender issues and the relationship between polygamy and poverty. Government was initially arguing that the very poor have seen an improvement in their living standards. The results of the PPA challenged this. The PPA process has initiated the government's increased involvement in the work of the NGOs.	NGOs are now increasingly more accepted as part of the development process.	The PPA process has contributed towards increased donor coordination
South Africa	The PPA highlighted the various dynamics of the decisionmaking process, coping strategies, seasonality, intra-household gender relations and the constraints of access to services. The problems of paying for school fees at a time when income was short were also highlighted through the PPA.	Too early to assess	Too early to assess	Too early to assess	Although the initial stakeholder workshop was time consuming and problematic to convene, there were many advantages which became apparent as the process evolved. The workshop identified the most appropriate approach and methodology. As a result, the PPA was both rapid and efficient. Good-quality reports have been submitted. The management of the process by the local consulting firm was transparent and effective. Thus, stakeholder involvement from the beginning, was an important step.
Swaziland		Too early to assess	Too early to assess	Too early to assess	

215

Annexe 2: *(Continued)*

Country	Value added through the PPA information	Impact upon the World Bank	Impact upon the borrower	Impact upon other institutions	Lessons learnt
Tanzania	Both the PA and the PPA estimated that the number of 'poor' in the rural areas was approximately 50% of the population. The PPA highlighted a larger proportion of these poor households being female headed. Whereas the PA focused upon consumption and expenditure, the PPA used criteria as defined by the poor such as feelings of powerlessness and hopelessness. In addition, many problems were gender specific: the women identified food, water and health as their main problems, whereas men identified transport, farming and drunkenness.	The financial-sector reform is using the same methodology. The information from the PPA is reflected in the PA. Evidence of policy impact is, however, as yet limited.	Government was initially cautious but became more receptive as it understood the value of the approach. The PPA highlighted the capacity of the poor to analyse their own problems.		More time and resources are required in order to promote a longer process which would lead to a greater understanding of poverty and its links to policy. This requires a shift in focus at all levels. Teams could be located at the field level. Coordination by one person in Washington proved difficult. The resident mission in Tanzania could be strengthened to take the initiative. Skilled people in the analysis of poverty could be located within the resident mission. To increase the capacity of the mission, training in best practice of qualitative-information gathering could be conducted and tool kits be provided.

Togo	Sample not nationally representative. Interviewees were approximately half male and half female. Results were not all disaggregated by gender.	There was limited impact on the Country Assistance Strategy because the PPA was completed afterwards.	Within country it is too early to assess the results.	Other donors are also promoting the use of qualitative techniques, such as the UNDP. The PPA assisted in building dialogue between the Bank and other donors.	Difficult for researchers to analyse and organize information in the field within the limited time frame. As such, some analysis may not have been accurate and it was not written in a way which was easy to understand.
Uganda	Men and women were consulted but the information was not disaggregated.	The PA was written by the PPA manager and thus the qualitative information was incorporated. The Ugandan PPA was one of the first in the Bank and it initiated Bank-wide discussions on the value of qualitative data.			
Zambia	Information detailed and comprehensive. Disaggregated by gender where appropriate. Such issues as school fees and the timing of their payment were highlighted through qualitative analysis.	The PA has a detailed action plan which incorporates some of the recommendations of the PPA. Specific elements which influenced the action plan included the emphasis on rural-infrastructure investments and urban services. The poverty profile, especially community-based identification of the ultra poor, coping strategies, safety nets and targeted interventions were also influenced by the PPA.	Government was influenced by the priorities expressed by the poor in the ranking exercises. The Ministry of Health has been using the results of the PPA and the PA in developing policy. In the Ministry of Education, a new policy is in preparation with reference to the timing of school fees. Positive feedback has been received from the communities in the PPA on the functioning of the emergency safety net during the southern Africa drought of 1992.	The NGO, PAG, has been developed into an effective policy-oriented institution. The capacity of the NGO has been built. It is, however, now dependent on government and donors for future sustainability and its capacity requires further strengthening.	Feeding information back to the communities and promoting ongoing dialogue should be part of the design of the PPA. Information from the PPAs could then be used to develop action plans and not just be extracted.

217

Annexe 2: *(Continued)*

Country	Value added through the PPA information	Impact upon the World Bank	Impact upon the borrower	Impact upon other institutions	Lessons learnt
Latin America and the Caribbean					
Argentina	NA	PA has already been completed. There is great potential for the results to be integrated into other Bank programmes due to the team ownership in the Bank.			Issues of ownership in the Bank context are relevant. From the beginning the PPA was planned and prepared through the adoption of an inclusive, consultative approach within the Bank.
Brazil					
Costa Rica	The BA highlighted the linkages between home ownership and status in society. Family was viewed as the most important institution and in times of stress people relied on their families for support.	Delay in the analysis and dissemination of findings has meant that the impact within the Bank has been limited to date.	Government was eager to disseminate the results but it took nine months for the Bank to grant permission	Too early to assess	The terms of reference state that the information from the PPA belongs to the Bank and permission is therefore required before disseminating it. This caused a delay of nine months. A clear dissemination strategy should be defined as part of the PPAs design.
Ecuador	Quality of information is good. The results fed directly into the type of questions analysed in the quantitative survey.	The PA information has been strongly reflected in the Country Assistance Strategy. Several sector divisions have started sector studies as prepartion of operations based on the PA results.	Although the government was not included in the process of the PPA and PA, the results of the PA have impacted upon the county's perceptions of its priorities through the final PA. Such issues as access to secondary schools and off-farm rural markets, previously not in the poverty debate in Ecuador, were placed on the agenda. The PPA work has initiated dialoque between	The NGOs in-country have increased their capacity to conduct qualitative surveys. UNICEF used the PPA methodology to evaluate the impact of their programme.	There were advantages in Ecuador of the qualitative assessment preceding the quantitative assessment. The qualitative information was used in the design of the quantitative survey. The PA manager should be closely involved in the whole process. However, a greater understanding of the qualitative research techniques from the beginning would have enhanced the results. As such, it is proposed that the preparation of the team involved in the PPA and PA is clearly thought through for each team and each country. The results should be analysed by someone who has an understanding of the country and its

Guatemala	The findings of the PPA have recently been published in a book and follow-up studies are underway on such issues as gender, indigenous issues and rural-urban dichotomies.
Mexico	The quality of the PPA was mixed. The information was not adequately ranked. However, it was gender specific, which added value. The report found that the women of Mexico City were unwilling to leave their houses and go to work. Since they did not have tenancy rights they were afraid that their houses may become occupied. In the northern areas it was easier for women to obtain jobs than men. This was challenging the traditional gender roles as many men found themselves out of work. Conflict within the household had become a major issue.

Annexe 2: *(Continued)*

Country	Value added through the PPA information	Impact upon the World Bank	Impact upon the borrower	Impact upon other institutions	Lessons learnt
Europe and Central Asia					
Armenia	The qualitative information assisted in the analysis of the results of the quantitative surveys. The PPA highlighted that there are a great variety of coping strategies, in addition, the limited trust in local government and the lack of respect for the private sector became apparent. This explained why many were reluctant to become involved in private-sector activities.	Too soon to assess	Results will be disseminated at a seminar in March 1996		If there had been adequate resources and time, the PA should have been integrated with the Social Investment Fund
South Asia					
Pakistan	The PPA highlighted the fact that the poor spent a large proportion of their income on health. The poor felt that social services were of an inadequate standard and there existed a lack of accountability to the communities. Many income-earning opportunities were lost through ill-health.	The awareness of some Bank staff of the information contained in the two PPA studies is limited.	Limited	Limited	Key stakeholders were consulted throughout the preparation of the PA. The resident mission helped in organising the workshops. Some felt that although the consultations were fairly extensive, the final document did not reflect the views of the majority.

Abbreviations
BA   Beneficiary Assessments
COD Country Operations Department
PA   Poverty Assessment
PPA Participatory Poverty Assessments

220

Annexe 3

Key Findings and Policy Recommendations from the South African PPA

JULIAN MAY

Many of the findings of the South African PPA (SA-PPA), and the policy analysis which follows from these findings, are unique to the South African situation. As most people would be aware, the system of apartheid implemented by previous governments acted as one of the most important ways in which poverty was generated – through the active dispossession of assets, neglect and discriminatory practices in almost all aspects of life. The transition to the current democracy was based on a broad mobilization of the people and communities of South Africa, and widespread activism. The consequence of these forces means that the communities in South Africa are perhaps unusually organized while being simultaneously fragmented and prone to conflict. It means also that the current government is perhaps especially responsive to the recommendations of policy researchers, willing to change existing or adapt new policy, and sympathetic to participatory-based research. Broader lessons can, nonetheless, still be learnt from the SA-PPA. A history of aggressive or predatory state action is common in many developing countries, as is a process of democratization.

This section presents, therefore, some of the key messages, and suggested policy interpretations from the SA-PPA. The list of key messages is clearly not exhaustive, and not all policy debate is covered. As such, the section is best seen as a contribution towards an on-going interpretation of PPAs in South Africa and elsewhere.

Pensions and other welfare payments

South Africa is fortunate in that there is a working social pensions and welfare system which has always had a universal, if not an equitable coverage. These welfare payments emerged as a particularly important theme in several of the PPA studies. It is apparent that, without pensions, many households and communities would collapse. Pensions are shared, and are used to invest in the development of household assets, and their utilization. Pensions are, moreover, very frequently a primary source of support for grandchildren, with the pensioner acting as child carer in the absence of the child's parents. This has freed both parents, or a single parent, to engage in other activities, principally a job search.

To an extent, then, pensions help to make old people secure in the family, or enable them to leave households if they so choose; as such, they give the elderly some measure of control over their own lives. At the same time, the elderly have become targeted by other members of the family as being the sole source of a cash income, particularly in rural areas. Demands may, in consequence, be placed on the elderly to share their income in return for family support. Isolation from family and community support was listed by the elderly as their biggest concern. Despite pension income, pensioners are, as a result, still defined as poor in most communities; indeed, old people themselves see care from their family as the most important element of well-being.

Pensions: policy issues

An obvious policy recommendation is that the pension system, vital as it is to combating poverty, must be strengthened and sustained. The additional resources required to support this need not be prohibitive. Options exist to make the system more efficient and its resources more effectively used. These include:

○ integrating the pension-delivery systems with other financial schemes so as to allow the pension money to be expended over the month, and to allow savings to accumulate;
○ eliminating corruption within the service; even where this is not present, the efficiency of delivery needs to be improved;
○ exploring new options for improving efficiency and sustainability, for example, the introduction of a contributory scheme. This would mean that more South Africans would be able to save towards their own old age.

At the same time, measures will be required to ensure that pensions do not become the key instrument for poverty alleviation, which results in the elderly becoming over-burdened with the needs of others in the household, with ambiguous benefits. Other welfare instruments should be sought, and promoting the well-being of children would seem to be a worthwhile next step.

The welfare of children

Although only one study focused specifically on children, the conditions faced by the young in poor households in South Africa was repeatedly stressed in the SA-PPA. In the absence of an effective child-care system, children are being abused and neglected on an unacceptable scale. Aspects of this crisis visible in the material include:

○ sexual abuse, including rape, and children being forced into prostitution;
○ fractured and unstable families: step-parents are often mentioned by children as a source or threat of abuse, including the sexual abuse of girls by step-fathers;
○ alcohol abuse by parents which leads to child abuse; and
○ children not being continuously parented or schooled as they are frequently moved around due to crisis or as a coping strategy for poverty.

The result of is this is that the home is not a safe place for many children, who opt instead to leave and to live on the street. These children have become actors in their own right, taking decisions which they believe best suit their circumstances. Some of the decisions have obvious long-term negative consequences, such as glue-sniffing as a way of dealing with the cold, or abuse. Despite this, children expressed their independent needs throughout the research, including safety, access to various kinds of services and access to income.

Social security for children and families: policy issues

From the above, it is clear that children's well-being is in crisis in South Africa and that this should be viewed as a critical issue for the country's long-term development as well as a current welfare issue. The social security system for children is weak and dysfunctional and places an unreasonable burden on vulnerable children and single mothers. The problem has two components:

(1) *parental maintenance*: the state places the responsibility on women for obtaining support from unwilling fathers, which they are unable to do. In the process they are exposed to the risk of physical abuse, and discrimination from a corrupt and inaccessible judicial system; and
(2) *welfare payments*: the system is hard to access and the response time is unacceptably slow, leaving vulnerable families without support of any kind for extended periods.

Many vulnerable children get no support and unemployed parents have no way of obtaining the basic minimum resources necessary to support their children. In practice, the pensions received by grandparents and great-grandparents are often the sole source of survival for such children.

A multi-sectoral response, which includes the following elements, is needed:

○ an assertive intervention in nutrition;
○ the overhaul of the judicial system to reduce the burden on single mothers for obtaining support from fathers;
○ addressing problems of delivery in welfare support to single mothers;
○ the rehabilitation of the family from the long-term impact of the abusive society which has characterized South Africa, and which at the level of communities runs the risk of continuing to be a feature of the country;[1] and
○ efforts to raise public awareness of the extent of child abuse so as to stimulate a coordinated response from government and civil society.

Despite this crisis in the welfare of children, children were frequently seen as the family's way out of poverty through their education and the jobs which it was hoped would result from education.

Education and training

Education was repeatedly stressed as the main way out of poverty, and as the strongest felt need by almost all groups. Within this, communities articulated two separate types of need: (i) for quality basic education for their children; and (ii) for effective skills training to improve employment chances for adults.

Crèches also emerged as a priority need for many rural women. The benefits of crèche provision were seen to include: improved nutrition; reduction of the time burden for women, and the creation of extra employment opportunities; and the establishment of a local source of employment.

The amount and timing of school fees are, however, a significant barrier to accessing education. Fees are currently a one-off lump-sum payment. Although comparatively modest, this amount is frequently beyond the means of poor households which often have to fall into debt in order to meet the payments. Examples reported in the PPA included women still repaying loans obtained for school fees eight months after incurring the debt. The quality of education and the education facilities remained, in addition, a serious concern to parents and children. This was particularly so on farm schools where the facility is funded and managed largely by the farmer.

A specific difficulty for girls related to a reported high level of teenage pregnancy. This usually resulted in the girl having to leave school, either to seek employment or because the family were unable or unwilling to take care of the child.

Education: policy issues

Given that education is perceived as critical and is aspired to by the poor themselves, access to quality education should be facilitated by a range of measures, amongst them:

○ the staggering of school expenses to relieve the burden of a single major payment which currently often falls in the lean season when people are least able to meet such expenditure;
○ skills training for adults which links to opportunities available in poor areas, and which builds on what people are currently doing or are able to do, while bridging the gap with other training currently on offer;
○ development of sex-education programmes in schools;
○ improved access to crèches because of their important development functions; and
○ improved access to schools in rural areas which are not farm-based and tied to the employment situation of the parents.

Such measures should not add to the time burden of women.

Training: policy issues

The provision of education obviously goes beyond the formal education system. Vocational training is also required. This should not be based on gender or any other stereotype. Part of the trap in which the poor are caught is that 'ghetto' people are taught 'ghetto' skills, skills which are, by their nature, capable of generating only low incomes. In the past, women trained to do women's jobs, rather than to acquire skills which lead to productive income-generating activities. Training should, therefore, be linked to the local economic-development strategy of an area. It should ensure that the skills learnt yield significant returns, and should include design, management and marketing.

To ensure that training in all of the services needed in rural and other areas can be adapted to suit local economic-development initiatives requires gaining leverage over service providers. Local initiatives need to gain control over training to make it locally specific. These requirements could possibly be met through the provision of service centres. One example, which could be implemented immediately is training in agricultural economics for agricultural extension officers. In addition, training which needs to be coherent in both urban and rural areas should emphasize the identification and development of comparative advantages.

Although training should be demand led, recognition must be given to the fact that many individuals and communities lack the capacity to take such initiatives. As a result, it is important to disseminate information, a process which may well be a local income-generating activity itself. One example of this is the translation of policy/development documents into local languages.

Health

A striking element of many of the studies related to the poor health of the poor. Reports documented people suffering from poverty-related illnesses, or from ill-health resulting from working conditions. Key messages included:

○ state health services do not function well and do not reach the poor;
○ health is a seasonal issue; and
○ the poor face a variety of barriers in accessing public health services, including: poor staff attitudes (rudeness etc.); costs of transport and physical distance; hours of opening; and the high costs of treatment. As a way of dealing with this, the poor use a variety of sources of health care, including traditional healers, herbalists and self-medication.

Health: policy issues

Policy shifts should ensure that health planning takes into account the specific problems the poor face in trying to access quality health services in different areas and environments, as stated above. Health planning needs also to recognize the informal sources, as well as public health provision, used by the poor. Support to these services may be required; more importantly, referral knowledge needs to be transferred so that informal leaders can refer cases which they are unable to assist into the formal health system.

AIDS/HIV is a critical issue for poverty-alleviation policy. Poor females are particularly vulnerable to AIDS because of the frequency with which prostitution is a survival strategy for women and girls, and through the sexual behaviour of their partners. The poor fear particularly the social isolation that AIDS leads to, as this undermines their use of kin and social networks, one of the critical ways in which they survive. The causes of AIDS, and the assistance required by those affected, is poorly understood by poor communities.

Specific policy issues relating to health and AIDS/HIV policies on health education and STD prevention need to take into account the particular vulnerabilities of poor females; in addition, programmes for counselling and treatment need to address the fear of social isolation which leads many households and individuals to hide the fact of infection.

Nutrition

The lack of access to adequate and appropriate food is obviously a critical aspect of poverty. Findings from the SA-PPA indicated that preparing food is time-consuming, and time is a scarce resource for poor women; furthermore, food supply/nutrition are seasonal issues in that cash flows, expenditure requirements and home-production vary month by month. The importance of women's' control of their own income for nutrition management is related to this. Nutrition education is, interestingly, recognized as being important by communities and poor individuals.

Nutrition: policy issues

Nutrition training should be directed to the whole family, not only to women. Women have, however, more capacity to improve nutrition when they have more control over their own income, and the nutritional status of the household is directly linked to the high labour and time burden experienced by women.

The seasonality of food supply/nutrition, which varies according to province and region and therefore requires local-level planning (e.g. labour-intensive public works directed at the lean season) must be recognized. Training needs also to note the extremely complex household structures of the poor, and that training will therefore have to be directed at the family, rather than at specific care-givers.

Institutions

The policies of apartheid have impacted on institutions and their ability to function. As a result, institutional mayhem prevails in much of government and civil society, both in terms of structures and capacity to deliver. Much of this can be ascribed to the differing pace of change of various institutions and systems. In certain areas of critical importance to the poor there is considerable inertia, meaning that the poor are still experiencing the same problems and obstructions as before the political transition commenced (e.g. welfare system, judicial system, agriculture). There is, however, no functioning system of local government at present. Numerous reasons exist for this, although it is particularly noteworthy that: newly elected representatives in democratic bodies often lack training and skills; the poor have been disempowered by the entrapping institutions and processes of the era of 'total onslaught', especially in the ex-bantustans and white-dominated farming areas; and static forms of local government, such as the traditional authorities, have become entrenched.

The result of this is that the poor do not know where power is to be found, nor what it has on offer. Institutional structures are, furthermore, opaque and disempowering. Of particular concern is the fact that communities are fractured; they cannot be assumed to be homogeneous and unified for purposes of planning. This is compounded by the fact that information flows between the poor and policymakers are distorted at best, and non-existent at worst.

Institutions: policy issues

Despite the many problems associated with institutional structures in post-apartheid South Africa, there are important and valuable organizations functioning among the poor, controlled and operated by the poor themselves, for example: care groups, civics, village health workers. To take advantage of these, a culture of active citizenship should be promoted. This would include:

○ training for newly elected officials;
○ measures to promote the democratization of the institution of traditional authorities;
○ schools to be used as a site for learning citizenship;
○ clear specification of where power is and how to access it, targeted information to be taken further by unions, religious groups, NGOs, civics etc.;
○ bold administrative reform which gives incentives to good-practice 'role models'; and
○ promotion of one-stop service and information centres.

Agriculture

Despite the low estimates of the contribution made by agriculture to the income of rural households, the SA-PPA suggests that agriculture is a relatively important source of livelihood for many rural people. Poor women in particular value subsistence agriculture even though they recognize that this is a high-risk and time-consuming activity. Multiple-cropping farming systems are important for the food security of many poor South African households. As one example, gardening is undertaken as a hedge against the lean season. As a result, it serves a vital supportive function at particular times of the year. To be sustainable, and to have the maximum effect, water availability is critical.

Despite this, input supply systems (chemicals, fertilizers and finance) are weak or non-existent. In particular, in the absence of crop insurance, the use of credit is seen to be risky as households might be required to sell off assets if crops fail due to drought. As a result, even where credit may have been available, cultivators were reluctant to incur debt.

Security of tenure is seen to be essential by rural households living in both areas of tribal tenure and on white farms. Extension and training are also seen by the poor as important, but the current agricultural extension system does not deliver to the poor and is perceived by them to be useless.

Agriculture: policy issues

From the policy perspective, it is important that agriculture is recognized as integral to the livelihoods of the rural poor, and that farming and gardening are seen to be highly valued by women as a form of economic opportunity/ income which they can control. The agricultural household must, however, be recognized as a complex system. This means that public policy must be geared to the realties under which the poor live, recognizing that: agriculture is not a full-time occupation; and that women perform most agricultural activities.

A starting-point would be the unification of the extension system as a matter of priority so as to make information and resources more accessible. Information and assistance must be based upon the complex cropping systems which are used by the poor. In addition, bold measures are needed to solve the inappropriate R&D system. Specifically, the agricultural R&D system needs to be opened to other disciplines, including sociologists, economists and networks of professionals and project-based people. Within this, vocational training for agriculture and R&D in agriculture should be systems-oriented and participatory, taking into account the realities under which the poor practise agriculture;

Labour markets

Poor people do not have secure jobs and poor communities are characterized by the widespread absence of the formally employed. Poor people instead undertake numerous, small, often dangerous jobs, both in terms of the likelihood of injury and of its consequences (loss of livelihood, frequently without compensation).

The poor are subject to seasonal stress, even when employed. Farm work is also moving from permanent to seasonal and casual employment. The poor are, furthermore, employed largely by the marginally less poor. Many poor people, especially women and children, engage in prostitution and are therefore vulnerable to STDs and AIDS. Unemployment for men is more than the loss of income, and has significant social costs in terms of the potential for violence and gender conflict.

It is not surprising, therefore, that poor people consistently expressed the need for reliable, secure forms of income. Children's education, and therefore children's future engagement in the labour market, is perceived by the poor to be their major way out of poverty/future investment for security;

Promoting local economic activity

Local economic activity which provides additional income is clearly important for poor households. Energy-draining, lost-cause attempts at promoting income generation should not, however, be encouraged; support should rather be given to women to enable them to improve the return from the activities which are they are undertaking. Those should also try to take advantage of economic opportunities in small towns, as well as linkages to larger cities through migration.

Service fees

User fees, such as school fees, should not be lump-sum payments, and should be staggered through the year. Specific attention should be directed towards avoiding payments in January/February. There are other periods of seasonal stress, however, which are largely determined by the nature of local agricultural and economic activity. This varies by area, as well as by settlement type. It is also worth noting that urban areas also experience seasonality.

Subsidizing of rural areas

Many communities require a significant degree of subsidization as they are unable to generate the revenue base from which to pay for their own development. Subsidies such as the Homestead Subsidy would make a profound impact on the lives of the poor. The proper mechanisms must, of course, be put in place to ensure that these reach the poor; specific attention must be given to ensuring that the intended beneficiaries know about the subsidy and how to acquire it. Communities are unaware of the policies which have been fashioned to assist them, of how to activate these and of how to push for changes if they are inappropriate. Mechanisms will be required to ensure that these subsidies are spent in the rural areas.

Community banking

Appropriate, properly-funded local financial institutions are required to extend credit, take deposits and foster investment. These may be fashioned around the needs of specific interest groups but will require that the organization be accessible and be able to deal with numerous small transactions and operate with innovative forms of surety. This will necessitate keeping down transaction costs. Cognizance must also be taken that even a simple form of 'bank', the *stokvel*, can be denied the poor due to rigidity in the rules.

One possible form of organization may be through credit unions linked to places of employment, or to participation in specific development projects.

Making development user-friendly

Development information flowing down to communities, and flowing up from communities to civil servants needs to be made user-friendly. The capacity of ensuring adequate information transfer should be built into a department's routine functioning as a priority.

Information transfer must be given priority by the top management of line departments, and the provincial and local authorities. Finally, it is important that an effective government information-delivery mechanism is established which translates and disseminates information, and retains a specific focus on the poor. Existing services may need to be fundamentally restructured to ensure that this is achieved.

Recognizing shifting dynamics in gender relations

The SA-PPA illustrated clearly that gender is a significant factor in South Africa in terms of limiting options, determining access to resources and setting roles and responsibilities, both within the household and between the household, the community and the workplace. Gender is, however, by no means a simple issue, in which all women are merely worse off than all men. A far more worrying issue is the absence of useful social and economic roles for men in the face of high unemployment, and their marginalization. This can have severe negative implications for women and children in terms of the risk of domestic violence, drains on household resources, and interference in decisionmaking and time. The impact on women who are employed appears to be ambiguous, with some women succeeding in gaining control over the affairs of the household, others being able to establish their own 'male-free' households, and others continuing to subsidize men. Targeting assistance should not aim simply at delivering forms of aid which help women, but at assistance which ensures that gender roles and responsibilities are beneficial to all individuals within the household.

Recognizing the significance of seasonality

Seasonal stress in terms of income, expenditure and nutrition forms a significant aspect of poverty in South Africa. By scheduling public-works programmes at those times of the year in which such stress occurs, the greatest impact can be achieved. It is, however, important that the significance of seasonal patterns in labour demands be recognized, as this often occurs at the same time as income needs are greatest, and resources are least available. Seasonal stress will also vary by region and by climatic zone. As a result, the implementation of programmes will need to be determined at a provincial or sub-regional level.

Areas for future research

It should be noted that the PPA itself was a limited exercise, both in terms of its spatial focus and the number of research initiatives which were undertaken. As a result, many issues are under-represented because of the sample, area and theme. In particular, the following can be identified as important gaps which would need to be filled before a comprehensive view on poverty in South Africa can be generated from the basis of participatory research:

o the urban poor within metropolitan areas, in particular the major centres of Durban, Johannesburg and Cape Town. While information was gathered concerning a segment of this group – the street children – it is evident that there are a number of other vulnerable groups in the metropolitan areas, including the adult homeless, refugees from violence, the recently urbanized and the long-term unemployed; and
o institutional arrangements within community-based organizations, and the relationships between CBOs and stakeholders with the community.

Possible areas of focus for a second round of the PPA include:

o the poor in provinces not covered by this study;
o the livelihoods of the poor in major urban centres;
o the specific problems people have in accessing high-quality basic-education services;

o the specific problems poor people have in accessing high-quality basic-health services;

o the specific problems the poor have in using the justice system to make claims;

o traditional aspects of claiming child maintenance;

o longitudinal studies which draw in more life histories and information concerning household members in the broadest possible sense;

o research on the long-term unemployed; and

o research on mothers and daughters, considering the aspirations that each have.

Notes

Chapter 3   Using PRA for agricultural policy analysis in Nepal: the Tarai Research Network Foodgrain Study

1. Given that resources were insufficient to establish a network that would cover the whole country, the reasons for concentrating on the Tarai are not difficult to see. Not only is it the country's granary, but returns to resources invested in information collection are likely to be relatively high, given the region's flat topography and relatively easy communications. For the future it remains at least as important to find ways of collecting similar information in the hilly and mountainous parts of the country, not least because they are food-deficit areas and people are generally poorer than they are in the Tarai. The logistical problems are such, however that they could not be tackled with the quite modest level of resources presently available for the purpose.
2. Visual methods have transpired to be extremely appropriate to group interviews with farmers; more traditional data instruments seem more suited to individual interviews with literate, town-based informants. For example, when a study of constraints on agricultural marketing was launched, the TRN used questionnaires to interview wholesalers, hoteliers, hauliers and traders. What is important, regardless of the method used to gather information, is an attitude of respect, politeness, transparency and appreciation towards informants.
3. The *Bikram Sambat* is the main calendar used in Nepal. Like its western equivalent it has 12 months, but these run from mid-month to mid-month according to the western equivalent, and the year begins in mid-April.
4. This is the number of crops harvested per annum. It is measured by a multiple-cropping index (MCI), where a single crop system equals 100 per cent. For a particular plot the MCI will be a multiple of 100 per cent, reflecting single, double or triple cropping, but when the index is averaged over a larger unit, such as a farm or village, indices like 171 per cent become possible.
5. The six villages in this diagram depict the three main foodgrains (summer paddy, wheat and summer maize) in both rainfed- and irrigated-production conditions. Within this framework they were chosen so as to provide a reasonably representative cross-section.

Chapter 4   Coping with cost recovery in Zambia: a sectoral policy study

1. A previous piece of work carried out with a team from the University of Dar Es Salaam had provided a 'people-oriented' report on macro-economic and political liberalization in rural Tanzania. A subsequent study in the same series has investigated rural democratization through the Law of Popular Participation in Bolivia. See Booth (1995 and 1996).
2. The PAG is a registered NGO that was formed by John Milimo and his collaborators in 1995. It aims to secure a permanent capacity in Zambia for field studies and training services in PRA and participatory assessment. It is receiving core start-up funding from Sida through Zambia's Social Recovery Project, Phase 2.

Chapter 5   Designing the future together: PRA and education policy in The Gambia

1. The other authors of this chapter like to thank Mary O'Reilly-de Brun for drawing together the contributions from four people on three continents. The authors would also like to thank Haddy Sey for her assistance during the 1995 PRA fieldwork session in Busura.
2. We were excited by what seemed to us an historical confluence of events: developments in economics, anthropology, philosophy, education and indeed even physics were all leading inexorably to a recognition of new non-linear approaches to development, the crucial importance of understanding social factors in project design, the value of multiple-stakeholder perspectives, the anthropologists' emphasis on an emic approach, and the educators' current robust debate on the ontological and epistemological foundations of qualitative research methods. In other words, we were on the road to PRA, which draws on all of these.
3. Two of us, Eileen Kane and Mary O'Reilly-de Brun, are anthropologists; Lawrence Bruce is a development administrator and Deputy Project Director of the Projects Implementation Unit of the Ministry of Education, The Gambia.
4. We were guided by Michael Quinn Patton's (1990) book on this; for example, adding to the cluster sample some statistically (or other) 'typical' places, 'deviant' places, and places where 'if it will work here, it will work anywhere'.
5. People were asked which household they belonged to, and facilitators quickly circled these on the well-being card-sort lists. If there were any gaps, it was a simple matter to ask if representatives from the 'missing' category of household could be invited to join us.
6. Our teams have always contained trained statisticians and mathematicians who have subsequently fallen in love (no other phrase will do) with PRA. A high point of one project was eight researchers shouting competing algebraic formulae for scoring, each excitedly reverting to a different Eritrean language, to the innumerate English-speaking-only anthropologist.
7. Even the elder among us, who had raided and plundered many a community in her day, did not fancy a repetition of the same in her sunset years (the youngest of us has an MA in theology and had reached the same conclusion, perhaps by a more edifying route).
8. Since we had last worked with them, they had used the strategy on other aspects of community development. They now had a bus service, a school garden, a credit scheme, a functioning bridge, and funds from two international donors.
9. Participatory learning and action.
10. Another interesting gender-inflected insight was that men tended to identify solutions that required 'outside help' more often than women, who seemed more proactive and creative in their resolution of problems.
11. This set of comments deserves a chapter in itself, but saying 'we don't need theory' is a theory in itself, and is untenable; the theory is there alright, but one is just accepting it without question. Of course people should bring their own cultural insights, world views and cognitive systems into the knowledge-getting process, but is refusing to explore these with them the best way of doing this? How do we work together to learn from one another's models of reality? Do we make them explicit or do we bank entirely on serendipity?
12. An excellent article on this subject is Jamieson's 'The Paradigmatic Significance of Rapid Rural Appraisal', Proceedings of the 1985 International Conference on Rapid Rural Appraisal, University of Khon Kaen, Thailand.
13. This section was written by Lawrence Bruce.

14. The Gambia Education Policy 1988–2003 aims at increasing access to, and improving the quality, relevance, equity and sustainability of the education system. The principles laid down in the education policy are very much in line with the objectives and strategies adopted at the International Conference on Education For All, held in Jomtien in 1990. The 'Education For All' mid-decade review in August 1995 set the stage for the renewal of education policy, aimed at contributing to poverty alleviation and the promotion of integrated human development through the provision of quality basic education, appropriate skills, and human-resource production and expansion.

Chapter 6   Can policy-focused research be participatory? Research on violence and poverty in Jamaica using PRA methods

1. In undertaking the PRA special acknowledgments are due to the following: overall responsibility for the project in UWI was provided by an advisory project committee chaired by Dr Barry Chevannes. Other members were Professor Don Robothom, Dr Anthony Harriott, Frances Madden and Horace Levy. The research was carried out collaboratively with a team of researchers from the Centre for Population, Community and Development (CPCD), Department of Sociology and Social Work, University of the West Indies (UWI), Mona. Horace Levy was the CPCD coordinator, and the team members were: Sean Ffrench, Charmaine Harris, Herbert Gayle, Jennifer Jones, Pauline Kidd, Arthur Newland, Angela Stultz-Crawlle, Imani Tafari Ama and Wilfred Talbert. Their field reports and synthesis analyses provided rich source material. Meera Shah, from IDS, University of Sussex, was an essential member of the research process, not only as the PRA trainer but also through her workshop report, which was of great assistance. Funding for PRA training and local fieldwork costs was provided by the British Overseas Development Administration, British Development Division in the Caribbean as a UK contribution to the preparation of the Jamaican Social Investment Fund.
2. The term PRA is used throughout, since this was a study using participatory rural appraisal methods in an urban context, and since the term participatory urban appraisal (PUA) has not as yet come into wide usage.
3. The Jamaican Social Investment Fund is funded from a number of sources: US$10 million from the Government of Jamaica (of which US$2.5 million is being provided from European Union counterpart funds); US$20 million loan from the World Bank; US$3 million grant from the Netherlands Government; and US$2 million from the OPEC Fund. The community projects are then funded through Social Investment Fund grants.
5. As Conyers (1982) aptly defined it, policy is about 'what to do', i.e. the process of social and political decisionmaking about how to allocate resources for the needs and interests of societies.
6. In a development agency that prioritizes the importance of measurement indicators, the issue of perception indicators is critical.
7. In addition, the different objectives of the two institutions participating in the study, the UWI and the World Bank meant that two reports where written. This section refers only to the World Bank document whose target audience was policymakers, as against UWI's' report which was intended for researchers and NGOs.

Chapter 7   Village voices challenging wetland-management policies: PRA experiences from Pakistan and India

1. The views expressed in this chapter are those of the authors and are not necessarily endorsed by the organizations they represent. Authors are listed in alphabetical order: Biksham Gujja is Manager, Freshwater Programme, WWF-

International, Gland, Michel Pimbert is Director of WWF-Switzerland, Geneva and Meera Shah is a visiting scholar at IDS, Sussex.

Chapter 8   The use of RRA to inform policy: tenure issues in Madagascar and Guinea

1. Freelance consultant based at 7118 Maple Avenue, Takoma Park, MD 20912 (USA). Phone/Fax: (301) 270–4785. Email: KSFREUD@AOL.COM.
2. I served as a consultant to both these projects, participating in the project design, training participants in RRA and leading the first of the case studies in each country.
3. In both cases, other donors were pursuing these more traditional approaches. In Madagascar, for example, the World Bank was strongly advocating private-land titling and was implementing a pilot programme during the period that the LTC research project was being carried out. In Guinea, French advisors at very high levels were promoting a land code based on a model favoured by the French since colonial times.
4. Because there is a massive confusion over the terms RRA and PRA, let me just note here that these were definitely cases of RRA: the process was designed and carried out principally by outsiders to the communities where the studies took place. Villagers participated with enthusiasm and sagacity in the activities proposed by the teams and they knew from the outset that the purpose of the exercise was to ensure that their views and situations were reflected in debates over national resource-management legislation. While it was not the primary purpose of the studies, in almost all cases I think it can be argued that these activities were empowering to the populations that hosted them. They were integrally involved in the research process and in some cases in later workshops to present the findings, and there were numerous examples of how the RRAs had spin-off activities in these villages that either addressed immediate concerns or enabled the populations to present their worries more effectively to local government officials.

Chapter 9   Scottish forestry policy u-turn: was PRA behind it?

1. *The Scotsman*, 27 April, 1996.
2. Since this chapter was written and presented as a paper at the IDS international workshop on PRA (13 May 1996), it has become apparent that this policy change has had little influence on the thinking and practice of the officials in the Forestry Commission (Sept. 1996).
3. All the thoughts in this chapter related to the difficulty of describing and documenting non-linear phenomena, uncertainty and complexity were inspired by the writings of the authors Daniel McNeill and Paul Freiberger (1993), and Ian Stewart (1989).
4. Adapted from Stewart (1989) p.83.
5. Adapted from ibid.
6. Adapted from the words of Max Panck, in Daniel McNeill and Paul Freiberger (1993) p.60.

Chapter 11   Introduction

1. In recognizing the need to draw in stakeholders from every constituency, the PPA also aims to promote participation in poverty assessments (PAs) beyond the level of the primary stakeholders (the intended beneficiaries) to include the secondary, or institutional, stakeholders (the actors in civil society and government) (Norton and Stephens, 1995: 4). Inclusion of secondary stakeholders aims 'to promote consensus, ownership and commitment to the analytical conclusions

and strategy identified among key actors whose support will be necessary for successful implementation'.

2. Just as it is increasingly recognized that the dynamics of poverty can only be understood through local poverty analysis, so too is there a clear need for an understanding of local perceptions of problems and priority interventions. PPAs create greater awareness of local observations of existing delivery mechanisms, such as micro-lending schemes or social services, and whether they are accessible to the poor. They provide, in addition, a broad-needs assessment of future project interventions as prioritized by local beneficiaries.

3. See World Bank (1992).

4. Personal communication, Caroline Robb.

5. By concentrating on the relationship between the changing environment and asset ownership, the PPA emphasizes vulnerability as a dynamic notion in contrast to poverty as a static concept. The PPA highlights that fixed income-based measurements of poverty are unable to capture the complex external factors that affect the poor, nor the diversity of their responses to economic difficulty. Critically, it shows that the poorest are not necessarily the most vulnerable, as they may have or be developing an asset portfolio that increases their security over time. The non-poor are, similarly, not necessarily the least vulnerable, as strategies to increase income in the short term may damage their asset base in the long term.

6. Hanmer *et al.*, (1996) argue that the conventional 'money-metric' approach to poverty analysis is both unnecessary and inadequate. The main alternative method, which defines poverty in relation to assets and/or attributes, is a more powerful analytical tool: 'Moreover, this alternative approach lends itself to a view of society in which individuals fall into socioeconomic groups which are defined by individual characteristics, as distinct from the model to which the World Bank has frequent recourse, which eliminates structure and postulates in its place a distribution across the population as a whole of whatever one-dimensional metric is adopted' (ibid: 8.4).

7. Shaffer (1996) argues that their fundamentally different epistemological underpinnings prevent effective synthesis of the two frameworks.

8. Over 150 organizations and individuals, encompassing NGOs, CBOs, academics and development workers, were contacted with regard to submitting proposals to take part in the South Africa PPA – *SA PPA Newsletter* (1995).

Chapter 13   The impact of PRA approaches and methods on policy and practice: the Zambia PPA

1. The team members were: S. Chimuka, N. Bubala, M. Nabanda, V. Mbewe, C. Njobvu, F. Kondolo, P. Ponga, S. Chama, and C. Kalamwina.

2. There was some variation in the quality of reporting. One group had to function without the team leader for three of the five sites, which had an impact on the functioning of that team.

3. From *Zambia Participatory Poverty Assessment Field Guide*, 1993.

4. Notably, the first and second phases of the Social Recovery Fund-sponsored Beneficiary Assessment, 1992–3.

5. See Andrew Norton and Thomas Stephens (1995). In due course this chapter will be updated with comments from co-author Dr John Milimo.

6. Participatory Assessment Group, May 1995, *Participatory Monitoring in Zambia*.

Chapter 14   Whose PPA is this? Lessons learned from the Mozambique PPA

1. Although the PPA has had measurable impact, it would be premature to evaluate the overall policy outcomes since the work is still at a relatively early phase (Phase I nearing completion as of May 1996).

2. Draft summary of Phase I activities, CEP, UEM, Maputo, December, 1995.
3. In the Zambia PPA, the urban field-site reports were without exception weaker than the rural reports. To have strengthened them, more attention to a separate but inter-linked urban PPA research agenda, and to the PRA methods to match those issues, would have been necessary during the design stage and the training workshop.
4. Although both the PAU poverty assessment and various Bank operations have also been subject to delays.
5. For example, district- and provincial-level planning units and some of the local NGOs were keen to receive information on measurable physical indicators of poverty (such as shops, clinics, schools, boreholes) which encouraged the generation of endless lists with very little analysis.

Chapter 15   Kicking down doors and lighting fires: the South Africa PPA

1. The whole development process would be guided by PRA principles, attitudes and behaviour, with methods appropriate in the ongoing development process used at various points. If done outside of a development process, PRA loses its effectiveness. Information shared during PRA sessions can be used by outsiders if the community or participants understand the purpose for which the information will be used and give their permission for its use (neither simple nor straightforward).
2. Reconstruction and Development Programme is the flagship policy of the Government of National Unity which seeks to rebuild South African society through economic growth based upon the simultaneous redistribution of the benefits of such growth. Up until April 1996, the RDP was planned and coordinated through a special office established under Minister without Portfolio, Jay Naidoo. This position was removed, however, and the functions of the RDP office have been split between Deputy President Thabo Mbeki and the Ministry of Finance.
3. As DRA was a very small organization, it did not anticipate that it would be conducting the research but rather facilitating it and synthesizing the results.
4. Two selected research teams, an NGO and an academic, withdrew from the process. The NGO could not take part as the community it was working with denied permission for the study. Its members feared exploitation. The academic could not take part as she could not meet the deadline.
5. The policy- and report-writing workshop was attended by one or two researchers from each of 11 of the 12 participating research teams. Both workshops were timed more or less to coincide with the beginning of the fieldwork and report-writing stages, respectively. That research teams were commissioned in three stages meant, however, that some, notably the four commissioned last, could not take part in these training workshops.
6. It is possible that some analysis was done by poor people who were part of the research process. We are not familiar enough with the details of each research process to indicate whether, or the extent to which this may have occurred.
7. The MC recognized these filters. In an attempt to reduce them, it requested raw field data to be annexed to reports, so that it could refer to the original data on which research reports were based.
8. The recent closure of the RDP office in South Africa has ended an opportunity for a more holistic approach to policy formulation. It is to be hoped that recent initiatives for provincial-level development strategies might ensure the continued development of policy at a more local level.
9. As such, we would welcome critical discussion of the process, which could improve future projects attempted on similar lines.

10. A literature review of existing qualitative research in South Africa was compiled, a stakeholder workshop was successfully convened and facilitated, and a manual of methodologies was drawn up.

Chapter 16   PPAs: a review of the World Bank's experience

1. This PPA review has been based upon a desk study as part of Phase 1. Phase 2 will include some in-depth analysis at the country level in order to evaluate the PPAs from the perspectives of the other stakeholders.
2. Annexe 1 refers to the to the various management and organizational issues. The column describing the levels of participation has limited value and is indicative only. To be more accurate, a multiple-stakeholder analysis of participation using the stakeholders' own indicators would be required. The diversity of experiences of the PPAs has been impacted upon by many factors including the context in the World Bank and in-country. This is detailed in Table 2.4 as are the methodologies employed to elicit the views of the poor. Annexe 2 focuses on the value added through the analysis of qualitative indicators, obtained through the PPA. In addition, an attempt has been made to analyse the impact on the World Bank's and borrower's country programmes and policies. In some cases, it has been too early to assess the impact. In others, the impact of the PPA alone had been difficult to isolate from other factors. Policy change and attitudinal shifts may be viewed as part of a complex social process, and it is often difficult, therefore, to isolate the impact of the PPA.
3. Although there were many limitations to these early PPAs their significance lies in their being the first to use qualitative data in the analysis of poverty.
4. All references to Mozambique are based on Chapter 14.

Chapter 17   Some reflections on the PPA process and lessons learned

1. Chapter 17 has benefited greatly from comments made during the IDS workshop.
2. The balance of recommendations of the World Bank Africa Region Task Force (World Bank 1996a: 111–12) for future action in poverty reduction mostly concerned future process. The main substantive recommendation of the report, however, highlighted the need for a future operational focus on rural infrastructure, which had clearly derived mainly from the PPAs.

Chapter 18   Introduction

1. Contrast, for example, the rationalist and incrementalist models of development policy: the former model (summarized by Carley, 1980; Walt, 1994) is based on the premise that complex social problems can be solved by systematic analysis leading to comprehensive planning, a conceptual approach that underpins the policy analysis and planning techniques of most international development agencies; the latter, on the other hand, promotes methods capable of recognizing and responding to 'uncertainty, detecting and correcting errors, generating and using knowledge as experiments progress, and modifying actions as opportunities and constraints appear during implementation' (Rondinelli, 1983: 14).
2. We are grateful to Neil Price for his valuable insights on the policy process.
3. 'Triangulation', seeking multiple perspectives, is a term that should apply not just to enquiry, but should extend to policy-influencing strategies.

Chapter 19   How are local voices heard by policymakers

1. In order for a village to receive land title, a LUP exercise had first to be carried out in order to provide specific development plans for the village lands that come with the title.

2. As with conflict resolution, communication is critical to the success of merging discourses. Johansson (1994: 3) describes a 'cross-cultural communication' where a 'modern, western logic meets with customary and local mental models of how the world works'.

Chapter 20   Getting policymakers to move the bricks around: advocacy and participatory irrigation management in India

1. Although concentrating on Anil Shah's role in facilitating the scaling-up of PIM cannot possibly do justice to his enormous contribution to the scaling-up of participatory processes more generally (particularly in wastelands and forest management), both as director of the Aga Khan Rural Support Programme and later as chairman of the Development Support Centre, as well as in his earlier function as a high-ranking Indian government official, I believe the PIM experience in Gujarat illustrates very clearly how policymakers can more effectively be approached to 'move the bricks around' (i.e. make those specific policy changes that are indispensable for participatory processes to spread).
2. Chapter 20 was written by someone who interviewed Anil Shah. Some of the views expressed may not necessarily be shared by him equally emphatically.

Chapter 21   Challenges in influencing public policy: an NGO perspective

1. There is an NSG for Joint Forest Management in India, which provides support to innovative initiatives and research, and a forum for exchange and dissemination of experiences and ideas. Similar NSGs for the watershed development and the Participatory Irrigation Management are under consideration.

Chapter 22   Towards community-sensitive policy

1. The Minister of Health, known personally by one colleague at the UCBHCA secretariat, officially opened the 1994 AGM by appealing to UNICEF and other donors to consider favourably the case of the association, which had just lost UNICEF support for its running costs. He stressed that this was a unique national network representing the interests of NGOs and CBOs working in primary and community-based health care. The UNICEF country representative who was present at the opening ceremony expressed her organization's commitment to the continual support for the association's initiatives, while reminding the association's members of UNICEF's decision to change its mode of support from grants to contractual arrangements.
2. There are up to 14 000 parishes in Uganda, each containing between three and six villages. Each level of local council has community representatives who deliberate on local development issues, including community-needs assessment and identification of resources.

Chapter 23   The research process: sustaining quality and maximizing policy impact

1. An important distinction is drawn here between the term 'methodology', which describes research traditions such as PRA, and the term 'methods', which describes individual tools or techniques that make up a research methodology.
2. 'Sharing our Experience: an appeal to donors and governments', a statement of the South–South Behaviour and Attitudes Workshop, Bangalore and Madurai, June 1996.

3. Originally labelled 'naturalist' by Lincoln and Guba (1985); these authors later preferred to use the label 'constructivist' (Guba and Lincoln, 1989).
4. Criticism of large-scale questionnaire surveys has been consistent and widespread among the 'participatory community'. On a broad level, critics argue that the survey is merely 'convenient and compulsive' (Mukherjee, 1995: 21) providing a common language and a commensurable data set to a self-perpetuating research industry (Chambers 1994a: 13–14). More specific difficulties cited include quality control, ensuring longitudinal comparability, finding comparable control areas and explaining multiple causality (Chambers, 1978; Gill, 1993; Mukherjee, 1995).
5. During a participatory village survey in Gujarat, for example, Jodha (1988) elicited that households whose well-being had declined in terms of per capita income were in fact better off according to 37 out of 38 of their own criteria of well-being, which included independence from patrons, mobility, security and self-respect.
6. The Madagascar and Guinea case studies (Chapter 8), demonstrate, for example, that the punctuation of field studies with regional workshops served not only to disseminate research results but to triangulate these findings by asking workshop participants for feedback. In the Jamaica case study (Chapter 6), focus-group discussions with a range of stakeholders following the field studies served a similar purpose.
7. See also Denzin (1978).
8. See also Kidder (1981).
9. See also Eisner (1975).
10. See also Halpern (1983).
11. Shah (1993) describes the use of impact diagramming with different groups for assessing the impact of participation and village institutions on local livelihood in Bharuch District, Gujarat, India. This method can be sequenced with visual interactive questionnaires, a group process of developing and conducting questionnaires in which issues to be studied and the methods and symbols to be used for information collection and analysis have been finalized by the participants themselves. This leads in turn to open-ended interviews with households, allowing participants to explore variables not initially included in the questionnaire process, and to corroborate or correct information collected. Sharp differences emerged in the indicators of change as perceived by local people and the outside professionals.
12. Five districts shown by the WMS to be the poorest in Kenya were selected (along with two later additions), and five clusters in each district then chosen by simple random sampling. Each cluster contained one village or part of a village, which then became the 35 sampled villages for mapping and inclusion in the PPA (Narayan and Nyamwaya, 1996: 10).
13. The results showed, for example, that 42 per cent of the population in Kwale district were 'Very Poor' compared to only 7 per cent in Busia district; similarly, gender disaggregation by headship revealed, for instance, that 77 per cent of female household heads in Kwale were 'Very Poor' compared with only 17 per cent of female heads in Busia (Narayan and Nyamwaya, 1996: 23).
14. SARAR is a community-based and participatory methodology that builds on local knowledge and strengthens local capacity. SARAR's approach combines generation of data with strengthening of group abilities to assess needs, identify priorities, establish goals and design action plans to be implemented and monitored. Certain tools, such as pocket charts, story with a gap, flexiflans and three-pile sorting cards are unique to SARAR (World Bank, 1996b: 183, 193–4).
15. A key challenge for the trainer is to teach participatory research principles through allowing people to 'discover' them, rather than falling into a lecture mode, a challenge with a philosophical basis common to the Freirian and Critical Theory schools of thought (Freire, 1970; Habermas, 1972, 1990). See Chambers (1995) for an elaboration on this.

16. For discussion of the principles shared by participatory research approaches see Grandstaff *et al.*, 1987: 9–13; McCracken *et al.*, 1988: 12–13; Gueye and Freudenberger, 1990: 10–19; Chambers, 1992: 13–15.

17. See for example, *Face to Face* (1996b): 'It is more important for each person and each group to invent and adapt their own approach, methods, sequences and combinations, than to adopt a ready-made manual or model. Let a thousand flowers bloom (and why only a thousand) and let them be flowers which bloom better and better, and spread their seeds'.

Chapter 24   Analysing participatory research for policy change

1. This paper draws extensively on experiences with research teams and colleagues in a number of countries and institutions. In particular, I should mention the staff of the Participatory Assessment Group, Zambia; the Centre for the Development of People (CEDEP) Ghana, and the participants at the Report Writing Workshop for the South Africa PPA, co-ordinated by DRA, Durban, in 1996. In terms of individuals who have contributed to the ideas presented here key contributors included David Korboe, Tony Dogbe, John Milimo, Ellen Bortei-Doku Aryeetey, Dan Owen, Caroline Moser, Jeremy Holland, Tessa Marcus, Julian May, Heidi Atwood, Amani Abou-Zeid, Nagwa Riad and Paul Francis. I am indebted for long-term support during the process of undertaking the PPAs and ideas, as well as for comments on a draft, to Robert Chambers. Responsibility for the views presented, of course, rests with the author.

2. Attwood and May (Chapter 15) describe the tension between policy research and the basic principles of PRA in terms of a set of oppositions, between on the one hand a viewpoint which stresses localized results, direct linkages, on-the-ground complexity, and project-based action (PRA) and on the other the requirements of policy research for generalized results, indirect linkages to action, abstraction and broad policy directives.

3. While the primary objective of policy research is not local-level empowerment, a concern that direct benefits can be brought to participating communities can be integrated into any participatory-policy research exercise. In the South Africa PPA and in the later phases of the Ghana PPA a principle was adopted by the research teams whereby communities were only selected if structures existed which could take forward the results of the research in a long-term process for the participants.

4. There are exceptions to this, for example using social maps for basic population information, or enumeration of social categories which may be consistent within a given culture (e.g. disability).

5. See Welbourn (1991) for an excellent description of this process.

6. While these texts usually pay lip-service to the 'multi-dimensional' character of poverty, in practice the structure of the analysis is dominated by a single indicator (household consumption).

7. For two different formulations on this see Swift (1989) and Moser (1996).

8. See Putnam (1993).

Chapter 25   Participation, policy and empowerment

1. IDS workshop participants identified a range of motivations which fell short of encompassing the principles of PRA, including: a 'favour' to the poor, a 'good thing to do', less problematic, cheaper, or simply a way of getting papers published.

Annexe 3

1. Children continue to be victims in the on-going violence which characterizes many areas of South Africa.

References and Sources

Absalom, E., R. Chambers, S. Francis, B. Gueye, I. Guijt, S. Joseph, D. Johnson, C. Kabutha, M. Rahman Khan, R. Leurs, J. Mascarenhas, P. Norrish, M. Pimbert, J. Pretty, M. Samaranayake, I. Scoones, M. Kaul Shah, Parmesh Shah, D. Tamang, J. Thompson, G. Tym and A. Welbourn (1995) 'Sharing Our Concerns and Looking to the Future', *PLA Notes* 22 (February) 5–10.

Action Aid (1992) *Participatory Rural Appraisal: Utilisation Survey Report, Part I, Rural Development Area, Singhupalchowk*, Monitoring and Evaluation Unit, Action Aid-Nepal, PO Box 3198, Kathmandu.

Adams, A., R. Das Roy and A. Mahbub (1993) 'Participatory Methods to Assess Change in Health and Women's Lives: an exploratory study for the BRAC–ICDDR, B Joint Project in Matlab', Research and Evaluation Division, Bangladesh Rural Advancement Committee, Dhaka and Harvard Center for Population and Development Studies, Cambridge, MA.

Bhatnagar, B. and A. Williams (eds) (1992) 'Participatory Development and the World Bank: potential directions for change', World Bank Discussion Paper 183, Washington DC: World Bank.

Blackburn, J. with J. Holland (eds.) (1998) *Who Changes? Institutionalising participation in development*, London: IT Publications.

Booth, D. (1995) 'Bridging the 'Macro'–'Micro' Divide in Policy-oriented Research: two African experiences', *Development in Practice*, Vol. 5, No. 4.

Booth, D. (1996) 'Micro–Macro Bridging Without Loss of Quality: a Swedish itinerary', summary of presentation to the Structural Adjustment Forum, Nottingham University, UK, 10–12 April (available from author, CDS Swansea; e-mail d.k.booth@swan.ac.uk).

Booth, D., J. Milimo, G. Bond, S. Chimuka, K. Liywalii, M. Mwalusi, M. Mwanamwalye, E. Mwanza, M. Nabanda, L. Peme and A. Zulu (1995) *Coping with Cost Recovery: a study of the social impact of and responses to cost recovery in basic services (health and education) in poor communities in Zambia*, Stockholm: Sida; reprinted 1996 as Working Paper 3 of the Sida Task Force on Poverty Reduction (available from Policy and Legal Affairs Department, Sida, S–105 25 Stockholm, Sweden).

Carley, M. (1980) *Rational Techniques in Policy Analysis*, Gower Press.

Carvalho, S. (1994) *Social Funds Guidelines for Design and Implementation*, Human Resources Development and Operations Policy, Working Paper, July, Washington DC: World Bank.

Carvalho, S. and H. White (1997), *Combining the Quantitative and Qualitative Approaches to Poverty Measurement and Analysis: The practice and the potential*, Technical Paper 336, Washington, DC: World Bank.

References and Sources

Chambers, R. (1978) *Rural Poverty-oriented Monitoring and Evaluation: simple is optimal?* Rome: FAO.

Chambers, R. (1983) *Rural Development: putting the last first*, London: Longman.

Chambers, R. (1989) 'Editorial Introduction: vulnerability, coping and policy', *IDS Bulletin* 20(2):1–7.

Chambers, R. (1992) 'Rural Appraisal: rapid, relaxed and participatory', *Institute of Development Studies Discussion Paper No. 311*, University of Sussex: IDS.

Chambers, R. (1993a) *Challenging the Professions. Frontiers for rural development*, London: Intermediate Technology Publications.

Chambers, R. (1993b) 'Experience with Alternatives to Questionnaires', a note prepared for IIED/IDS workshop on 'Alternatives to Questionnaire Surveys', 26 October 1993.

Chambers, R. (1994a) 'Participatory Rural Appraisal: challenges, potentials and paradigm', University of Sussex: IDS.

Chambers, R. (1994b) 'Participatory Rural Appraisal (PRA): analysis of experience', *World Development* 22(9), 1253–68.

Chambers, R. (1995a) 'NGOs and Development: the primacy of the personal', IDS Working Papers No. 14, January.

Chambers, R. (1995b) 'Poverty and Livelihoods: whose reality counts?', *IDS Discussion Paper No. 347*, University of Sussex: IDS, January.

Chambers, R. (1997) *Whose Reality Counts? Putting the first last*, London: Intermediate Technology Publications.

Chambers, R. and I. Guijt (1995) 'PRA – Five Years Later. Where are we now?', *Forests, Trees and People Newsletter*, No. 26/7: 4–14.

Clarke, J. D. and L. Salmen (1993) *Participatory Poverty Assessments: incorporating poor people's perspectives into poverty assessment work*, Washington DC: World Bank.

Conyers, D. (1982) *An Introduction to Social Planning in the Third World*, Chichester: John Wiley and Sons.

Cook, T. D. and D. T. Campbell (1979) *Quasi-experimentation: design and analysis issues for field settings*, Chicago: Rand McNally.

Cornwall, A., I. Guijt and A. Welbourn (1994) 'Acknowledging Process: challenges for agricultural research and extension methodology' in I. Scoones and J. Thompson (ed.) *Beyond Farmer First: rural people's knowledge, agricultural research and extension practice*, London: ITP, pp. 98–117.

Cusworth, J. W. and T. R. Franks (eds) (1993) *Managing Projects in Developing Countries*, Longman.

Denzin, N. K. (1978) *Sociological Methods*, New York: McGraw-Hill.

Eisner, E. W. (1975) 'The Perceptive Eye: toward the reformulation of educational evaluation', *Occasional Papers of the Stanford Evaluation Consortium*, Stanford CA: Stanford University, mimeo.

Face to Face (1996a) 'PRA in Nepal: talking, doing, being', No.7, March.

Face to Face (1996b) 'Start, Stumble, Self-correct, Share', No. 13, March.

Freire, P. (1970) *Pedagogy of the Oppressed*, New York: The Seabury Press.

Gill, G. J. (1991) 'But how does it compare to the REAL data', *RRA Notes* 14: 5–13.

Gill, G. J. (1992) *Policy Analysis for Agricultural Resource Management in Nepal: a comparison of conventional and participatory approaches*, Kathmandu: Research Support Series No. 9, Ministry of Agriculture/Winrock International, July.

Gill, G. J. (1993) 'OK, The Data's Lousy, But Its All We've Got (Being a Critique of Conventional Methods)', *Gatekeeper Series* No. 38, London: International Institute of Environment and Development, Sustainable Agriculture Programme.

Gill, G. J. (1996) *Maintaining the Granary: foodgrain production and productivity in the Nepal Tarai*, Kathmandu: Winrock International *Policy Analysis in Agriculture and Related Resource Management*.

Glassco, L. and Y. Ishihara (1995) *What Does PRA Tell Us About Poverty That Conventional Methods Do Not? The case of Zambia*, Unpublished MPhil, 24 April.

Grandstaff, S. W., T. B. Grandstaff and G. W. Lovelace (1987) 'Summary Report', in *KKU Proceedings*, 3–30.

Grindle, M. S. and J. W. Thomas (1991) *Public Choices and Policy Change. The political economy of reform in developing countries*, Baltimore and London: John Hopkins University Press.

Guba, E. G. and Y. S. Lincoln (1989) *Fourth Generation Evaluation*, London: Sage.

Gueye, B. and K. Schoonmaker Freudenberger (1990) *Introduction à la Methode Accelerée de Recherche Participative (MARP)*, Centre de Recherches pour le Developpement International, BP 2435, Dakar, Senegal, October.

Gujja, B. *et al.* (1996) 'Participatory Management Planning for the Keoladeo National Park, Bharatpur India', WWF and Forest Department, Rajasthan, draft report on PRA workshop held at KNP from 20 November – 5 December 1995.

Habermas, J. (1972) *Knowledge and Human Interests*, London: Heinemann.

Habermas, J. (1990) *Moral Consciousness and Communicative Action*, Cambridge MA: MIT Press.

Halpern, E. (1983) *Auditing Naturalistic Inquiries: the development and application of a model*. Unpublished doctoral dissertation, Indiana University.

Hanmer, L., G. Pyatt and H. White (1996) *Poverty in sub-Saharan Africa: what can we learn from the World Bank's poverty assessments?* Institute of Social Studies, The Hague.

Hill, M. (ed.) (1993) *The Policy Process: a reader*, New York: Harvester.

Hill, P. (1986) *Development Economics on Trial: the anthropological case for a prosecution*, Cambridge: Cambridge University Press.

Hlabisa PRA Training Report (1995) August.

Hulme, D. (1994) 'Social Development Research and the Third Sector: NGOs as users and subjects of social inquiry', in D. Booth (ed.) *Rethinking Social Development: theory, research and practice*, Harlow: Longman, pp 251–78.

IDS Bulletin (1989) 'Vulnerability: how the poor cope', Vol. 20, No. 2, April.

IDS (1994) *Poverty Assessment and Public Expenditure: a study for the SPA working group on poverty and social policy*, University of Sussex: IDS, September.

References and Sources

IIED (1994) 'Rapid and Participatory Rural Appraisal', *RRA Notes* 21 1 November.

Inglis, A. (1991) 'Harvesting Local Forestry Knowledge: a comparison of RRA and conventional surveys', *RRA Notes* 12: 32–40.

Inglis, A. (1992) *A Tale of Two Approaches: conventional questionnaire surveys vs PRA*, Rural Development Forestry Network Paper 14c, London: Overseas Development Institute.

Jodha, N. S. (1988) 'Poverty Debate in India: a Minority view', *Economic and Political Weekly*, Special Number 2421–8, November.

Johansson, L. (1994) 'Interactive Multimedia Technology and "Instant Video" in Rural Development', *Forests, Trees and People Newsletter*, Uppsala, Sweden: IRDC, Swedish University of Agricultural Sciences.

Johansson, L. and A. Hoben (1995) 'RRAs for Land Policy Formulation in Tanzania', in *Forests, Trees and People Newsletter*, No.15/16, 26–31.

Johnson, R. J., D. Gregory and D. M. Smith (ed.) (1986) *The Dictionary of Human Geography*, 2nd ed., Oxford: Basil Blackwell.

Kabeer, N. (1996) 'Agency, Well-being and Inequality: reflections on the gender dimensions of poverty', *IDS Bulletin* 27(1): 11–22.

Kane, E. and M. O'Reilly-de Brun (1993) 'Bitter Seeds: girls' participation in primary education in The Gambia', Washington DC: World Bank, Africa-Sahelian Department, Population and Human Resources Division, draft.

Kidder, L. H. (1981) 'Qualitative Research and Quasi-experimental Frameworks', in M. B. Brewer and B. E. Collins (ed.) *Scientific Inquiry and the Social Sciences*, San Fransisco: Jossey-Bass.

Korboe, D. (1995) *Extended Poverty Study (PPA Phase 3): access and utilisation of basic social services by the poor in Ghana*, UNICEF.

Kumar, S.(ed) (1996) *ABC of PRA: attitude, behaviour, change*, a report on the South–South Workshop on PRA: Attitudes and Behaviour, Bangalore and Madurai, 1–10 July, organized by ACTIONAID India and SPEECH.

Leiss, S. and J. Gage (1995) 'Tenure Security in Madagascar', *Land Tenure Center Newsletter*, No. 73, Fall.

Lincoln, Y. S. and E. G. Guba (1985) *Naturalistic Inquiry*, London: Sage.

McCracken, J. A., J. N. Pretty and G. R. Conway (1988) *An Introduction to Rapid Rural Appraisal for Agricultural Development*, London: IIED.

McNeill, D. and P. Freiberger (1993) *Fuzzy Logic*, New York: Simon and Schuster.

May, J. with H. Attwood, P. Ewang, F. Lund, A. Norton and W. Wetzal (1996) *Draft PPA*, Data Research Africa.

Miles, M. B. and A. M. Huberman (1984) 'Drawing Valid Meaning from Qualitative Data: toward a shared craft', *Educational Researcher*.

Moser, C. (1993a) 'Urban Social Policy and Poverty Reduction', *TWURD Working Paper No. 10*, Washington DC: World Bank.

Moser, C. (1993b) *Gender Planning and Development: theory, practice and training*, London: Routledge.

Moser, C. (1996) 'Confronting Crisis: household responses to poverty and vulnerability in four poor urban communities', ESD Studies and Monographs Series No. 7, Washington DC: World Bank.

Moser, C., J. Holland and S. Adam (1996) 'The Implications of Urban Violence for the Design of Social Investment Funds: a case study of the Jamaican SIF', *Infrastructure Notes*, Washington DC: TWU, World Bank, December.

Mukherjee, N. (1992) 'Villagers' Perceptions of Rural Poverty through the Mapping Methods of PRA', *RRA Notes*, No. 15 (May): 21–6.

Mukherjee, N. (1995) *Participatory Rural Appraisal and Questionnaire Survey (Comparative Field Experience and Methodologival Innovations)*, New Delhi: Concept Publishing Company.

Mukherjee, N. (1996) 'Resolving People–Sanctuary Conflict in Protected Areas: Kushiara Village, Mirzapur', *Economic and Political Weekly*, 27 January: 197–9.

Narayan, D. and D. Nyamwaya (1996) *Learning from the Poor: a participatory poverty assessment in Kenya*, Environment Department Papers No. 034, Environmentally Sustainable Development, Washington DC: World Bank.

New ERA (1995) *A Participatory Poverty Assessment Study in Selected Communities of Tanahu and Ilam districts*, New ERA: Maharagunj, PO Box 722, Kathmandu, Nepal, October.

Norton, A. and P. Francis (1992) *Proposal for a Participatory Poverty Assessment in Ghana*, mimeo.

Norton, A., D. Owen and P. Francis (1994) *Zambia Participatory Poverty Assessment*, Vol. 5 of the Zambia Poverty Assessment, Washington DC: World Bank.

Norton, A. and T. Stephens (1995) *Participation in Poverty Assessments*, Social Policy and Resettlement Division, Washington DC: World Bank.

Norton, A., E. Bortei-Doku Aryeetey, D. Korboe and T. Dogbe (1995) *Poverty Assessment in Ghana using Qualitative and Participatory Research Methods*, PSP Discussion Paper Series No. 83, Washington DC: World Bank.

O'Reilly-de Brun, M. (1994) 'Tender Shoots: a case study of community mobilization and response to problems of girls' education in The Gambia', AF5PH, draft, Washington DC: World Bank.

Participation in Action (nd) 'Win-Win Trainings', Issue 5, 19 August.

Patton, M. Q. (1990) *Qualitative Evaluation and Research Methods*, 2nd ed, Newbury Park, California: Sage.

Pimbert, M. P. and J. N. Pretty (1995) 'Parks, People and Professionals. Putting "participation" into protected-area management', UNRISD-IIED-WWF. UNRISD Discussion Paper No 57, Geneva.

Pimbert, M. P. *et al.* (1996) 'Community-based Planning for Wetland Conservation: lessons from the Ucchali complex in Pakistan', Lahore: WWF and the Punjab Wildlife Department of the Government of Pakistan, 100pp.

Pretty, J. (1993a) 'Criteria for Trustworthiness: a note for the joint IIED/IDS Workshop on Altenatives to Questionnaire Surveys', Sussex: IDS, 26 October.

Pretty, J. (1993b) 'Alternative Systems of Inquiry for a Sustainable Agriculture', London: International Institute for Environment and Development, Sustainable Agriculture Programme.

Pretty, J., I. Guijt, J. Thompson and I. Scoones (1995) *Participatory Learning and Action: a trainers' guide*, London: IIED.

Putnam, R. (1993) 'The Prosperous Community: social capital and public life, *American Prospect*, Spring: 35–42.

Putnam, R. (1993) *Making Democracy Work: civic traditions in modern Italy*, Princeton: Princeton University Press.

Rajaratnam, J., C. Gamesan, H. Thasian, N. Babu and A. Rajaratnam (1993) *Validating the Wealth Ranking of PRA and Formal Survey in Identifying the Rural Poor*, RUHSA Department, Christian Medical College and Hospital, RUHSA Campus 632 209, North Arcot Ambedkar District, Tamil Nadu.

RAMSAR (1996) Recommendation 6.3 of the RAMSAR Convention of Contracting Parties, Brisbane, Australia, March.

Robb, C. (nd) 'Opening Up the Policy Debate: The Gambia's strategy for poverty alleviation', unpublished paper.

Rondinelli, D. A. (1983) *Development Projects as Policy Experiments*, London: Routledge.

SA PPA Newsletter (1995) Vol. 1 of 3, 21 August.

Salmen, L. (1995) *Beneficiary Assessment: an approach described*, Environment Department Paper 023, Washington DC: World Bank.

Schultz, T. P. (1989) 'Benefits of Educating Women', Background Paper Series, Population and Human Resources Department, Education and Employment Division, Washington DC: World Bank.

Shaffer, P. (1996) 'Beneath the Poverty Debate: some issues', *IDS Bulletin* 27, No. 1: 23–34.

Shah, A. C. (1991) 'Shoulder Tapping: a technique of training in participatory rural appraisal', *Forests, Trees and People Newsletter* 14 (October): 14–15.

Shah, M. K. (1996) 'Participatory Planning with Disaster Victims: experience from earthquake-hit areas of Maharashtra, India', Refugee Participation Network, Refugee Studies Programme, Oxford, UK: No. 21, April 15–17.

Shah, P. (1993) A note for the joint IIED/IDS workshop on 'Alternatives to Questionnaire Surveys', 26 October.

Shah, P., G. Bharadwaj and R. Ambasha (1991) 'Farmers as Analysts and Facilitators in Participatory Rural Appraisal and Planning', *RRA Notes* 13: 84–94.

Stegeborn, W. (1996) 'Sri Lanka's Forests – Conservation of Nature versus People', *Cultural Survival*, Spring.

Stewart, I. (1989) *Does God Play Dice*, London/New York: Penguin Books.

Stromquist, N. and P. Murphy (1995) 'Leveling the Playing Field', Economic Development Institute Studies. Washington, DC: World Bank.

Swift, J. (1989) 'Why Are Rural People So Vulnerable to Famine?' IDS Bulletin 20(2): 8–15.

UNDP (1996) *UNDP's 1996 Report on Human Development in Bangladesh. A pro-poor agenda, Volume 3: Poor People's Perspectives*, UNDP: Dhaka, Bangladesh.

Vigoda, M. (1993) 'Participatory Rural Appraisal in a Women's Health-education Project in Bangladesh', CARE-Bangladesh, GPO Box 226, Dhaka, January.

Walt, G. (1994) *Health Policy: an introduction to process and power*, London: Zed Books.

Welbourn, A. (1991) 'RRA and the Analysis of Difference', *RRA Notes* 14, December: 14–23.

Welbourn, A. (1993) 'PRA, Gender and Conflict Resolution: some problems and possibilities', paper presented at PRA and Gender Workshop, 6–7 December.

Welbourn, A. (1995) *Stepping Stones: a training package on HIV/AIDS, communication and relationship skills*, London: Action Aid.

Wildavsky, A. (1979) *Speaking Truth to Power: the art and craft of policy analysis*, Little Brown.

World Bank (1990) *World Development Report*, Washington DC: World Bank.

World Bank (1991) *Assistance Strategies to Reduce Poverty*, Washington DC: World Bank.

World Bank (1992) *Poverty Reduction Handbook*, Washington DC: World Bank.

World Bank (1994) *Zambia Poverty Assessment, Volume V: participatory poverty assessment*, Washington DC: World Bank.

World Bank (1995a) *Ghana, Poverty Past, Present and Future*, Washington DC: World Bank.

World Bank (1995b) *Seeing for Yourself: research handbook for girls' education in Africa*, Washington DC: World Bank.

World Bank (1996a) *Taking Action for Poverty Reduction in sub-Saharan Africa: report of an Africa region task force*, Human Resources and Poverty Division, Technical Department, Africa Region, Washington DC: World Bank.

World Bank (1996b) *The World Bank Participation Sourcebook*, Environmentally Sustainable Development, Washington DC: World Bank.

World Wide Fund For Nature and Development Perspectives (1996) 'Conservation with a Human Face', documentary video (22 mins).

Wuyts, M. *et al.* (1992) *Development Policy and Public Action*, London: Oxford University Press.

Index

local/poor 1, 65, 85, 91, 100–2, 125–6, 144, 156–7, 184
vulnerability 47, 56, 93, 109, 188–9

water 32, 59, 186
see also drought; irrigation; rainfall; wetlands
weaknesses 128–9
wealth-ranking 107, 109, 174, 175, 190
wetlands 10, 57–9
wheat 20, 21
win-win 154
women 31, 37, 39, 40, 49, 138, 223–6
see also circumcision, female; domestic violence; dowry; gender; girls' education; invisibility

work *see* labour
working groups 86, 159, 166
workshops 55, 68–9, 121, 124, 125, 126, 127, 155, 167, 170
World Bank 33–34, 44–6, 112–18, 185, 187, 196, 199, 211–20
PPAs 91–101, 103, 121, 131–42, 201–10
WWF 57, 58, 65

yields 20–6, 85

Zambia 9, 138, 146, 149, 179, 191, 197–8, 207, 217
cost recovery 28–30, 195
PPAs 94, 95, 103–11, 133, 143–5, 177, 182, 186, 196